Modern Banking in the Balkans and West-European Capital in the Nineteenth and Twentieth Centuries

Modern Banking in the Balkans and West-European Capital in the Nineteenth and Twentieth Centuries

Edited by

KOSTAS P. KOSTIS

Routledge
Taylor & Francis Group
LONDON AND NEW YORK

First published 1999 by Ashgate Publishing

Reissued 2018 by Routledge
2 Park Square, Milton Park, Abingdon, Oxon OX14 4RN
711 Third Avenue, New York, NY 10017, USA

Routledge is an imprint of the Taylor & Francis Group, an informa business

Typeset in Sabon by Manton Typesetters, 5–7 Eastfield Road, Louth, Lincolnshire, LN11 7AJ.

A Library of Congress record exists under LC control number: 98029823

ISBN 13: 978-1-138-32370-4 (hbk)
ISBN 13: 978-1-138-32371-1 (pbk)
ISBN 13: 978-0-429-45125-6 (ebk)

Contents

List of Figures and Tables

Figures

Tables

Preface

This volume originated in the Athens conference on Modern Banking in the Balkans and West-European Capital, organized in January 1997 by the Hellenic Bank Association and the European Association for Banking History on the occasion of the 70th anniversary of the Hellenic Bank Association.

Some of the papers published here were presented at the conference, while others were written especially for this publication. I owe an important debt to all the volume's contributors, as well as to G. Alogoskoufis, Philip Cottrell, G. Dertilis, C. Holtfrerich, and Alice Teichova who, as commentators during the conference, greatly enriched its proceedings and results.

I would like also to thank Prof. Dr Manfred Pohl, Executive Member and Deputy Chairman of the European Association for Banking History, for his invaluable support in organizing the conference and the publishing of this volume, and Ms Emma Johnston for her assistance in coping with many practical problems. Many thanks are also due to Caroline Cornish for her help with the editing of this volume.

To John Manos, General Secretary of the Hellenic Bank Association, we owe the initial idea of the Athens conference; he supported the venture by all means at his disposal and, most especially, by his deep conviction that the history of banking is an integral part of banks' activities.

Finally, I would like to thank the Hellenic Bank Association and its President Th. Karatzas, Governor of the National Bank of Greece, for sponsoring the conference.

Kostas P. Kostis

Introduction

Kostas P. Kostis

> A specter is haunting Western culture – the specter of Balkans. All the powers have entered into a holy alliance to exorcise this specter: politicians and journalists, conservative academics and radical intellectuals, moralists of all kinds, gender, and fashion. Where is the adversarial group that has not been decried as 'Balkan' and 'balkanizing' by its opponents? Where the accused have not hurled back the branding reproach of 'balkanism'? (M. Todorova)[1]

In search of foes, as well as of fields in which to develop its crusading spirit, following the role it considers its own on the stage of international politics, the West was to discover, after the collapse of the so-called socialist regimes, with mixed feelings of fear, surprise and contempt, that the Balkans were still in place.

The 50 years that have elapsed since the Peninsula last appeared in the European scene as the 'Balkans' have been no more than an interlude in a long-term attempt to describe and understand this corner of Europe, which somehow failed to meet any of the stereotypes descriptive of 'the European'. The politically correct attempts to rename this world South-east Europe instead of the Balkans, in the hope that a change of name would bring about a change of reality, failed; the governments of the countries in this area continue to hold 'Inter-Balkan' conferences and its academic community still publishes 'Balkan studies', without shame.

Meanwhile, and following 1989, the West was to realize that the Balkans constituted yet another potential field of glory, since the newly formed states were in need of financial assistance in order to survive and of political counselling if they were, in turn, to benefit from the 'end of history'. An 'end of history', however, that was to prove closer to an apocalypse, as Bosnia and Albania demonstrate, than to the paradise promised by the advocates of neo-liberalism.

Nevertheless, there have been many attempts to find ways out of this predicament: international meetings have succeeded one another and many European and American projects have been suggested to help solve the political and financial problems of the area and to support the best ways to achieve Europeanization. In good faith, notwithstanding the political returns and economic benefits, the West, with its protean presence, has left no stone unturned in striving to banish from its borders a problem that irritates by its very refusal to be contained by its locale of birth.

In strategies for the economic recovery of the Balkan states, the banking factor is seen as, and undoubtedly is, fundamental. Most Balkan countries' economies are disorganized and the living standards are extremely low. Hopes of improvement are based on an influx of western capital and on a banking financing of the economy that will allow these countries' integration in the international labour division, benefiting from their comparative advantages, whatever these may be. Even in the case of the most developed of the Balkan countries, Greece, the problem remains the same: to meet the requirements for its participation in the European Economic and Monetary Union, the country needs foreign capital and the increasing number of West-European banks working in Greece shows that the interest in such ventures is mutual.

Taken as a whole, these are hardly new problems: almost a century ago, for Balkan countries struggling to survive in a world that was becoming increasingly competitive as it marched towards the First World War, foreign capital and West-European banks appeared to be the only means to ensure rapid modernization, seen, at the time, as the building of an elementary economic infrastructure and powerful armies.[2]

Things may be different today, but, just as one cannot imagine pre-First World War Balkan antagonisms without considering the oppositions of the banking groups of West-European countries, so one cannot understand actual Balkan reality without taking into consideration the choices implemented in the well-guarded offices of western banks in the Balkan capitals. This becomes obvious in countries like Greece, for example, where, while the policy of a 'strong' drachma constituted the cornerstone of the convergence policy of the country's governments towards the European Economic and Monetary Union, the pressure exercised by foreign banks and foreign capital movements has recently resulted in the abandonment of this policy and in the drachma's devaluation. The situation is far more critical for the other Balkan countries, where the economy is far from meeting even the elementary needs of their populations: the transition to a stable and modern financial system demands conditions that are unattainable without the contribution of foreign capital.[3] However, the latter does not seem very willing to assume such a role unless the Balkan governments adopt certain measures, which cannot easily be implemented owing to the domestic political situation.

This volume attempts to follow the role of western, and especially West-European, capital in the constitution of modern banking systems in Balkan countries and in the economic development of these countries. Its contents, which cover a wide range of subjects and sometimes express diverging opinions, can be seen to raise five kinds of issue, namely:

1. The extent to which West-European capital has penetrated the different Balkan countries.
2. The strategic choices of this capital regarding the banking sector.
3. The new techniques and ideas introduced or imposed by West-European banks.
4. The existence of an inter-Balkan integration facilitated by the penetration of West-European capital and the creation of inter-Balkan financial networks.
5. The impact of West-European banking on the economic development of the area.

The papers published here offer answers to almost all the questions and certainly raise new issues for discussion. Nevertheless, none of the contributions explicitly approaches a problem raised by the title of the volume, although all of them seem to deal with it with an astonishing conformity; the concept of modern banking is considered by all contributors as self-evident and thus requiring no definition or clarification.

There is no need to insist on this question. I only wish to point out that none of the papers deals with the pre-1860 period and I believe this is no coincidence. Modern banking in the Balkans emerged during the last decades of the nineteenth century and it has to be related to the increasing internationalization of the Balkan economies, one aspect of which is the increasing presence of West-European capital.[4]

I believe that an important turning point for the Balkan economies was the year 1863, when the Ottoman Imperial Bank was created by a group of English bankers to play the role of a bank of issue, but also to fulfill a key role in the penetration of West-European capital in the fertile and still unexploited territories of the Ottomans, which then included a great part of the Balkans.[5] As by then the financing of the imperial needs was in the hands of the Greek, Armenian and Jewish bankers of Istanbul[6] who, using West-European capital, realized high profits from the endless need of the Ottoman government for funds, the establishment of the Ottoman Imperial Bank marked the first efforts towards some kind of rationalization of the financial and monetary system. Although, in the short term, the Ottoman Imperial Bank's success in achieving this goal is doubtful, it nevertheless succeeded by its presence to introduce some rules of the game and if not to eliminate certainly to control, to a certain degree, the role of local bankers in Ottoman finances. In addition, new financial techniques, accompanying the public borrowing and the financing of public works, especially railroads, were introduced which very soon spread to all the Balkan states.[7]

The neutralization of the Black Sea and the internationalization of the Danube after the Treaty of Paris (1856) also contributed to the opening of the Balkan peninsula to West-European interests and began to render its markets attractive. From this point onwards changes in the banking reality of almost all the Balkan countries become more and more important and this is why I think we should keep the year 1863 as the starting point of our investigations. Although the same changes in some other Balkan areas came much later and at a slower pace than in the Ottoman Empire it seems that these changes were heavily dependent on the management of the public debt.[8]

However, if we take the 1860s as the upper limit of our chronological horizon, we should also add that the turning point of the banking sectors of the different Balkan countries, with the emergence of the 'new bank', comes later. This bank, with an extended branch network which tried to attract national savings and make them productive, made its appearance in the Greek case, for example, only in the last years of the nineteenth century and became an important factor in the economic life of the country, under the tutelage of French capital, in the first decades of the twentieth century.[9] And as far as I can judge from the studies published in this volume, this holds for the other Balkan countries too, national differences considered, of course.

By proposing a kind of periodization, I do not mean that we should deal with the Balkans as an entity. On the contrary, I strongly believe that such an entity has never existed and I doubt whether it will now. In his contribution (Chapter 11), Professor Lampe underlines the fact that 'Neither of two Yugoslavias formed during the twentieth century was able to integrate its previously disparate regions into a single, modern economy.'[10] If this holds for the separate countries, what could we say of the whole Peninsula? And what was the role played by banks and foreign capital? The Greek experience of the early twentieth century shows that the Greek banks, and especially the 'enfant gâté' of the French Haute Banque, the Bank of Athens, avoided investments in Greece and oriented themselves towards the Middle East, where the possibilities for high profits were greater than in Greece and the other Balkan countries.[10]

Of course, no one could deny the existence of a division of labour, even in an elementary form, in the Balkan regions occupied by the Ottoman Empire. But this reality breaks down, first with the creation of the Balkan national states and then with the penetration of West-European capital which disorganized the economies and, profiting from this, incorporated different areas into its orbit to various degrees. Professor Jacques Thobie has demonstrated in a way that leaves little margin for doubt the political and economic fragmentation caused by foreign capital in the Ottoman Empire in the early twentieth century.[11]

Some thirty years ago, Professor Ljuben Berov impressively mapped out all the intersecting West-European banking networks in the

Balkans.[12] This mapping merely showed, in my opinion, the sophisticated business methods used by the West-European bankers to make the Balkan economies dependent on western economies, not the existence of an inter-Balkan economic space, which could support the idea of elementary economic integration among the national economies of the area. On the contrary, the East-Mediterranean area, as Professor Hadziiossif demonstrates convincingly in his contribution (Chapter 9), formed a rather unified economic space with free movement of people and capital; however, this was so because the area was part of the Ottoman Empire.

The Balkans as an economic entity has never existed, unless during the period of Ottoman domination. Even the use of the word Balkans, with its pejorative connotations, appears with the penetration of West-European capital; the subsequent emergence of this world on the European horizon was treated sometimes with sympathy, sometimes with curiosity and most of the time with arrogance and contempt. Perhaps today, when the term Balkans carries, once more, the same connotations as in the early twentieth century, we could for the first time see some attempts towards an increasing economic cohesion in the Balkans. This view is built upon the increasing penetration of Greek banking and other enterprises in contiguous Balkan countries as well as on the timid intentions declared by some governments of the area. But the political rivalries, so intense in the area, convince me that all these efforts and good intentions cannot lead to the creation of a common Balkan destiny.

If it is true – as Ludwig von Mises, cited by Professor Lampe, states – that the socialist states of the Balkan peninsula broke down because of their inability to allocate capital rationally,[13] then it is just as true that none of the contemporary Balkan economies, whatever name we wish to give them, can allocate resources rationally either. The extreme example of Albania underlines this reality.[14] Besides, it would be a great mistake to ignore the fact that there is no pure sphere called economy, separated by a live-wire fence from the domain of politics. The history of the Balkans has made this sufficiently clear for anyone to argue that the foreign financing of the national economies was more a matter of bargaining between banks and ministries of foreign affairs than a purely economic transaction. H. Feis, a pioneer in the study of the political dimensions of European foreign investments, used to say of railway building in the Balkans: 'in such a world even the laying of a mile of track is an action disputed in a dozen Foreign Offices'.[15]

No doubt the relations between banks and ministries of foreign affairs were never simple and uniform, thus offering space for manoeuvre for national governments whenever competition between West-European states was revealed.[16] But as we approach the First World War these possibilities decrease and raising a loan in the international capital market becomes more and more a matter of foreign policy. Almost all the papers in this volume converge in emphasizing the importance of the political factor in foreign capital's penetration in the Balkan countries; Dr G. Kronenbitter's contribution (Chapter 10) in particular is invaluable in underlining this political-financial aspect of Balkan history in all its complexity.[17]

If we cannot find an economic entity called the Balkans, we should not forget that the economies of the Peninsula do have features in common. All of them are latecomers to economic development and they share common experiences. And if the direct presence of West-European banks varies according to the economy, their indirect presence is almost the same everywhere. The public debt and its administration for unproductive purposes constitutes a common element in their histories, in addition to the state bankruptcies, formal or informal, which, in turn, fostered the contempt of West Europeans for the people living in this part of Europe. Behind the public borrowing we can see the West-European banks and the high interest rates of public loans, which were 4 and 5 per cent higher than those of public loans in the so-called developed countries.[18] And a major part of these important sums was directed toward West-European industries for military orders, especially in the years which preceded the First World War.[19]

The capital exported by West-European countries to the Balkans before the First World War is estimated at 1 250 million dollars, a far from negligible sum.[20] We know, however, that the economic development of the Balkan countries did not profit proportionally to the possibilities offered by the influx of such a sum. What happened is very accurately described by H. Feis when he wrote of the public debt of Serbia: 'Any independent state can buy enough rope to hang itself, if it will pay enough.'[21] Only Romania among the pre-war Balkan countries avoided insolvency and foreign financial supervision, probably because of its oil industry which offered the possibility for a faster development and a more equilibrated foreign balance. All the other countries were forced, though in different ways and through different means, to submit to the limitation of their sovereignty by some kind of international financial control: the Ottoman Empire in 1881, Greece in 1893, Serbia in 1896 and Bulgaria in 1902.

Modern banking in the Balkan countries, with the possible exception of Romania, undoubtedly emerged through the management of their public debt; it is thus undeniable that the so-called modernization of the banking sector in the Balkans owes a lot to West-European capital. Professor Edhem Eldem's contribution (Chapter 3) supports this view for the Ottoman Empire and the role played in it by the Ottoman Imperial Bank and Dr A. Kostov (Chapter 4) is of the same opinion for the Bulgarian banking system. We could add the example of the inter-war period when the re-incorporation of Bulgaria, Greece, Romania and Yugoslavia in the international capital markets required them to reorganize their central banks according to contemporary central banking standards defined by the experts of the Financial Committee of the League of Nations and representatives of the West-European central banks.[22] In my opinion, however, all these examples underscore the fact that modernization is not an inherent element of Balkan societies and economies: it occurs under pressure from the international environment and cannot be considered identical to economic development. M. Palairet's recent book on the economic development of some Balkan countries during the nineteenth century emphasizes the economic stagnation observed during the institutional transformation of these countries following West-European standards.[23]

But if we agree, with some reservations of course, on the modernizing role of West-European capital, we should immediately add that the cost of this modernization was extremely high and for this reason weighed heavily on the economic development of the area. This is not a moral issue but one of the contradictions common to all the states of the Balkan peninsula, a contradiction that has now become evident.

If the activity of West–European banking in the financing of public debt is well known and more or less uniform for all Balkan countries, its capacity to penetrate Balkan economies directly, that is by creating branches or subsidiaries, varied according to the resistance and the power of the domestic financial and social structures. Christian Bichi's contribution (Chapter 2) emphasizes this point by presenting the social conflicts aroused by the competition between foreign and domestic investors for the creation of a bank of issue in nineteenth-century Romania. And the strategies of the West-European banks were adapted to these realities. In some cases, the weight of the West-European banks in a country's banking sector was important as in the cases of Romania and the Ottoman Empire. In other cases it was, at least in terms of percentages, minor, as in Greece. In the latter, the appearance of the Banque de l'Union Parisienne was realized only in a period when the National Bank of Greece's position was weak, because of the employment of the major part of its assets in public loans, which thus left space for the activities of other banking institutions.[24] And, of course, the Greek economy held no particular interest for French capital. However, a Greek bank was always a very efficient tool for West-European penetration into areas inhabited by orthodox populations such as the Middle East and the Ottoman Empire. We could make the same observation concerning the attitude of the German banks and the non-Muslim bankers of the Ottoman Empire in order to underscore the extreme adaptability of the West-European banks in their efforts to conquer the market.

This adaptability is extremely well described by Professor Giannitsis in his paper on the changing nature of the internationalization of the postwar Greek financial system (Chapter 8). In some cases the penetration of foreign banks in the Balkan economies met with strong resistance, and unpredictable results: the efforts of the foreign banks, first American then West European, to establish branches in Greece in the 1960s were very badly received by the Greek banks. The final result of the negotiations between domestic and foreign banks and governments was the near elimination of competition between the two groups of banks, with the foreign banks working in conditions of high profitability offering their services to the foreign enterprises working in Greece, and the domestic banks keeping their positions in the domestic market more or less unchallenged and continuing to profit from their high oligopolistic structure.[25]

In contrast to these different forms which the West-European banks adopted in order to establish themselves in South-east Europe, their attitudes towards direct investments were uniform. According to some estimates, the West-European capital invested in Serbian industry before the First World War did not exceed 3–5 per cent of government loans. Of this low percentage, 5–6 million dollars were invested in copper and iron-ore mines and in the logging of chemical industries. In Bulgaria and Greece the situation was much the same, except that there were no profitable mines to invest in; in the Ottoman Empire at the end of 1913 direct investments in industry represented £3 959 000 while the total presence of foreign capital is estimated at some £216 505 000.[26] Romania was the sole exception because of its oil industry which was very attractive to foreign investors. It seems that pre-war Romania profited from this advantage to achieve a more rapid industrialization than that of the other Balkan countries.[27] The situation during the 1920s seemed to have changed, as Table 1 shows us, but not in ways that would indicate any particular interest of West-European capital in investing in the industrial sectors of the Balkan countries.

In all these cases, West-European banks or their domestic agents showed a natural preference for monopolistic situations which could guarantee them high profits and low risks. An example of this attitude was the financing of the railways. The impact of railways on national economies was unexpected. Railway construction was quite independent of the economies' overall level of development: this is clear for the Greek and Ottoman/Turkish cases, but it is true also for Serbia and

Table 0.1 Distribution of foreign capital in the Balkan countries according to occupation, late 1920s (percentage)

Country	Public finances	Trade	Banking	Insurances	Public works	Industry	Other
Yugoslavia	67.7	3.3	6.4	0.1	1.9	20.2	0.4
Romania	74.6	0.8	1.8	0.3	0.8	22.1	0.2
Bulgaria	82.6	2.0	2.8	0.1	—	12.2	0.3
Greece	70.7	7.7	7.1	—	7.3	3.5	3.5
Turkey	54.0	3.0	7.2	4.0	23.0	5.0	3.8

Source: L. Berov, 'Le capital financier occidental et les pays Balkaniques pendant les années vingt', *Études balkaniques*, 2–3, 1965, p. 142.

Bulgaria whose core railway system was the famous Berlin–Bagdad line built to support the German Drang nach Osten.[28]

The Balkan economies today face up to almost the same kinds of problem, in a far more difficult context than before the First World War: I am not among the optimists and I do not believe that the presence of West-European banks, even in the case of Greece which has the advantage of belonging to the European Union, ensures the achievement of the economic targets of every country. Especially in periods of crisis, their presence tends to be very disturbing for the maintenance of the sensitive equilibrium of balances of payments. The Greek example of the last years and the failure of the strong drachma policy is indicative. Fortunately, most of us are historians and we are not under any obligation to propose economic policy measures. But I believe that everybody would agree, and all the contributions indicate it in their own ways, that the relation of West-European capital and banking with the Balkan countries has been extremely ambiguous. Although its presence was identified with periods of economic development, it is at the same time very doubtful whether West-European capital supported or obstructed such development.

Notes

1. M. Todorova, *Imagining the Balkans*, New York and Oxford: Oxford University Press, 1997, p. 3.
2. J.R. Lampe and M.R. Jackson, *Balkan Economic History, 1550–1950. From Imperial Borderlands to Developing Nations*, Bloomington, Ind.: Indiana University Press, 1982, pp. 159 ff.
3. R.W. Anderson and Ch. Kegel, *Transition Banking. Financial Develop-*

ment of Central and Eastern Europe, Oxford: Clarendon Press, 1998, pp. 1–30.

4. I.T. Berendt and G. Ranki, *The European Periphery and Industrialization, 1780–1914*, Cambridge: Cambridge University Press, 1982, p. 101. The same phenomenon can be seen in the major changes observed during the same period in West-European banking structures, R. Cameron, *La France et le développement économique de l'Europe, 1800–1914*, Paris: Seuil, 1971 (1st American edition 1961); D. Landes, 'Vieille banque et banque nouvelle: La Révolution Financière du dix-neuvième siècle', *Revue d'Histoire Moderne et Contemporaine*, 3, 1956, pp. 204–22.
5. On the Ottoman Imperial Bank see the most recent publication of A. Autheman, *La Banque Impériale Ottomane*, Paris, 1996.
6. On the role played by Greek bankers of Istanbul and the influence of the Ottoman Imperial Bank on their activities see H.A. Exertzoglou, 'Greek banking in Constantinople, 1850–1881', thesis submitted for a Ph.D. degree, King's College, London University, 1986.
7. Cameron, op. cit., pp. 169–71.
8. For reasons of accuracy we should add that the first joint-stock bank was established in the Ionian islands, then under British protectorate, in 1839. Two years later the National Bank of Greece was created to assume the role of a bank of issue for the Greek Kingdom. The Ionian Bank was a purely English bank and part of the share capital of the National Bank of Greece belonged to West-European investors, although very soon, when the fashion of philhellenism was extinguished, they pulled out of participation in the bank.
9. K. Kostis, V. Tsokopoulos, *The Banks in Greece, 1898–1928*, Athens, 1988, pp. 42–51 (in Greek).
10. The main reason for the collaboration between the Bank of Athens and the Banque de l'Union Parisienne was, according to the French Ambassador in Athens, the high yields of the Egyptian stock market, while the interest for doing business in Greece was very limited, see Kostis and Tsokopoulos, op. cit., p.135. See also the remarks made by J. Bouvier, *Un siècle de banque française*, Paris: Hachette, 1973, pp. 235–6.
11. J. Thobie, *Intérêts et impérialisme français dans l'Empire Ottoman (1895–1914)*, Paris 1977, pp. 704ff.
12. L. Berov, 'Le capital financier occidental et les pays Balkaniques pendant les années vingt', *Etudes balkaniques*, 2–3, 1965, pp.139–69.
13. J.R. Lampe, p. 186, this volume.
14. The first foreign banks, for example, which hastened to establish branches in Albania after the collapse of the communist regime were suspected of money laundering as well as those that arrived in the country later, see M. Vickers and J. Pettifer, *Albania. From Anarchy to a Balkan Identity*, London: Hurst and Co., 1997, p. 240. The same phenomenon is also observed in other countries.
15. H. Feis, *Europe. The World's Banker 1870–1914. An Account of European Foreign Investment and the Connection of World Finance with Diplomacy before the War*, New York and London, 1930, p. 293.
16. R. Poidevin, 'Les intérêts financiers français et allemands en Serbie de 1895 à 1914', *Revue historique*, 232, July–September 1964, pp. 49–66.
17. See also the contribution of A. Kostov, Chapter 4 in this volume.
18. See, for example, Kostov, op. cit.

19. According to one estimate, from 1879 to 1893 when Greece went bankrupt, the Greek state had borrowed 755 million francs which were approximately spent in the following way: 389 million for servicing the foreign debt, 121.7 million to pay off past debts, 100 million for war furnitures, 120 million for public works and 25 million for commissions, currency exchange differences, etc., see D. Georgiadès, *La Grèce économique et financière en 1893*, Paris, 1893.
20. Berendt and Ranki, op. cit., pp. 82–3.
21. Feis, op. cit., p. 263.
22. C. Evelpidis, *Les Etats Balkaniques. Etude comparée politique, sociale, économique et financière*, Paris, 1930, pp. 346–7 and A. Plessis and O. Feiertag, Chapter 13 in this volume. On the problem of modernization see also G. Pagoulatos, Chapter 6 in this volume.
23. M. Palairet, *The Balkan Economies c.1800–1914. Evolution without Development*, Cambridge: Cambridge University Press, 1997.
24. Kostis and Tsokopoulos, op. cit., pp. 37ff.
25. K. Kostis, *Collaboration and Competition. The 70 Years of the Hellenic Bank Association*, Athens, 1997, pp. 99ff. (in Greek).
26. S. Pamuk, *The Ottoman Empire and European Capitalism, 1820–1913. Trade, Investment and Production*, Cambridge: Cambridge University Press, 1987, p. 66.
27. Berendt and Ranki, op. cit.
28. L. Papagiannakis, *The Greek Railways (1882–1910). Geopolitical, Economic and Social Dimensions*, Athens, 1982 (in Greek); B.C. Gounaris, *Steam over Macedonia, 1870–1912. Socio-economic Change and the Railway Factor*, East European Monographs, New York: Columbia University Press, 1993; D. Quataert, 'The age of reforms, 1812–1914', in H. İnalcık and D. Quataert, *An Economic and Social History of the Ottoman Empire, 1300–1914*, Cambridge: Cambridge University Press, 1994, pp. 804–15; I.T. Berendt and G. Ranki, *Economic Development in East-Central Europe in the 19th and 20th Centuries*, New York and London: Columbia University Press, 1974, pp. 75–8.

PART I
National Experiences and West-European Capital

CHAPTER ONE

Foreign Capital in the Bulgarian Banking System, 1878–1944–1997

Ljuben Berov

Before the First World War

The first steps taken by foreign capital to penetrate the credit relations of some Bulgarian regions took place on the eve of Bulgarian liberation from Turkish domination. The first bank actually to achieve this penetration was the Ottoman Bank. This bank, created by English-French capital, apart from its central office in Istanbul, also founded a branch in Plovdiv, a town in South Bulgaria, at the beginning of the 1870s. It was a branch operating with a maximum of 1–200 000 French francs, which at first financed the export trade in this region. From 1882 onwards it also began practising mortgage credit. After a temporary lull in its activities (1885–89), the Ottoman Bank created four new branches and two 'correspondents' offices', which usually had at their disposition 10–15 million francs, a capital mainly originating from their own resources. The activity of these branches by the end of the 1880s outmatched the scale of operations of the Bulgarian National Bank.[1] This development though did not last long, since during 1895–96 the Ottoman Bank after speculation with Turkish and South-African securities suffered great losses and therefore oriented itself towards liquidation, which was completed in 1899. That was, for Bulgaria, the first edifying example of a bank that collapsed because it deviated from its basic functions of financing and reimbursing, and occupied itself with speculation with securities.

Shortly after the founding of the first branch of the Ottoman Bank, many attempts were made to create banks with foreign capital in Bulgaria. Table 1.1 shows the attempts made in the years 1878–95.

These, though, were mere attempts. The first successful step, apart from the one by the Ottoman Bank, was taken in 1901 in Sofia, and was the founding of the Targovska banka (Commercial Bank) with Austro-Hungarian capital. Three branches were also founded in the country. In December 1905 the bank was renamed Banque Générale de Bulgarie, now having established five branches in the country, and possessing a share capital of only 2 million golden leva or golden francs. This capital was raised to 5 million leva in 1905.

Table 1.1 Attempts made to create banks with foreign capital in Bulgaria, 1878–95

Year	Capital
1878	Austrian
1880	German
1881	Banque de Paris et de Pays-Bas
1884	French and Russian
1889	French
1891	Austrian
1892	English, German and Russian
1895	Russian

A similar case was the founding of the Kreditna banka (Credit Bank) in Sofia, with German capital which mainly originated from shareholders of Diskonto Gesellschaft and the Bleichröder banking house. This German capital amounted initially to 3 million golden leva. Two branches were also established in the towns of Varna and Rousse.

The Balkanska banka (Balkan Bank) appeared in Sofia at the beginning of 1906, and also founded seven branches and agencies around the country. Its capital initially amounted to 3 million Bulgarian leva and was raised to 6 million leva during 1911. Its shareholders were mainly the Wiener Bankverein, the Crédit Anversois and the Banque de l'Union Parisienne.

The interest rate in Bulgaria at the time was two to three times higher than the interest rate in Western Europe. During that period the three large commercial banks with foreign capital in Sofia were able to profit from large credits granted by their central offices in Paris, Vienna, Berlin, Anvers, and so on. These credits surpassed by two to three times the amount of their own capital. Also, during 1911, three banks with a paid capital plus reserves of 15 million golden leva had in their disposal 52 million leva from local deposits and foreign credits. They accounted for a profit of 1.29 million francs, and distributed annual dividends of 5–8.5 per cent.

It should be mentioned here that up to 1912, the leva as the Bulgarian national currency, which contained 0.29g of gold, belonged to the Latin Monetary Union and was completely equal to the French golden franc which was the basic currency in Europe at the time. According to its actual purchasing power in 1911, the Bulgarian leva (or the French franc), equalled approximately 1.7 of today's US dollars.

Several specialized banks were also founded in Bulgaria during a six-year period (1905–11), all of which were mainly controlled by foreign capital. Among them, the following should be mentioned:

1. The Bulgarian Lottery Bank, with a French capital of 3 million francs.
2. The Banque Commerciale et Financière des Balkans, with a capital of 3 million francs, mainly French and Russian plus a small Bulgarian contribution.
3. Bulgarska Ipotekarna banka, with an Austro-Hungarian capital of 5 million francs.
4. Generalna Ipotekarna banka na Tsartsvo (Banque Générale Hypothécaire du Royaume de Bulgarie), with French, Hungarian, German and Belgian capital of 3 million francs.
5. The two banks above merged in January 1912, thus forming the Crédit Foncier Bulgare which, apart from a capital of 20 million francs, comprised also Austrian and Russian capital.

As a result, three commercial and three specialized banks functioned in Bulgaria by mid-1912, possessing a foreign capital amounting to 28.5 million francs including reserves. Thus, the foreign capital surpassed the Bulgarian capital, which amounted, by this year, to 23 million francs.

Later, on the eve of the Balkan Wars and during the years following the First World War, banks with foreign capital in Bulgaria played an important role in financing the Bulgarian export trade, especially exports of grain. More specifically, these banks realized, at the time, almost half of the foreign currency sales and financed half of the Bulgarian trade. Large banks also pioneered the creation, already very common in Western Europe, of subsidiary enterprises and financial groups.

Efforts were made to facilitate foreign capital to penetrate the Bulgarian National Bank, which was created in 1879 as the country's state central bank. The first attempt was made by the Russian entrepreneurs Ginsburg and Poljakov with the official support of Russian diplomacy in 1879–80, but was unsuccessful. In 1882, after a suggestion made by foreign bankers, a draft concerning the new status of the Bulgarian National Bank was elaborated along with a proposal to reorganize the bank as a joint-stock company. In order to attract foreign capital, 66 per cent of this bank's shares had to be sold in public subscription. The project could not be realized because it received a negative response from the public as people believed that the Bulgarian National Bank should remain a state property. In 1884 the project was altered by proposals from other Austrian banks, but was once again rejected by the government. A similar attempt was made in September 1899, only this time help was offered by the directors of a group which, at the time, conceded a foreign loan to Bulgaria.

Other, unsuccessful efforts also took place during the 1880s to create a regional bank with foreign capital in the Bulgarian region of Eastern Roumelia, which at first was autonomous. Other attempts were made, aimed at creating an agricultural bank with foreign capitals, which would restructure already existing semi-cooperative financing funds in the countryside. These attempts, also unsuccessful, both occurred during the same period (1880–1883), and shortly after, in 1892.

During the war period, which consisted of the Balkan Wars (October 1912 to May 1913) and the First World War, which followed shortly after (July 1914 to November 1918), all banking activities of banks controlled by foreign capital were frozen. The only banks active were a branch of the Deutsche Bank, the Credit Bank and partially the 'Balkan Bank', all of which had their central offices in Sofia. These banks realized very limited operations, which concerned some military deliveries from Germany and Austro-Hungary to Bulgaria, and employed few employees. The General Bank was closed.

The 1920s

The interwar period, especially until November 1929, proved to be very controversial as regards development of foreign investors' intentions in Bulgaria,, both generally, and particularly in the banking sector. The first half of this period was quite an optimistic stage for foreign investments in Bulgaria. Afterwards came several years (1930–32) of fear and hesitations caused by Hitler's assumption of power, which created political uncertainty in Europe and resulted in pressure towards dictatorship in other countries, and the world economic crisis. During the following years, from 1932–33 till the Second World War, the prevailing part of foreign banking capital marked a quick retreat from Bulgaria. The final result of all these changes during the interwar period cannot be easily summarized, since many banks with foreign capital appeared suddenly on the market and just as quickly disappeared after some years.

Such optimistic behaviour of many foreign investors towards Bulgaria was apparent as early as the first years following the end of the First World War. It was apparent despite both political pressures attempted by left political forces in 1919, and the consolidation of Alexander Stambolyiski's regime as a government of the quasi-left, but also very controversial, Bulgarian Agrarian Union during 1920–23.

During these years, several more important new banks with foreign capital appeared in Sofia, the most influential of which was the

Italian-Bulgarian Commercial Bank. Its capital mainly originated in the Banca Commerciale di Milano and the Assiccurazioni Generali.[2] In a brief period of three years following 1919, this bank created a new financial group of ten related commercial and industrial companies. In 1923 it reached first place in the Bulgarian private banking system with granted credits of 797 million leva.

Apart from Italian capital, Czechoslovakian capital, partially in combination with English, was also active, thus creating the Prague Credit Bank. The first steps to form this bank were taken during 1914; in 1920 the bank was reorganized and later renamed English-Prague Credit Bank, which created a financial group of 11 industrial enterprises.

French capital, too, penetrated the Bulgarian banking system in 1917, creating the Franco-Bulgarian Bank for International Trade in Sofia. Formally founded in 1917, but reorganized in 1920, it was created in order to finance the export of Bulgarian tobacco, and was controlled by a mainly French capital that represented initially 50 per cent and later on 66 per cent of its share capital. It originated from the following second-class French banks:

1. The Crédit Français, in Paris.
2. The Caisse Commerciale et Industrielle de Paris in Paris.
3. The Crédit Foncier du Brésil et de l'Amérique du Sud in Paris.
4. The Banka Franco-Romana in Bucharest.

This bank also formed in 1921–22 a financial group of six commercial and industrial enterprises, with the United Tobacco Mills in Plovdiv at their head. This group played an important role in the creation of the most powerful postwar cartel in Bulgaria, the Tobacco Cartel.

Another attempt made by French capital, in cooperation with Belgian capital, resulted in the foundation of the French-Belgian Limited Joint-Stock Company in 1920. Its capital amounted to 20 million leva, 60 per cent of which came from the Crédit Foncier d'Algérie et de Tunisie in Paris, 35 per cent from the Banque Belge pour l'Etranger in Bruxelles and, finally, 5 per cent from the participation of Angel Kujumdgiiski, exercising a strong influence in the Jewish circles, as a Bulgarian banker. This bank had, by 1921, formed a financial group of nine industrial and commercial enterprises, and in 1923 was transformed to a joint-stock company, named French-Belgian Bank, in Sofia.

Further activity in the establishment of new banks controlled by foreign capital was demonstrated by several smaller foreign investors. This activity resulted in the formation of the following small banks:

1. The Bulgarian-American Bank in Sofia, with a capital of 3 million leva in 1922. It was formally created in 1911 and reorganized in 1920.
2. The Hungarian-Bulgarian Bank in Sofia, with a mainly Hungarian capital of 5 million leva in 1922. It was founded in 1921 and reorganized in 1922.
3. The Lozarska banka in Sofia (Winegrowers' Bank). This was a small bank with mainly Bulgarian and only a small percentage of English capital formed in 1922.
4. The Austrian-Bulgarian Credit Bank in Sofia. The nominal capital amounted to 20 million leva, but only 7.5 million was actually paid, originating partially from Austria and the USA.

None of these small banks had branches in the country, in contrast to the aforementioned large banks with foreign capital.[3] These four small banks lasted no longer than the second half of the 1920s and were of no importance to the country's banking system.

During the same period, the aforementioned large banks with foreign capital quickly revived and surpassed the scale of their pre-war activities.

The Balkan Bank, for instance, extended its local network of branches from four to nine branches and augmented its deposits from 11 million leva in 1911 to 337 million leva in 1922. French financial participation had increased too. The actual value of deposits in 1922 does not, indeed, compensate for the devaluation of the Bulgarian currency during 1921–22, but the ratio between the capital and the deposits was 1 : 3 in 1911, and reached 1 : 16 in 1922. That was definitely a success. Another successful step taken by the same bank was the creation of a large, considering the Bulgarian scale, financial group of 25 related industrial, commercial and insurance companies.

The General Bank in Sofia acted similarly, creating a financial group of 19 industrial, commercial, transport and insurance companies, but with a lower level of internal discipline.

The Credit Bank in Sofia, which was controlled by German capital, also revived after the war, but not completely, since Germany was defeated in the war. Up to 1922, it had organized a financial group of ten related enterprises, but in 1923 its leaders decided to cease further participation in new related companies.

Thus the influence of foreign capital in the Bulgarian banking system during the period between the first years following the end of the war and 1923 had considerably increased, as compared to the pre-war years. The actual sum (in golden francs) and the percentage of foreign capital was twice as large in 1923 as in 1911. This influx of foreign capital in Bulgarian banks was due to increasing differences between the higher level of interest rates in Bulgaria and their low level in Western Europe, and was observed after the rapid depreciation of the Bulgarian currency. Of course, these higher interest rates also entailed higher credit risk in a country where political problems had to be resolved by a military *coup d'état* and a bloody uprising in September 1923.

One more result of foreign capital penetration in the country's economy was that: after the creation of financial groups, either small or larger, around the nucleus of pre-war or postwar foreign capital-owned banks, finally seven financial groups functioned in Bulgaria under the predominance of foreign capital. Each group included 6–25 related[4] enterprises or subsidiary companies. Most of the latter were industrial companies, since despite the pressure applied during the postwar period to almost all developed countries by the generally destructive economic crisis, a specific conjuncture in Bulgaria during 1920–23 created the prerequisites for an intensive increase in national industrial production. Although there was an orientation towards industrial enterprises, there was no actual strategy elaborated by foreign capital concerning the country's economic future. It was simply a result of the banks' limited and cautious financing during these years, since all banks in Bulgaria had to avoid paper money, due to the continuing postwar depreciation of the national currency.

These seven financial groups under the control of banks with foreign capital included 90 middle-sized industrial and commercial enterprises, which represented about 40 per cent[5] of the country's private industrial production and 55–60 per cent of the country's exports. Some branches[6] of Bulgarian industry were almost completely controlled by these financial groups.

Financial groups with Bulgarian capital appeared, too:

1. The group associated with the Bulgarian Bank, consisting of 35 related companies.
2. A smaller group associated with the Bulgarian Commercial Bank in Sofia and Russe, with 15 related companies.
3. A similarly smaller group associated with the Girdap Bank in Russe, with five related companies.

Most of the companies controlled by these financial groups, though, were of secondary importance. The organizational ties in these financial groups were looser in comparison to the groups associated with banks with foreign capital.

Thus, foreign capital had the opportunity to rule over a great part of the country's economy, even though the ties between the industrial or commercial enterprises controlled by these groups and the seven aforementioned large banks were not so firm and direct. Not only was this an opportunity to manage either directly or indirectly the existing important enterprises, but these groups also had power over the economic strategy of the country by taking decisions such as creating or enlarging large enterprises or refusing finance to a certain branch. The decentralization of that power in seven financial groups was quite fortunate for the country, since if it were to be centralized it would illegally replace the country's government. The foreign investors' and the country's interests could, of course, be concordant, but they could also be contradictory.

The creation of financial groups was introduced as a new organizational form of higher level management of part of the pre-existing large-scale national capital. During the 1920s it was a privilege of the aforementioned large foreign capital banks. These new management forms, though, were just in an early stage, since either the control of a certain bank over all the related companies in its financial group was not absolute, or the group composition was not very stable because some groups received credits from two competing banks, or even because the bank managers were neither theoretically nor practically qualified, etc. But this situation was inevitable in the case of a relatively new national capitalistic system such as that in Bulgaria.

After the summer of 1923 inflation in Bulgaria continued to increase, but already at a slower pace, especially after 1926. Both the interest rates in Bulgaria and the gap between them and the West-European rates began to decrease. During the second half of the 1920s the influx of western capital continued, however at a lesser rate and without establishing new commercial or specialized foreign capital banks.

The unique exception was the creation of the partially state-owned Mortgage Bank in Sofia in 1928. It was an exception because it was not a completely specialized bank. It united the rest of the unrealized assets of some pre-war foreign capital banks in Sofia, which were already liquidated, along with the support of certain new capital. It was founded on concession principles with a paid capital of just 3.3 million Swiss francs. Of this capital, 60 per cent originated in the participation of the banks that had issued the Bulgarian state loans of 1926–28, whereas the remaining 40 per cent came from the participation of the state, the Bulgarian Agrarian Bank and other Bulgarian banks and insurance companies. After three years, the bank's resources doubled due to a loan contracted abroad with the guarantee of the state. The foreign capital was supplied by Blair & Co. in New York, Lazard Brothers in London, the Banque de l'Union Parisienne in Paris and the Banque Belge pour l'Etranger in Brussels, along with the lesser participation of the Schweizerische Bankgesellschäft in Zürich, the Amsterdamsche Bank in Amsterdam, and so on.

Another case that was, in part, an exception during the same period was the participation of French capital from the Banque de Paris et des Pays-Bas in the pre-war large bank named Bulgarska Targovska Banka in Sofia (Bulgarian Commercial Bank), which, till 1926, possessed only Bulgarian capital, to the extent of 25 per cent of Bulgarska's share capital. This French bank also took part as a shareholder in two basic subsidiary enterprises under the control of the Bulgarian Commercial Bank and more specifically the Badashte coal mine and the Adree power station with 18 and 20 million leva respectively.

A certain regrouping during the same period (the second half of the 1920s) of already existing foreign capital banks should also be mentioned. In 1926 two banks, the Balkan Bank and the French-Belgian Bank, merged under the name of Balkan Bank in Sofia. The foreign capital structure engaged by this consolidated bank remained as it was before the merger. Another similar 'one-coloured' case was the unification of the Credit Bank in Sofia with the branch of Deutsche Bank in Sofia, in mid-1929. Yet another merger occurred at the very beginning of the world economic crisis. After a decrease in French capital participation in the French-Bulgarian Bank for International Trade, the bank decided, in autumn 1929, to merge with the Bulgarian Bank in Sofia, which was controlled only by Bulgarian capital. This merger was realized at the beginning of 1930, along with the incorporation of other smaller Bulgarian banks under the name Saedineni Bulgarski Banki (United Bulgarian Banks). The reasons for the decrease of French capital influence were not political, but originated in the significant losses this capital had suffered in the tobacco trade.

The influence exercised by foreign banks through their financial groups increased during the second half of the 1920s. This is shown by the fact that the sum of all account 'Participations' in seven large foreign capital banks in Sofia in 1929–31 had tripled in comparison to 1924. This increase also occurred because the amount of individual old joint-stock companies' capital was belatedly re-evaluated after the inflation was curbed from 1924–26. Such expansion, though, was not characteristic of all financial groups with foreign capital. The most active financial group at the time was the group associated with the Italian-Bulgarian Commercial Bank. It almost doubled, partially at the expense of enterprises belonging before 1925 to other financial groups, thus occupying in 1927–28 second place in the similar group ranking. The group directed by the French-Belgian Bank in Sofia also expanded, almost as greatly as the previous one, controlling additionally 13 new enterprises. As for certain other financial groups, the situation was as follows:

1. The expansion of the financial group controlled by the Credit Bank in Sofia and the General Bank in Sofia was not as extensive as the previous ones.
2. The financial group managed by the French-Bulgarian Bank for International Trade in Sofia experienced a small development.
3. The group directed by the Prague Bank in Sofia did not experience any changes.

During the same period changes also occurred in the nationality of the foreign capital engaged in the Bulgarian banking system, an example of which are the changes in the General Bank in Sofia. This bank was initially founded before the First World War, with as main shareholders the Banque de Paris et des Pays-Bas in Paris, with 58 per cent of the capital, the Banque Hongroise de Pest in Budapest, with 29 per cent of the capital, and the Österreichische Bodencreditanstalt in Vienna. Both the second and the third shareholders were only formally Hungarian and Austrian. The second one, after 1923, was closely related to an English financial pool composed of H.I. Schröder & Co., the Westminister Bank, the Continental Industrial Trust, the Middle European Corporation and Gullness Mahon & Co. in London at the head, plus the participation of Dillon, Read & Co. in New York, Continential Security Corporation in New York, the Schweizerische Bankverein in Zurich, Horre & Co. in Amsterdam, Hallgarten & Co. in Hamburg, and so on. The third shareholder was founded in 1864 as a bank for the Austro-Hungarian aristocracy, but was changed after 1918 to an international amalgam, with the participation of J.P. Morgan & Co. in New York, H.I. Schröder & Co. in London, the Amsterdamsche Bank in Amsterdam, the group Solvay in Brussels, and the Schweizerische Bankgesellschaft in Geneva, and so on.

Thus, during the second half of the 1920s, foreign capital expansion in the Bulgarian banking system continued, only at a reduced rate. It should also be noted that certain foreign banks were more cautious, especially after 1927.

After the crisis

The period of optimism ended as soon as the first signs of the world economic crisis appeared in 1929. Of course, this crisis was a heavy blow for all banks in Bulgaria and especially for the foreign capital banks. These banks had experienced an important credit expansion during the second half of the 1920s, supported greatly by their head offices in Paris, Brussels, London, etc. Immediately, though, after the first days of the crisis, the head offices began to withdraw their credits from all the branches they had given them to, because this was also a crisis affecting the banks' liquidity both in Bulgaria and in all developed countries.

In 1931 all foreign capital banks in Bulgaria faced additional difficulties. After a temporary liberalization of the currency regime (1929–30), the country's central bank, the Bulgarian National Bank, was forced to return to a very restrictive currency legislation, from October 1931 onwards. This was very unpleasant for all banks in the country, including Bulgarian banks. However, it mostly affected the large foreign capital banks because of their higher level of involvement in foreign trade, operations concerning other currencies, interest or dividend payments abroad, and so on.

In the meantime, the general economic and political orientation of the country had gradually begun to change. After the German–Bulgarian clearing agreement in 1932, the country's economic orientation towards Germany became quite apparent. Hitler's coming to power after 1933 was also connected with a political reorientation in Bulgaria, but it was not so evident at first. In addition to that, there were certain hesitations concerning relations between the two countries, as King Boris II attempted to manoeuvre between Western Europe and Germany. Certain wealthy circles in Bulgaria feared this reorientation. Thus, due to all these changes, all western capitals were withdrawn from Bulgaria. This withdrawal began in 1932–33, intensified during 1935–37, and was very apparent in the attitude of almost all banks and enterprises with western capital on the eve of the war.

The most characteristic example during that period was the conduct of the General Bank in Sofia. In 1934 the bank's management openly confirmed that the effect of the country's orientation towards Germany was negative. Due to one aspect of this negative effect, the financing of the greater part of foreign trade was concentrated under the control of the Credit Bank in Sofia. The increase in paper currency, as a result of the German–Bulgarian clearing and the yet unknown fears of an economic crisis, led the merchants to trade in cash, and to avoid both the bill credit operations and any help offered by the banks. In fact, the General Bank obtained a mediating position in the French–Bulgarian clearing; this was, however, quite an insufficient compensation. On that account, the bank's board of managers attested that: 'under these unfavourable circumstances ... the bank cannot function normally'. Count M. Kasteras, the bank's general director, also had personal experience of such a negative appraisal, having been affected by some orders concerning the currency given by the Bulgarian National Bank.

Under these circumstances, the bank's management gradually altered its line of activity. Since the very end of 1931 and the beginning of

1932, the bank had adopted a policy leading to a restriction of credit activity and a decrease in investments. The average banking rate diminished from 8.48 per cent in 1928 to a mere 4.47 per cent by the autumn of 1932. The sum of deposits in the bank, after a brief period (1929–32) during which it temporarily increased from 137 to 314 million leva, indicated a diminution due to the competition of other banks offering higher deposit interest rates (5 per cent). The deposits in foreign currency from patron banks decreased further.

Restricting credit activity is a policy not only apparent in the premeditated withdrawal of bank deposits. At the time, the bank also quickly reduced its investments in bills and debit accounts, always keeping a greater part of its available means either in cash or in deposits in the Bulgarian National Bank. Thus, during 1929–36, and according to the bank's balances, the total of deposits diminished from 318 to 216 million leva, the discounted bills and credit accounts diminished from 384 to 216 million leva, but the available cash increased from 32 to 53 million leva.

In addition, the bank began at the same time to liquidate some of its subsidiary industrial enterprises. In 1932 it attempted to sell its four affiliated milling works in Sofia and Varna; however, this operation stopped in the second half of the 1930s due to juridical difficulties. Similar to this policy was the bank's reorientation concerning two other large enterprises after 1932, the sugar refinery in the village Kaialy in the region of Burgas and the enterprise for glue and fertilizers production[7] in Kostinbrod near Sofia. In this process towards liquidation the following steps were taken:

1. In the spring of 1933 the General Bank sold its own shares in the papermill to the stock company Madara.
2. In the autumn of 1934 the directors of the head office in Sofia and the branches in Plovdiv, Russe, Varna and Burgas were instructed not to participate in 'financial deals' (meaning capital participation) and to restrict themselves to the sphere of 'purely commercial credit'.

Another aspect of the tacit policy aimed at limitation and liquidation of the bank's activity in Bulgaria was the merging of the General Bank with the French-Belgian Bank in Sofia. This merger was achieved with help from the Banque de Paris et des Pays-Bas and the Hungarian Commercial Bank of Pest in Budapest, which guaranteed liquidity concerning the assets of the General Bank. The bank formed by this merger was controlled by a capital of 51 million leva which was twice as small as the capital controlling each one of the two former banks. The General Bank also attempted in 1936, unsuccessfully this time, to merge with the Bulgarian Commercial Bank. This effort was supported by the Banque de Paris et des Pays-Bas which participated in both banks.

Another bank with French and Bulgarian capital that adopted an even more definite policy aimed at the restriction and liquidation of its activities was the French-Belgian Bank in Sofia. After an increase in 1928 its capital reached 150 million leva. This new capital consisted of interlocked interests of certain West-European financial groups with French and Austrian capital at the head, as well as some American shareholders led by the Irving Trust in New York since 1938. It was a creation of mainly West-European banks, which had no interests in Germany and were not concerned with the German penetration of the Balkans. Among the financial groups that were either directly or indirectly shareholders of the French-Belgian Bank in Sofia financial centres under Jewish direction, predominated, such as the Westminster Bank in London, the Österreichische Creditanstalt für Handel und Gewerbe in Vienna, the branches of Rothchild in Paris and Vienna, the families of Samuel,[8] the family Bleichröder, the corn trade company L. Dreifuss, Angel Kujumdgiiski, etc. Because of the anti-Semitic policy adopted by Hitler, these individuals could not be indifferent to Bulgaria's economic and political subordination to Germany.

As already said, the policy adopted by the French-Belgian Bank in Sofia was quite similar to that adopted by the General Bank in Sofia. Analysis of the bank's archives shows that its executive committee strictly followed directives given by the main shareholders in Paris and Brussels in order to decrease the bank deposits. Thus the deposits diminished from 634 million leva in 1930 to 82 million leva in 1940, mostly due to the drawing back of short-term credits from the patron banks. The allotted credits decreased proportionally more than the deposits, from 679 to 72 million leva respectively. The bank strove to keep a higher liquidity in cash, as well as in deposits within the National Bank, or as state bonds.

The capital controlling the bank was also reduced due to two decisions following one closely after the other. The first decision was made by the board of managers in February 1934 and resulted in a reduction from 150 to 75 million leva; the second one in December 1936 resulted in a further reduction from 75 to 50 million leva. This reduction was motivated by a devaluation of the stocks or assets that were losses made by Cogefita.[9]

In the process of liquidation and limitation of the bank's activities, the following steps were also taken:

1. The bank's branches in the province were limited from 11 branches to one branch.

2. The bank attempted in 1934 to sell the gold it possessed in Sofia (which had a value of 1.2 million francs), but did not receive the necessary authorization.
3. It also tried to transfer part of its capital abroad by illegal means, using Cogefita as a canal through which foreign currency was smuggled during 1936–37.

The actual reasons for which the bank adopted such a restrictive policy were political. It is true that in the minutes of a management meeting in 1934, the Belgian delegate A. Callens is reported to have given only one reason: 'the patron banks do not intend to augment their engagements in Central and Eastern Europe in view of the ever increasing difficulties in the transfer of capitals'.[10] However, the real reason is the negative attitude of the bank's managers towards Hitler's regime in Germany and its followers in Bulgaria; this attitude is demonstrated by the directive in 1935 to abolish the credits of all enterprises under German influence such as Koralovag in Varna, Granitoid in Temelkovo, Rella & Neffe in Sofia, the Bulgarian Credit Bank in Sofia, Staer in Sofia, and so on.

During the 1930s the gradual liquidation of the French-Bulgarian Mortgage Bank continued. Until 1939, the bank realized two-thirds of the initial sum of the allotted mortgage loans. During 1939 it passively kept all collected instalments in cash, while transferring a part of them to France by compensation deals.

Another bank with partial foreign participation that hurried to liquidate its operations in Bulgaria was the Mortgage Bank in Sofia. In 1935, the bank's shareholders decided on this liquidation, after negotiation with the state. In 1936, after the active mediation (and commission) of the French-Belgian Bank in Sofia, the capital controlling this bank was bought back for 5.3 million Swiss francs.

As a result of both the withdrawal of western capital from Bulgaria, and, partially, of the strengthening of the state-owned bank Bulgarian Credit, during the 1930s the system consisting of financial groups with western capital[11] practically disappeared. Along with the limitation of the activity of the large banks, the ties between them and the groups either loosened or disappeared. Almost all of the initially related enterprises in these groups became independent both from the banks and from foreign capital, usually because foreign capital of western origin withdrew not only from all banks, but also from almost all related enterprises. The orientation towards the liquidation and limitation of activity in Bulgaria was most consistently adopted by Swiss and Belgian capital. French capital, too, adopted this policy; however there were more exceptions, since at that time, in certain circumstances, it was not easy to find a new buyer for an investment in Bulgaria so as to repatriate the money to France. As concerns English and American capital, the policy adopted was not so strong.

It is quite difficult to gather full statistical data about changes in the amount and the initial level of dependence concerning all foreign capital withdrawn from West-oriented financial groups in Bulgaria during the 1930s. Nevertheless, the scale of this withdrawal can roughly be demonstrated by the official statistical data concerning the sum of all foreign capital participation in Bulgarian joint-stock companies in a ten-year period (1931–1941). According to these data:

1. Belgian capital participation diminished from 724 to 62 million leva (11 : 1).
2. Swiss capital participation decreased from 547 to 48 million leva (11 : 1).
3. French capital participation was reduced from 389 to 128 million leva (3 : 1).
4. English capital participation diminished from 114 to 23 million leva (5 : 1).
5. American capital participation doubled.

However, it is true that three financial groups controlled by foreign capital managed to survive during the 1930s. These were the groups directed by the Credit Bank, the English-Prague Bank and the Italian-Bulgarian Commercial Bank. German and Italian capital, though, could not compensate for the retreat of western capital. After 1933 and Hitler's coming to power, the whole German economy was totally oriented towards a new world war. Consequently the German banking system could not afford to export capital without hesitations. This also applied to the Czechoslovakian banking system, which experienced serious new problems due to the pressure applied to it by Hitler's imperialistic policy. Thus it could help the English-Prague Bank in Sofia no longer. Italian banking capital, very active during the 1920s, remained utterly passive after the crisis of 1929–33 because all large banks in Italy suffered great losses during this period and did not have the necessary strength to export any more capital, since capital was engaged in certain state projects either in Italy or in the newly conquered Ethiopia.

It is debatable whether the aforementioned withdrawal was spontaneous or premeditated, or whether its prevailing motives were political or economic. Economic motives cannot always be distinguished from political motives as is apparent in the relations between Bulgaria and Germany during this period. However, in many cases the motives are evidently political. The negative attitude of western investors towards Bulgaria was not connected as directly with general political considerations as it was with their personal fears of interference in their immediate interests, due to the foreseen worsening of the conditions of their activity in Bulgaria, a result of anti-Semitic policy in both Bulgaria and Germany. The prevailing part of the withdrawing Belgian, French, Swiss and partially English capital was in fact connected with just several large collaborating financial groups,[12] with many Jewish shareholders. Thus arose in a private way a, more or less, common standpoint concerning the necessity of withdrawing from Bulgaria and the Balkans, as a future pro-German region. This viewpoint was not demonstrated in the form of circular letters or agreements but was a tacit and informal organization through which the financial groups attempted to rescue their own capital in a threatened area.

During the years of war following September 1939, and especially after the beginning of German operations against Greece and Yugoslavia in the spring of 1941 and Hitler's invasion of Russia in June 1941, the Bulgarian economy was in a very difficult situation since industrial and agricultural production had decreased. In addition, this period was marked by the isolation of foreign trade, a hard state regimentation in the country's economy and inflation, all of which combined with political pressures. Under these circumstances, the activity of all the banks in general, even of those controlled by German or Italian capital, was very limited. The French-Bulgarian Bank in Sofia was practically idle during 1941.

It could be stated as a conclusion concerning the entire period between the end of the nineteenth century and the Second World War that, as a whole, foreign capital in Bulgaria participated quite positively in the development of the country's economy. Apart from realizing its profits, which was inevitable, it contributed, first, to the modernization of the emerging national banking system, second, to the lowering of the rate of interest and, third, to the country's industrialization. Furthermore, it introduced new organizational forms for the country's large-scale capital management. This positive contribution was effective only as long as the currency regime in the country remained liberal and allowed capital to move freely, imported or exported from Bulgaria. After the introduction of a rather severe currency regime in Bulgaria in October 1931, the positive effects of western capital ceased. However, the relative economic activity in Bulgaria revived despite the withdrawal of western capital from the country.

After the Second World War

After the *coup d'état* with the help of the Soviet army on 9 September 1944 and following several transitional years of political compromise and hesitations during 1944–47, the Bulgarian communist party oriented itself, by the end of 1947, towards an open political offensive and quickly began 'the building of a socialist society' according to the Soviet model. From then on the facts remain as follows. The parliamentary opposition was eliminated after several months, and, finally, was naturally liquidated. In December 1947 all banks and industrial enterprises were nationalized, as, later, were all other sectors. So began the socialist period in which foreign capital had no place in the country's banking system. What remained of the German and Italian capital was quickly liquidated according to the terms of the peace treaty. The French-Bulgarian Bank too, was, liquidated after an agreement between France and Bulgaria.

After political change in 1989 the banking system was reorganized according to the new law concerning banks and credit activity established in 1991, which allowed for the creation of banks controlled by foreign capital. Foreign banks or branches were temporarily privileged, since they had the right to a more liberal registration without obligations such as setting apart the legally compulsory reserves in the central bank of the country or obtaining the legally minimum amount of paid capital in leva. They could not, though, be members of the Association of Commercial Banks; however, a breakthrough is expected regarding this problem.

As concerns private Bulgarian banks partially controlled by foreign capital, the first to appear in Sofia in 1994 were the Bulgarian-Russian Investment Bank and the Corporative Bank. The following banks appeared during the next two years:

1. 1995: the Bavarian-Hungarian Bank in Sofia and branches of the Ionian Bank, the Hios Bank, the Greek National Bank and the representative office of the Agricultural Bank of Greece.
2. 1996: branches of the Reifeisen Bank, the Credit-anstalt Investment Bank, the Eurobank, the Société Générale, the Bulgarian Investment Bank, the Banque Nationale de Paris and the Dresdner Bank.

Thus in November 1997 14 banks controlled by foreign capital were present in Sofia, controlling 5 per cent of the deposits and 16 per cent of the capital of all commercial banks in the country.

The tendency lately is clearly towards an increase in foreign capital participation in the country's banking system. Some private banks have increased the proportion of foreign capital in their registered capital, such as the Bulgarian-Russian Investment Bank and the Bulgarian-American Investment Fund. Other banks such as the Teximbank and Sveti Nikola are aimed at selling, completely or partially, their shares to foreign investors. There are certain investors seriously interested in buying all the shares of banks that are facing quasi-failure such as the Stopanska Bank, the Business Bank, the International Bank for Investments and Development, Slavjiani, etc. The only Bulgarian bank whose shareholders do not agree with attracting foreign investors is the Central Cooperative Bank.

Foreign capital participation in Bulgaria's banking system is presently expected to increase greatly due to changes in the state sector concerning the particular system. There is pressure from the IMF for all Bulgarian state commercial banks to be sold by the end of 1998. Certain steps have already been taken for the United Bulgarian Banks, the Hebros Bank, the Express Bank and the Post Bank. As concerns the bank Biochim, there are no potential investors. Some shares belonging to state banks have already been sold by the intermediary investment firm Hedjer in Sofia. Preparations have also been made since winter 1997 to sell the Bulbank,[13] the most powerful state commercial bank.

In the near future, the predicted intensification of competition in the bank services market in Bulgaria can be considered a threat to the existing Bulgarian banks. For the time being competition is still in its initial stage. Almost all Bulgarian banks function at great costs, with high tariffs as compared to the services they provide. As things are now it would be illusory to believe that they could possibly compete with western bank institutions in a free Bulgarian market.

If the tariffs for bank services were to be reduced and the approach to new markets and new resources enlarged, it would be an important and positive result of the presence of foreign banks in Bulgaria. However, that would be possible only in a context of a liberal currency regime, such as that existing before 1926.

Notes

1. Bulgaria did not at the time have any larger banks.
2. Assiccurazioni Generali was later renamed Societa di Credito Mobiliare et Immobiliare, in Lugano.
3. In 1922 the Balkan Bank had nine branches, the General Bank four, the French-Belgian Bank three and the Credit Bank two.
4. Related either through financing dependence, or through participation of individual bank directors or shareholders, as members of the board of directors of a given related company.

5. Not including the state-owned coal mines in Pernik, Bobov Dol and Maritza.
6. These branches included the production of sugar, salt, spirits and cigarettes, the export of tobacco, eggs and poultry, shipbuilding, etc.
7. The later Works N. Chilov.
8. Samuel was one of the founders of the Royal Dutch Shell.
9. The abbreviation for Compagnie Générale Financière de Tabac. It was founded as a credit syndicate responsible for the distribution of risks taken in order to finance the tobacco trade, along with the participation of the Société Générale de Belgique, the Sherman Corporation, etc.
10. *Central State Archives,* No. 292/1–59, p. 73.
11. Which consisted of the financial groups around the General Bank, the Balkan Bank, the French-Bulgarian Bank for International Trade and the French-Belgian Bank.
12. The Société Générale de Belgique, the Banque de Paris et des Pays-Bas, the Banque de l'Union Parisienne, Lazard Frères, Rothchild, etc.
13. The former Bulgarian Foreign Trade Bank.

CHAPTER TWO

Foreign Banks in Romania: A Historical Perspective

Cristian Bichi[1]

Creation of the banking system (1865–1918)

Intensification of economic activity in the Romanian principalities following the Adrianople Treaty (1829)[2] enhanced the need for capital and made imperative the establishment of a modern credit system. Since 1832 several proposals had been submitted concerning the setting up of a bank of issue, as well as other credit institutions, but they would come into being only after the creation of the modern Romanian state subsequent to the unification of Wallachia with Moldavia on 24 January 1859.

It is worth mentioning that as early as the first few decades of the nineteenth century a clash of opinions was aroused concerning the role of foreign capital in the creation of the Romanian credit system. Accordingly, large landowners favoured the establishment of a bank of issue and a rural credit institution, with foreign capital, while the emerging bourgeoisie supported the setting up of the two institutions with domestic capital. As further developments prove, the bourgeoisie standpoint won eventually. One main reason for this state of affairs was the painful experience of the first Romanian bank of issue, the National Bank of Moldavia, established in 1856 by the Prussian banker Al Neuland, by means of German, English, French and Romanian capital, which went bankrupt two years later because of mismanagement and involvement in speculative actions.

The first modern commercial bank was established in the Romanian principalities in 1865 under the name of Bank of Romania. The bank was organized as a limited joint-stock company, with subscribed capital worth 25 million French francs. The Bank of Romania was set up as a bank of issue and commercial bank by English and French investors who governed the Banque Impériale Ottomane. In 1869 the Romanian Government – under pressure from the domestic bourgeoisie – revoked the Bank of Romania's monopoly of issue. Accordingly, this institution operated further as a private commercial bank until its liquidation in 1948 by the communist regime.

Establishment of a modern-type banking system, designed to replace the money lenders and trade houses that had developed healthily before the mid-nineteenth century, was a slow process until the setting up of the National Bank of Romania,[3] on 17 April 1880. During 1866–80 only two long-term credit institutions were established, the Rural Credit Bank (1873) and the Urban Credit Bank (1874), and a commercial bank – Marmorosch Blank & Co. (1874). It should be mentioned that the two credit institutions were based exclusively on domestic capital, unlike the commercial bank which had both foreign and domestic capital stakes.

The National Bank of Romania was established at the initiative of the Liberal Party with a view to granting credits in high demand after the Independence War (1877) and providing financial stability for the country. The National Bank of Romania was designed not only to play the role of state financing and note issue, but also to perform purely commercial banking functions. In compliance with provisions of the law governing its establishment, the new banking institution was a joint-stock company, with the Romanian government holding one-third of the capital stock, and domestic shareholders holding the remainder. These provisions precluded foreign shareholders from owning any interest in the National Bank of Romania's capital, closely following the principle of domestic control over the national economy required by the liberals. In 1901, in the wake of withdrawal of the state from the partnership, the National Bank of Romania became a private institution, enjoying special privileges from the Romanian government, especially the monopoly of issue. Under the Liberal Party's control, the National Bank of Romania played a significant part in the foundation of the Romanian modern-type banking system and contributed to the strengthening economic position of the Romanian bourgeoisie.

The economic progress that accompanied consolidation of the Romanian state and the support provided by the National Bank of Romania accelerated the establishment of private commercial banks, especially during the period that preceded the outbreak of the First World War. The number of commercial banks increased to 215 in 1914, from three banks in 1880, 27 in 1900, and 197 in 1913. If the setting up of the National Bank of Romania and long-term credit institutions was done only with domestic capital, in turn, foreign capital would be involved substantially in the creation of new private commercial banks. Accordingly, in 1914, 40 per cent of Romanian commercial banks' capital was held by German, Austrian, French, Belgian and English banking institutions.

On the eve of the First World War, the Romanian banking industry was highly concentrated, being dominated by nine leading commercial banks (of which eight banks were located in Bucharest) called 'the big Romanian banks'. In 1913 these banks held 70 per cent of total commercial bank resources, while 188 small and middle-sized banks held the remainder of total resources. Taking into account the origin of the capital, the composition of the group of 'the big Romanian banks' was as follows: four banks with national capital (Banca Agricola, Banca Comertului din Craiova, Banca Romana de Scont, Banca Romaneasca); four banks with foreign capital (Banca Generala Romana, Banca de Credit Romanesc, Banca Comerciala Romana, Banca Romaniei); one bank with foreign and domestic capital (Marmorosch Blank & Co.).

The originating shareholders of the banks with foreign capital are listed below:

- The Banca Generala Romana (Romanian General Bank) was established in 1897 by a German financial group including Diskonto-Gesellschaft and Solomon Bleichröder following the takeover of two Bucharest banking houses: Ghermani si Fratii Elias.
- The Banca de Credit Roman (Bank of Romanian Credit) was set up in 1904 by the Viennese banks Länderbank and Niederösterreichische Escompte-Gesellschaft.
- The Banca Comerciala Romana (Romanian Commercial Bank) was founded in 1906, with Austrian, French and Belgian capital held by the Anglo-Österreichische Bank, the Wiener Bankverein in Vienna, the Banque de l'Union Parisienne in Paris and the Crédit Anversois in Antwerp.
- The Banca Romaniei (Bank of Romania) was established in 1865 by the Banque Impériale Ottomane in London and Paris; in 1903 this bank became a branch of the Bank of Romania Ltd, set up in London in 1903 by the same Banque Impériale Ottomane.

As far as the Marmorosch Blank & Co. Bank is concerned, it became a joint-stock company in 1905, with subscribed capital from the Pester Ungarische Commercial Bank of Budapest, Bank für Handel und Industrie (Darmstädter Bank), Berliner Handelsgesellschaft of Berlin, Banque de Paris et des Pays-Bas in Paris and bankers Mauriciu Blank and J. Marmorosch.

The importance of foreign capital in the Romanian banking system on the eve of the First World War is proved also by data referring to the position of the nine biggest banks during 1911–14 (Table 2.1). The table shows that to the end of the period under review, foreign-controlled banks held a larger weight as regards both own funds and other liabilities. In 1914, for example, own funds of banks with foreign interests totalled 106.8 million lei, much more than the value of own funds held

Table 2.1 Liabilities of the nine biggest commercial banks in Romania (thousand lei)

Banks	1911				1914			
	Own funds (capital + reserves)	Percentage of total	Other liabilities (deposits, central bank refinancing, other creditors)	Percentage of total	Own funds (capital reserves)	Percentage of total	Other liabilities (deposits, central bank refinancing, other creditors)	Percentage of total
Banks with foreign capital	69604	65.15	257037	66.44	106845	56.05	348538	56.24
Banks with domestic capital	37254	34.85	130001	33.59	83773	43.95	271168	43.76
Total	106858	100.00	387038	100.00	190618	100.00	619706	100.00

Source: BNR, *Contributii la problema reorganizarii creditului in Romania* (Contributions regarding the issue of the reorganization of the credit system in Romania), vol. 1, Bucharest, 1938, p. 59.

by banks with Romanian capital, that is 83.7 million lei. The indicator 'other liabilities' also shows the pre-eminence of banks with foreign capital which held 348.5 million lei (56.24 per cent) of other liabilities of the nine banks analysed totalling 619.7 million lei. This state of affairs is explained by the fact that, due to high interest margins,[4] the banks with foreign interests were able to attract sizeable short-term loans from abroad. These banks were also considered reliable institutions by the public; this perception enabled these banks to build a strong saving deposits base. In turn, the Romanian banks failed to attract deposits in large amounts because of the illiquidity of their assets and, consequently, they had to rely heavily on the rediscount facilities of the National Bank of Romania, offered at interest rates of 5–6 per cent.

The characteristic feature of banks established before the First World War was that they were involved in the active fostering of industry, agriculture and commerce by direct intervention in these fields; not only did they lend, they also become large equity-holders in industrial and commercial companies.

The policy of building up industrial holdings was promoted mainly by the big banks, especially by the foreign-controlled banks. In this respect, V. Slavescu,[5] a leading liberal theoretician, remarked:

> Almost all the big banks in Romania understood the utility of their involvement in industrial and commercial activities and tried to control the most important enterprises in these areas ... It could be observed, however, that mainly the banks with foreign interests seem to be those that were more active in this direction, which is so profitable.[6]

The years 1918–44

Accomplishment of the union of the historical Romanian lands into a national state in 1918 brought about important changes to economic life. The Romanian financial system developed significantly; banking institutions of the new territories – Transylvania, Bukovina and Bessarabia – added to the banks existing in the Old Kingdom. The years that followed witnessed rapid development of financial capital in Romania, with foreign-owned banks playing a significant role during this period too.

Penetration of foreign capital into the Romanian banking system developed during the intra-war period against the background of intense ideological debates concerning the economic development pattern to be followed by new Romania. The main doctrines in this respect were neo-liberalism, peasantism and social democracy.

The neo-liberalism represented the interests of the industrial and financial bourgeoisie, politically represented by the Liberal Party and grouped around the National Bank of Romania and the Banca Romaneasca.[7] The liberals backed up the need for developing industry with a view to rapid streamlining of the national economy and protecting the country's independence. To this end, they pushed for the creation of strong Romanian banks in order to back the drive for industrialization. Unlike classic liberalism, which emphasized the freedom of the individual, the Liberal Party[8] and its theoreticians were in favour of an active state policy, which should foster economic life. Under the slogan 'through ourselves', the neo-liberals were also advocates of a 'policy calling for limitations on foreign investment and for ensuring the predominance of the Romanian capital in all the branches of the economy and individual enterprises'.[9]

In contrast to the liberal doctrine, peasantism advocated the preservation of the agrarian structure of the Romanian economy. The peasantists also considered that Romania did not possess enough capital to make use of all its natural resources and to rebuild its economy. Thus, the National Peasant Party,[10] which politically stood for the ideology of peasantism and protected the interests of the petite and middle bourgeoisie, especially from the countryside, adopted the policy of 'open gates' facilitating penetration of foreign capital in the Romanian economy. As regards the social-democrats, they were in favour of foreign capital inflows in Romania provided that a substantial part of profits would be reinvested in the national economy.

The evolution of the Romanian banking system during the interwar period can be divided into three main stages. The first (1919–28) is known as the 'country's reconstruction' period. The second (1929–33) was marked by the Great Depression. The final stage (1934–44) was characterized by determined efforts to regulate and supervise the banking system and by increased state intervention.

Period of the country's reconstruction

Soon after the end of the First World War, Romanian legislation for nationalization of goods belonging to the citizens of defeated countries was implemented and monetary unification was accomplished (1920) by the withdrawal of rubles (in Bessarabia) and crowns (in Transylvania and Bukovina). The nationalization process in the banking area led to the takeover of the enemy's foreign capital participation (German, Austrian and Hungarian capital) by the Romanian and allied countries' investors. Accordingly, the German and Hungarian capital participations in Marmorosch Blank & Co. passed into Romanian and French hands, while participations of Austrian banks in the Banca de Credit Roman and the Banca Comerciala Romana turned into French and English participations and French and Belgian participations, respectively. Moreover, the German interests in the Banca Generala Romana, which during the war period served as a bank of issue for the occupation forces, were replaced by Romanian capital. Thus, in December 1919, the bank changed its name to the Banca Generala a Tarii Romanesti,[11] becoming the third bank in the hands of the liberal bourgeoisie.

During 1919–24, under the influence of the territorial increase, inflation and speculative activity, the number of banks increased considerably from 486 to 928. Stimulated by the official policy of fostering the development of the industrial sector and by the euphoric climate of peacetime, the banks expanded their loan portfolios and invested heavily in real estate and shares of private corporations; this policy placed many banking institutions in a non-liquid condition. The boom in banking activity was accompanied by a lax regulatory environment. In Romania, no special licence was needed to start a bank, either with domestic or foreign capital. Banks were subject to the general rules of the Commercial Code and no genuine supervision was exercised on them until 1934. As a result, many of the newly established banks lacked adequate capital and proper management. In the next years (1925–29), a period witnessing stabilization efforts, the business climate never regained the hectic tone of the inflationary period and the increase in the number of banks registered a slowdown. In 1928 there were 1 122 banks (the peak) and in 1929 they had decreased to 1 097. No change was brought to the banks' policy to promote growth of industry by rolled-over current account loans and by acquisition of equity stakes. Since the National Bank of Romania was containing the flow of credit in the economy in order to revalue the national currency, competition among banks for deposits became intense and lending rates rose tremendously up to 20 per cent. Accordingly, these high lending rates affected the repayment capacity of the banks' customers and prepared the seeds for the credit crunch to come together with the Great Depression.

During 1919–28, foreign capital invested in the Romanian banking system soared, as reflected by both the setting up of new banking companies with foreign interests and the increase in capital stakes in foreign hands in the existing banks. However, the weight of foreign capital in the banking industry decreased as a result of buoyant banks with domestic capital, governed mainly by liberals. In 1928 foreign capital invested in Romanian banks accounted for only 25 per cent of total share capital existing in the banking sector, as compared to 33 per cent recorded in 1923.

However, it should be noted that the increase in domestic banking capital was mainly the result of the creation of hundreds of small banks, which could not be serious competitors for the better capitalized foreign-controlled banks. As in the previous period, the banks with foreign interests continued to have an average share capital bigger than the average capital of all the banks.[12]

During the period under review, foreign banks entered in the Romanian banking system through several channels. Accordingly, they not only acquired shares in the subsidiaries belonging to banks from 'enemy countries', but also established new branches, set up subsidiaries as Romanian joint-stock companies and took over some small domestic banking companies.

During the reconstruction period, French and Belgian capital held a dominant position in the foreign banking capital. In 1928 French and Belgian investors had capital stakes in 20 Romanian banking institutions, with a capital base of more than 700 million lei. French banks enlarged their sphere of influence not only by taking over shares in three big banks,[13] but also by taking part in the formation or the increase of the capital of some banking companies, such as Banca Timisoara (1906), Banca Franco-Romana (1920), Banca Romano-Franceza in Iasi (1925) and Creditul Ipotecar Roman (1928). Belgian capital played a significant role by establishing a Bucharest branch of the Banque Belge pour l'Etranger in 1921. This branch was taken over in 1923 by the Banca Comerciala Romana, which concentrated Belgian capital interests in Romania.

The Hungarian and Austrian banks, which at the end of the war held important capital stakes in the Romanian banking sector, especially in Transylvania and Banat, managed to maintain their positions, to a large extent. However, the activity of their subordinated relatively small banking entities (mostly Budapest and Vienna banks' branches and subsidiaries[14]) did not expand too much in the reunited territories, as they were at a disadvantage in competing with the local banks or the large western capital-controlled banks. It is also of interest that following two successive capital increases, in 1928 and 1929, the controlling stake in the Banca de Credit Roman, passed to the Österreichische Creditanstalt, Vienna.

During the period under review, Italian capital started to exert a substantial influence following the establishment of the Banca Comerciala Italiana si Romana (Italian and Romanian Commercial Bank) in 1930 by the Italian Commercial Bank in Milan. This entity gradually became one of the biggest banks in Romania and supported actively the entry of Italian capital into several industrial activities through its branches and affiliates.

Table 2.2 Situation of the principal banks with foreign capital in Romania at 31 December 1928 (thousands lei)

Name of bank	Share capital	Participations	Credit balances on current accounts	Net benefits 1923–28	Dividends 1923–28 %
1. Banca Comerciala Italiana si Romana	100 000	—	1 352 161	140 236	12–15
2. Banca Comerciala Romana	100 000	27 303	1 339 340	88 144	10–15
3. Banca de Credit Roman	200 000	267 926	1 202 084	312 431	15–18
4. Banca Franco-Romana	120 000	103 242	280 299	79 514	11–12
5. Banca Marmorosch	125 000	385 694	2 307 970	343 675	20–24
6. Banca Chrissoveloni	350 000	389 263	1 561 912	275 898	12
7. Banca Industriala	100 000	1 539 843	1 821 822	50 353	0
8. Banca Comertului	100 000	85 637	514 997	138 231	21
9. Banca Moldovei	100 000	69 370	530 627	114 634	20
10. Banca Timisului	62 500	101 953	507 390	115 431	14–18
Total 10 banks	1 357 500	2 970 231	11 418 602	1 658 547	
All banks	10 000 176	3 589 603	17 205 487	8 827 773	

Source: C. Murgescu and N.N. Constantinescu (eds) *Contributii la istoria capitalului strain in Romania* (Contributions regarding the history of foreign capital in Romania), Bucharest: Ed. Academiei RPR, 1960, pp. 118–19.

As far as English capital is concerned, its position in the Romanian banking system strengthened as a result of both more intense activity of the Bank of Romania Ltd's branch and the establishment of the Banca Anglo-Romana (1921) and setting up of two branches by the Anglo-International Bank Ltd (1926).

Despite the 'nationalization (nostrification) policy' followed by Romania immediately after the First World War, German capital continued to operate within the Romanian banking system through the Dresdner Bank's branch[15] in Bucharest, established in 1918 during the occupation period.

Moreover, during 1919–28, Swiss, Swedish, Czech and Polish capital started to penetrate the Romanian banking system.

Table 2.2 shows selected financial indicators concerning the position of the main banks with foreign capital during 1923–28. It reveals that the strength of the banks with foreign capital when compared with the banks with Romanian capital was related not only to the size of their own capitals, but rather to the borrowed capitals which were attracted mostly through recourse to foreign credits. Accordingly, at the end of 1928, the first ten banks with foreign interests held 13.5 per cent of the banking system's share capital and they were making use of 66 per cent of amounts recorded under the banks' balance-sheet item 'Credit balances on current accounts'.

The crisis period (1929–33)

The economic crisis during 1929–33 heavily affected the Romanian banking system. The collapse of prices during the Great Depression had adverse effects on banks' portfolios, and depositors' confidence was sapped as a result of a new law which allowed banks to suspend payments, with no possibility for creditors to control the banks' activities. Foreign short-term loans, which represented substantial financial resources for large banks, started to be withdrawn at the end of 1929. This process accelerated after the collapse of the Austrian bank Creditanstalt in 1931. These developments triggered massive runs on the Romanian banks which resulted in the failure of large banking institutions: Banca Generala a Tarii Romanesti (June 1931), Banca Bercovitz (July 1931), Marmorosch Blank Bank (October 1931). The collapse of those banks also caused the crumble of several regional banks. Generally, banks with foreign interests were better able to cope with the shocks of the Great Depression than domestically owned institutions, but the massive capital flight triggered by the Creditanstalt crisis and the contagious effect on the Romanian banks naturally caused misgivings about the usefulness of foreign capital and heavy reliance on short-term (portfolio) inflows.

Period of the strengthening of the banking system (1934–44)

In order to strengthen the banking system, which was badly affected by the crisis, the Romanian Parliament passed the Law on the organization and regulation of banking commerce, on 8 May 1934. This law introduced detailed regulations regarding the setting up and operation of banking companies and stipulated creation of a Banking Council under the chairmanship of the governor of the National Bank of Romania, with a view to supervising banks' activities. Under the law, no bank could operate without a licence and special licences were needed for institutions to be allowed to collect savings deposits. Moreover, minimum capital requirements were established for different classes of banks in order to be authorized and their by-laws were subject to Banking Council approval. The 1934 law also provided for regular audits of banks by the Banking Council and imposed heavy penalties if the banking regulations were infringed. If the banks experienced large losses, the Council was empowered by the law to liquidate them. The banking law also introduced the obligation for banks to publish semi-annually their balance sheets in a standardized form. The main impact of the new law on foreign banks was the fact that they were no longer allowed to establish a business presence in Romania as a branch; they could enter the local market only by setting up a separate legal entity incorporated in Romania.

Pursuant to the 1934 law, the Romanian government, supported by the National Bank of Romania, was deeply involved in drafting measures for recovery of the banking system by liquidating non-viable credit institutions and merging institutions weakened by the crisis. Consequently, the number of banks diminished from 893 in 1933 to 523 in 1937 and 246 in 1944. This process led to both the concentration of capital in the banking industry and the increase in importance of eight large banks[16] located in Bucharest: Banca Romaneasca, Banca de Credit Roman, Banca Comerciala Romana, Banca Comerciala Italiana si Romana, Societatea Bancara Romana,[17] Banca de Scont a Romaniei, Banca Chrissoveloni and Banca Urbana. At the end of 1944 these banks held 39 per cent of own funds, 61 per cent of deposits and 77.6 per cent of current account credit balances of all commercial banks.[18] These banks, especially the first three institutions, held controlling stakes in many important industrial companies and in small and medium-sized banks.

It should be noted that following the changes in the capital structure of the Banca de Credit Roman,[19] the Banca Comerciala Romana[20] and the Banca Chrissoveloni[21] during the war period, German capital exerted partial or total influence in four out of the eight banks mentioned above. These four banks played a crucial role in the penetration of the Romanian economy by German industrial companies.

The communist era (1947–89)

Soon after the communists took power in Romania, according to Decree Law No. 197/1948 all Romanian and foreign-controlled banks were liquidated, except for the National Bank of Romania, the National Company of Industrial Credit and the Savings Bank.

The 1934 banking law was abrogated, with the remaining banks continuing their activity under the provisions of the Commercial Code and their specific laws. In the years that followed the Romanian banking system was organized as a mono-bank system, typical of a centrally planned economy. During a period of economic liberalization in the 1970s, two foreign banks were allowed to establish branches in Romania: Manufacturers Hannover Trust[22] and Société Générale, which still operate today.

The transition period (1990–97)

The process of creating a market-oriented banking sector in Romania began *de facto* in December 1990, when the National Bank of Romania spun off its commercial bank operations which were taken over by a newly created bank – the Romanian Commercial Bank. *De jure*, a two-tier banking system was established in April 1991, after the promulgation of the Law on banking activities (Law 33/1991) and the Law on the National Bank of Romania (Law 34/1991).[23]

The new legal framework bestowed 'universal attributes'[24] on the commercial banks, whereas the National Bank of Romania was granted a high degree of independence and made accountable only to the legislative body of the country. Since the passing of the new banking legislation the Romanian banking sector has expanded forcefully. While on 1 January 1990 there were only six banks in Romania, 41 banks were licensed as of 31 December 1996.

Of the total number of banks operating at present in Romania, 32 are domestic incorporated institutions and nine are branches of foreign banks. Apart from this, five representative offices of foreign banks are also active in Romania.

In December 1995 the participation of foreign investors in the Romanian banking sector represented 84 649 billion lei or 13.66 per cent of the total subscribed banking capital in Romania. The Romanian

Development Agency reported that it had registered, up to early 1996, 16 banks with foreign capital participation amounting to US$122 million. Foreign equity participation in Romanian incorporated banks ranges from 0.03 per cent to 99.90 per cent (ABN-AMRO).

In the last couple of years, major international banks (ABN-AMRO, ING Bank, Citibank) have established a business presence in Romania. There is also a growing interest from Greek banks in developing a presence in Romania, with four of them already in service or setting up operations.

It is worth noting that from the very beginning of the reform process the Romanian authorities have encouraged the entry of foreign banks into the domestic banking system in order to promote a competitive and modern financial system. Foreign banks can undertake operational activities in Romania in the form of wholly owned subsidiaries[25] or joint ventures with other foreign and/or local partners or branches.[26] The foreign-controlled banking entities have no restrictions on the expansion of their activities in the country or as regards the range of banking services they can provide.

While Romanian authorities adopted a liberal attitude regarding the licensing of foreign-controlled *de novo* banks, the role of foreign capital in the privatization of state-owned banks remained a sensitive and controversial issue. Until recently the progress of bank privatization in Romania was elusive due to a lack of political commitment. One reason for this state of affairs is the fact that many policy-makers fear foreign control of the national economy with the presence of large foreign banks as strategic investors. The new Romanian government, formed after the election in November 1996, has expressed a strong commitment to economic reform. One of the key elements of its economic programme is represented by the privatization of state-owned banks, and the participation in this process of large foreign investors, especially reputable financial institutions, is welcomed. By the end of 1997, Romania plans to privatize two state-owned banks.

Conclusions

In Romania the commercial banking system was created after the establishment of the Central Bank in 1880. Several banking institutions were set up by 1900, but the real growth in the banking system occurred from then until 1914. On the eve of the First World War, the Romanian banking system was fully developed and able to serve the credit needs of industry, trade and large agricultural landowners. Foreign capital played an important role in the creation of private banks and the development of the economy. The foreign-controlled banks attracted sizeable short-term foreign loans contributing to the establishment of modern industries, exploitation of natural resources and creation of infrastructure.

After the First World War, under national-oriented policies promoted by the Liberal governments, the weight of foreign capital in the banking system declined in relative terms. Despite this capital trend, the banks with foreign interests maintained significant positions in the banking system and were better able to identify profitable investments than their Romanian-controlled competitors. For five years starting in 1928 the Peasantist governments promoted an open door policy aimed at reintegration of Romania into the international financial circuit, and the presence of foreign capital investment in the domestic banking system was encouraged.

Amid the Great Depression, the banking sector felt the repercussions of the economic crisis due to its close links with industry, and some large banks failed. The foreign-controlled banks absorbed the shocks better than the Romanian banks, but the massive capital flight triggered by the crash of several leading western banks and the domino effect on Romanian banks caused mistrust about the usefulness, under any circumstances, of foreign capital.

After the communist period, foreign capital started to re-enter the Romanian banking system. New banks, partially or wholly owned by foreigners were established. The issue of whether or not to allow foreign ownership/control of the soon to be privatized state-owned banks has resurrected the old clash of ideas from the intra-war period regarding the role of foreign capital in the reform of the Romanian economy. While the acquisition of small equity positions by foreign investors is widely seen as a positive development, there are many policy-makers who argue that foreign control of the main Romanian banks should be discouraged on the grounds that it could affect independent strategic decisions in the national economy. As such opinions may have some real basis, the new government, which is currently in the process of drafting bank privatization law, is to weigh the cost and benefits of an open door policy in this period of economic transition.

Notes

1. The author, who is Advisor to the Governor of the National Bank of Romania, bears sole responsibility for the views expressed in the paper.
2. The Adrianople Treaty, ending the Russo-Turkish War of 1828–29, put an end to the effective Ottoman domination over the Romanian principalities (Moldavia and Wallachia). Under the Treaty, the principalities

obtained legislative and administrative autonomy and freedom of commerce was guaranteed.

3. At the time of its establishment, the National Bank of Romania was the sixteenth central bank in the world.
4. Interest rates on the short-term foreign loans were 2–4 per cent compared with the interest rates of 8–12 per cent on loans granted to Romanian companies.
5. V. Slavescu, *Marile banci comerciale din Romania* (The big commercial banks in Romania), Institutul de Arte Grafice 'Universala', Bucharest, 1915.
6. Slavescu continues: 'The fact that also the domestic banks, although weaker as regards their financial resources, tried to affirm themselves in these fields, makes us think that once consolidated they would enter, with even more energy and initiative in these large areas of activity.'
7. The Banca Romaneasca (Romanian Bank) was established in 1911 and has gradually become one of the biggest banks in Romania.
8. During the interwar period the Liberal Party governed the country from 1922–27 and from 1933–37.
9. Kurt Treptow (ed.), *A History of Romania*, Iasi: The Center for Romanian Studies, The Romanian Cultural Foundation, 1996, p. 397.
10. The National Peasant Party was in power during the years 1928–31 and 1932–33.
11. The Banca Generala a Tarii Romanesti merged with the Banca de Scont a Romaniei in 1941.
12. At the end of 1928 the average share capital of the banks with foreign interests was 48 132 075 lei compared with the average capital of all banks of 8 912 812 lei, C. Murgescu and N.N. Constantinescu (eds), *Contributii la istoria capitalului strain in Romania* (Contributions regarding the history of foreign capital in Romania), Bucharest: Ed. Academiei RPR, 1960.
13. Banca Comerciala Romana, Banca de Credit Roman and Marmorosch Blank.
14. Pester Ungarische Commercial Bank, Ungarische Allgemeine Credit Bank, Wienerverein, Anglo-Österreichische Bank, Merkurbank.
15. Under forced administration after the war, the branch resumed its activities in 1919 when the Romanian state obtained a comfort letter from the Dresdner Bank.
16. A large bank was defined as a banking institution having a capital of more than 100 million lei.
17. This bank was established in 1929 as a result of the transformation of the Dresdner Bank's branch in Bucharest into a Romanian legal entity. The capital of the new banking institution (250 million lei) was subscribed by the Dresdner Bank; the Commerz und Private Bank, Berlin; S. Japhet & Co., Ltd, London; the Amsterdamsche Bank, Amsterdam; Bankhaus J.H. Stein, Koln; and Bankhaus Simion Hirschland, Essen.
18. For a detailed account of the position held by these banks within the banking sector see C. Kiritescu, *Sistemul banesc al leului* (The monetary system of the leu), Bucharest: Ed. Academiei RSR, 1971.
19. In the wake of the nationalization of a great part of the share capital, besides the Romanian capital, the bank held only German capital represented by Reichs-Kredit Gesellschaft.

20. In the case of this bank, the French and Belgian interests passed to the Deutsche Bank.
21. The German interests in the Banca Chrissoveloni were represented by Berliner Handelsgesellschaft.
22. The branch is now part of the Chase Manhattan Bank network.
23. For a detailed account of the initial stage of the banking reform in Romania see E. Ghizari, 'Banking reform in Romania', in D. Kemme and A. Rudka (eds) *Monetary and Banking Reform in Post-communist Economies*, New York: Westview Press, 1992, pp. 115–22.
24. As a result of the promulgation of the Law on securities and stock exchanges in 1995, some functions of universal banking, such as brokerage activities, are no longer allowed to be undertaken by the Romanian commercial banks.
25. As Romanian entities, the subsidiaries have to pay in the same amount of initial minimum capital as other Romanian banks.
26. A branch of a foreign bank has no obligation to pay in initial capital in Romania.

CHAPTER THREE

The Imperial Ottoman Bank: Actor or Instrument of Ottoman Modernization?

Edhem Eldem

Several years of research and cataloguing in the Ottoman Bank archives[1] has enabled us to conduct a certain number of studies and analyses on various aspects of the bank's history and of its role and participation in the developments of the late-nineteenth and early-twentieth-century Ottoman Empire.[2] Most of these studies were aimed at either a general description of the archives and the material they contained or a rather specific analysis of certain series. What we intend to do here is to present a more synthetic analysis of the same material centred on the specific – yet somehow vague – notion of modernization in the context of the Ottoman Empire.

The argument that the Imperial Ottoman Bank was part and parcel of the modernization and westernization programme upon which the Ottoman state embarked in the nineteenth century requires little, if any, justification. What we intend to look into is rather the ways in which the Ottoman Bank has been involved in this process of modernization, namely as an (autonomous) actor, or as an instrument of the state (a function that does not preclude an active role).

The establishment of this institution in 1863 as a state bank fell in line with the aims of the *Tanzimat* reformers at establishing a state apparatus heavily inspired by the western model of the time and destined to provide the Empire with the infrastructure necessary for the gradual transformation of the whole system into a modern and rational one. In fact, one may even argue that within the general context of the *Tanzimat* movement the reforms pertaining to the financial system had been the hardest and slowest to come into being: the foundation of the Imperial Ottoman Bank in 1863 came as a belated attempt at solving the accumulation of nearly two decades of financial disorganization and difficulties, following – and despite – the unification of currency in 1844.[3]

If financial reform and reorganization had been slower to realize than other administrative transformations of the *Tanzimat* period, the reason has to be sought in the actual difficulties involved in such a process rather than in a relative ignorance or backwardness of the Ottoman state in things financial. In fact, quite to the contrary, most of the pre-*Tanzimat* reform movements in the Ottoman Empire, going as far back as the seventeenth century, had been strongly dominated by financial and fiscal concerns and the Ottoman governing élite had long shown its capacity for a proper understanding of the importance of these matters, or even for innovation in this domain.[4] In a sense, and somewhat paradoxically, one of the major impediments to the systematic adoption of a western-based or -inspired financial and fiscal system might well have been the existence of a strong and well-implanted Ottoman tradition in the field, making it all the more difficult to graft new elements onto a pre-existing structure.

Moreover, it is worth noting that the modernizing *Tanzimat* élites had not hesitated to introduce some innovations in the field, starting with the use of paper money (*kaime-i mutebere-i nakdiye* or *kaime*) as early as 1839,[5] the adoption of a bi-metallic decimal standard in 1844 and the establishment of a foreign currency regulating agency in 1845 (the Banque de Constantinople as it was named after 1847).[6] However, each of these measures had proved highly inefficient, mainly because most of these innovations had remained at the level of – often contradicting – half-measures: the uncontrolled issue of paper money had led to a disastrous depreciation of the *kaime*s while at the same time adding to the monetary chaos of the period; the 1844 monetary reform had been unable to eradicate the circulation of altered currency; and the Banque de Constantinople had been forced into bankruptcy by the government's demand for cash advances which the insufficient capital basis and local resources of the bank had been unable to meet.

The Crimean War constituted the *coup de grâce* to all dreams of finding local solutions to the Empire's chronic financial malaise. Under the enormous pressure of the war effort, alongside a predictable attempt at financing the war through new issues of *kaime*s, the Ottoman state had, for the first time in its history, resorted to foreign credit. The 1854 and 1855 loans of £3 million and £5 million organized by Dent, Palmers & Co. and the Rothschilds of London respectively had marked the starting point of a long series of debts contracted on the European markets. Local sources of credit – the banking houses of Galata – had by then proved to be incapable of meeting the growing needs of the state for cash: what was needed was a new and preferably autonomous financial agent that would organize the process initiated by the first foreign loan of 1854, especially with respect to the guaranteeing of the debt service, a *sine qua non* condition for the Ottoman state to obtain new loans from the financial markets of Europe.

As a financial broker of the Empire, the Imperial Ottoman Bank was without any doubt fulfilling the role of an instrument of modernization at the hands of the westernizing élites of the time. In that sense, the institution was part and parcel of the ongoing westernization programme; however, the question remains whether the Ottoman Bank was an instrument or really an actor in the process. The question is probably a false one, in many respects, subject to distortions due to the ideological implications of historiographical perceptions of the *Tanzimat* process and the involvement of western powers in it. It is thus typical that some historiographical trends, tending to depict the *Tanzimat* as a process of economic and social exploitation – a sort of semi-colonization – of the Empire by the West, will see in the Ottoman Bank an institution serving the interests of its London- and Paris-based capital. Within such a perspective, the Imperial Ottoman Bank, more than just an instrument of change, becomes an autonomous actor participating in the systematic destruction and dismemberment of the Empire.

Needless to say, this caricature of the parasitic institution greedily feeding on the Empire's indebtedness was far from depicting the much more complex reality. That the bank was controlled by foreign capital, and that the Empire was increasingly falling under the control and domination of western imperialist expansion was undeniably true, and, in that sense, it may be argued that the Imperial Ottoman Bank was in many ways involved in this process of exploitation. On the other hand, what seems to be often forgotten is that beyond its organic links to Paris and London through its shareholders and committees the Imperial Ottoman Bank was, first and foremost, a private venture, the main concern of which was profits on a long-term basis. This brought to the institution a high degree of autonomy, not only with respect to the Ottoman government which it was supposed to serve, but also *vis-à-vis* western governments whose policies did not necessarily coincide with its own interests.[7] With respect to the Ottoman government, the bank was therefore conscious of its responsibilities as a state bank and, as such, made use of its power and influence to maintain Ottoman creditworthiness above acceptable limits. Even though the bank realized substantial profits out of the sole servicing of the Ottoman debt, it was also aware that this dramatic situation could not go on indefinitely. In other words, the bank was conscious of the fact that its very existence, in the long run, was conditional on the survival of the Ottoman Empire and, preferably, on its capacity to break the vicious circle of indebtment it had been sucked into.[8] For the Ottoman Bank, a normalization of the Ottoman debt would bring about the normalization of its own activities as a commercial venture. Instead of mobilizing most of its resources in short-term advances to the government[9] or in the backing of foreign loans, it would be able to invest them in more productive ventures such as infrastructure investments or commercial banking in general. This in turn would trigger a substantial development of the market and economy, thus guaranteeing long-term returns of a more solid nature to the bank.[10] From its creation, the Imperial Ottoman Bank had, therefore, a 'developmental' vision of its role in the Empire – not unlike the Rostowian 'take-off' model of a century later – according to which a judicious injection of capital would hopefully lead to the transformation and growth of the economy.

This vision of coinciding interests between the bank and the Empire did not, however, exclude a latent conflict of sovereignty between the two with regard to financial matters. If the Imperial Ottoman Bank admittedly saw its role as a state bank as being essentially defined in terms of 'service' to the Empire, it nevertheless believed that its success depended to a large extent on its capacity to impose its conditions on the state it was supposed to serve. Thus, although theoretically an instrument of modernization and reform in the hands of the Ottoman government, the bank clearly thought that it was necessary that it should control the potentially reckless ways in which the government tended to borrow funds without making proper use of these resources in terms of sound economic investments.[11] The strong insistence, from the very start, that the bank should be administered by a committee nominated by the concessionnaires in London and Paris, and that the High Commissioner appointed by the Ottoman government should have absolutely no say on the administration of the bank were the first signs of this mistrust of the bank *vis-à-vis* the Ottoman government and its belief that it could act for the good of the Empire only if the preconditions of its autonomy – not to say its supremacy – were guaranteed.[12] The 1874 negotiations carried out in Paris with Sadýk Pasha, Minister of Finance, and the resulting amendments to the convention, dated 17 February 1875, only reinforced this impression, as the Ottoman Bank squeezed from an increasingly helpless Ottoman government additional prerogatives such as a full presence in the budget commission and an exclusive right to pre-emption for any loan contracted.[13] Paradoxical as it may sound, the Ottoman Bank was willing to become an instrument of the government, but only as long as it was given the rights and power of a full and autonomous actor. 'The White Bank's Burden', in the eyes of the Paris and London committees, deserved that much of a concession and sacrifice on the part of the Ottoman government.

In effect, however, the bank would never fully realize all the advantages it had obtained on paper from the Ottoman state. Until 1875 it was greatly absorbed by the effort of organizing foreign loans, and the

Ottoman government, taking advantage of the vagueness of the 1863 convention, was to a large extent able to play down the bank's potential influence by resorting to a wide range of competitors, all willing to grab their part of the profitable market of Ottoman loans. After 1875, and despite the amendments that gave it preponderance over potential competitors and control over the financial affairs of the Empire, the bank was faced with the financial insolvency of the state and with the extraordinary conditions of the war against Serbia and Russia. It felt forced to advance huge sums to the government, while the latter made sure, by all means, that the bank did not get full access to the documents and information that would have enabled it to exercise some control over budgetary and financial matters. It was only with the normalization of the situation after the creation, in 1881, of the Public Debt Administration that the Ottoman Bank came to a point where it could try to assert its influence and force the government into greater compliance with the 'rules of the game'. However, this time, the reemergence of a threatening competition, especially that of the combined political and financial power of Berlin and the Deutsche Bank, would once again provide the Ottoman government with sufficient space to manoeuvre away from total dependence on the Ottoman Bank.

A single example will best illustrate the awkward situation that had by then developed between the government and the Ottoman Bank. When, in 1896, the Ottoman government had asked for an advance of 150 000 lire to pay the arrears of its gendarmerie troops stationed in Macedonia, the bank, still waiting for an authorization from the committees, had soon discovered that the government had been proposed German financial support for the same purpose and had, in anticipation of this support, already started disbursing sums officially attributed to the servicing of the debt. Such blatant disrespect of agreements infuriated the bank, which immediately wrote a harsh and incisive letter to the Minister of Finance:

> We take the liberty of respectfully pointing to Your Excellency that the Imperial Government is following a very adventurous policy by refusing to support the constant efforts of the bank to maintain its credit on European markets and that it is precisely at the very moment that it [the Government] is looking into the possibilities of engaging in a very important financial operation that it is diverting from their [proper] destination funds attributed to the servicing of one of its loans.[14]

Everything in the tone carried a sense of superiority on behalf of the bank: arrogance, scolding, accusations of ingratitude, masked threats even. Yet there was little more that the bank could do beyond expressing its resentment and frustration; it had learned through experience to live with the somewhat whimsical and manipulative practices of the Hamidian regime and had no real power to impose its will on a government resourceful enough to play the German card anytime it felt it useful.

One understands easily therefore the enthusiasm with which the administration of the bank greeted the Young Turks revolution of 1908 and the proclamation of the Constitution. Hopes could now be nurtured of seeing the establishment of a regime more inclined toward an open – and budget-based – financial management, and the bank immediately expressed its wish to see its real role of a state bank – as it understood it – respected by the new system. Thus in a letter to the Paris Committee, Deffès, Director-General in Constantinople, declared that it was in the interest of the bank to support the new regime, even if this support should not, immediately, include financial support, for fear of German participation in the process.[15] A few days later, the bank officially contacted the Ottoman government via the Minister of Finance, expressing its desire to see the establishment of a true collaboration under the terms of the 1875 agreement.[16] However, the Young Turk regime, under the counsel of its Minister of Finance, Cavid Bey, soon proved to be even more willing than the Hamidian governments to use German, British and even French competition to curb the power and autonomy of the Imperial Ottoman Bank. The bank's hopes of finally establishing some kind of control over Ottoman finances soon disintegrated, and the Ottoman Bank gradually lost whatever leverage on the government it had been able to salvage until the First World War.

This brief overview of the relationship between the Imperial Ottoman Bank and the Ottoman state from 1863 to 1914 shows to a large extent – and contrary to widespread beliefs – that the bank behaved, overall, much more as an instrument of modernization serving the general purposes of the Ottoman government than as an autonomous actor with the force and prerogative of imposing its own will. Although the attitude of the bank may well have been – in fact was – much more 'paternalistic' in intent, its real potential turned out to be quite different, as it was time after time frustrated in its attempts to gain a stronger grip on Ottoman finances.

Does that make the Imperial Ottoman Bank a 'colonial/imperialist failure'? Not really, if one considers the fact that the whole process of Ottoman modernization entailed an inherent dependence on western control, be it political, economic, or even cultural. On the other hand, it is doubtful that the Ottoman Bank ever thought of itself as an instrument of colonization and imperialism, at least beyond the limits of the context – within the dominant discourse of the period concerned – of the 'evident' need for control over a yet 'immature' economy and society. What limited the possibilities of the bank really controlling the Ottoman government was the fact that the relationship between the two was much less unequal than may be thought, and that it was based much more on interdependence than on dependence alone. As long as profits flowed, and as long as its privilege as a state bank was not endangered by an attitude that might be perceived by the government as open negligence or infraction of its duties, there was little the bank could or indeed would do to change the *status quo*.

One might rightly argue that this compromising attitude was one of the main reasons behind the bank's general reluctance to engage in any form of investment or commercial operation without solid guarantees as to their returns. It is therefore more than probable that the bank's contribution to the 'real' economic development of the Empire lagged far behind its true potential, even after the 1880s when it had finally freed itself from the cumbersome burden of advances to the state. However, it should be noted that, even within the limitations imposed by this cautious attitude, the most important – or at least most interesting from the viewpoint of the social scientist – contribution of the Ottoman Bank to the process of change in the Ottoman Empire probably lies in its interface with the economy and society. The thousands of files relating to customers and employees of the bank tell a much livelier – and in many ways truer – story of the transformations undergone by the Empire, told with the neutrality of what we could best define as a recipient and a catalyst of modernization. A story which, at any rate, would by far exceed the scope of this paper.

Notes

1. The first phase of the project was initiated in 1989 under the collaboration of the Ottoman Bank (Osmanlı Bankası) and the French Institute for Anatolian Studies (Institut Français d'Études Anatoliennes) and involved the classification and cataloguing of historical archives kept at the archive building of the bank (Bulgur Palas, Cerrahpşa, Istanbul). This 'virtual' classification ended with the publication in 1994 of a detailed inventory of the archives (Edhem Eldem, *Banque Impériale Ottomane. Inventaire commenté des archives*, Istanbul: IFEA-Osmanlı Bankası, Collection Varia Turcica XXV, 1994). In 1997, approximately one year after the transfer of the Ottoman Bank from the French Paribas group to the Turkish Doğuş group, the new management of the bank decided to take up and expand the project, in association with the Foundation for the Economic and Social History of Turkey (Türkiye Ekonomik ve Toplumsal Tarih Vakfı) with the ultimate aim of setting up an autonomous unit under the name of the 'Ottoman Bank Historical Research Center'. The archival material has thus been transferred from Bulgur Palas to the previous location of the Beyoğlu (Pera) branch of the bank, now used for the

research centre. The project includes the classification of additional material pertaining to the 1933–96 period and of remaining archives transferred from the Anatolian branches of the bank. A great portion of these archives will be scanned and digitalized throughout 1998 and the research centre should be open to researchers by the end of 1998.

2. 'Osmanlı Bankası Arşivi ve Tasnif Çalışmaları Hakkında Bir Sunuş' (A presentation on the Ottoman Bank archives and their classification), *Toplum ve Ekonomi*, 3, 1992, pp. 5–12; 'Galata'nın Etnik Yapısı' (The ethnic structure of Galata), in *İstanbul*, 1, 1992, pp. 58–63; 'The Ethnic Structure of Galata', *Biannual Istanbul*, 1, 1993, pp. 28–33; 'Culture et signature: quelques remarques sur les signatures de clients de la Banque Impériale Ottomane au début du XXe siècle', *Études turques et ottomanes. Documents de travail n° 2*, June 1993 and *L'oral et l'écrit*, Paris, 1993, pp. 63–74; 'Batılılaşma, Modernleşme ve Kozmopolitizm: 19. Yüzyıl Sonu ve 20. Yüzyıl Başında İstanbul', (Westernization, modernization and cosmopolitanism: Istanbul at the end of the nineteenth and beginning of the twentieth centuries) in Rona Zeynep (ed.) *Osman Hamdi Bey ve Dönemi*, Istanbul: Tarih Vakfı Yurt Yayınları, 1993, pp. 12–26; 'Culture et signature: quelques remarques sur les signatures de clients de la Banque Impériale Ottomane au début du XXe siècle', in *Revue du Monde Musulman et de la Méditerranée. Oral et écrit dans le monde turco-ottoman*, 75–6, (1–2) 1995, pp. 181–95; 'Istanbul 1903–1918: a quantitative analysis of a bourgeoisie', *Boğaziçi Journal. Review of Social, Economic and Administrative Studies*, 11 (1–2), 1997, *Istanbul Past and Present Special Issue*, pp. 53–98. As part of the ongoing project we should finally mention the realization of an exhibition (17 December 1997–17 March 1998) under the title 'Glimpses from the Past. An Exhibition of the Ottoman Bank Archives' (Tarihten İzler. Osmanlı Bankası Arşivleri Sergisi) in collaboration with Şölen Bazman, Eray Makal (graphic design) and Cengiz Kabaoğlu, Zehra Tulunoğlu (architectural design) and the forthcoming publication of *A 135-Year-Old Treasure. Glimpses From the Past in the Ottoman Bank Archives.*

3. The 4 February 1863 agreement signed between the Ottoman government and the concessionnaires of the future Ottoman Bank clearly stated the following functions of the new institution, *Ottoman Bank Archives*, hereafter *OBA*, Legal Affairs Files, Certified copy of the 4 February 1863 agreement, February 1307/1892:

- The Ottoman Bank was to become the state bank of the Ottoman state.
- It would enjoy a 30-year privilege of issue for banknotes, against the obligation of holding half of their value in reserve during the first two years and one-third during the following years, while the state pledged it would refrain from issuing paper money.
- It would be managed by a committee nominated by the founders in Paris and London.
- It would conduct treasury operations on behalf of the state in those locations where it has branches, discounting notes issued by the Ministry of Finance.
- It would manage the internal and external debt payments of the Ottoman state, charging a 1 per cent commission for this service.

- It would become the official broker of internal and external loans contracted by the Ottoman state, against a yearly fee of £20 000.
- It would open a £500 000 credit to the Ottoman state at 6 per cent as a 'statutory advance'.

4. Fiscal transformations of the seventeenth and eighteenth centuries have been analysed by Halil İnalcık in his 'Military and fiscal transformation in the Ottoman Empire, 1600–1700', *Archivum Ottomanicum*, VI, pp. 283–337. For an excellent analysis of late-eighteenth and early nineteenth-century fiscal and financial reform in the Ottoman Empire, see Yavuz Cezar, *Osmanlı Maliyesinde Bunalım ve Değişim Dönemi*, Istanbul, 1986.
5. On the Ottoman paper money experiment, see Ali Akyıldız, *Osmanlı Finans Sisteminde Dönüm Noktası. Kâğıt Para ve Sosyo-Ekonomik Etkileri*, Istanbul: Eren, 1996.
6. André Autheman, *La Banque Impériale Ottomane*, Paris: Comité pour l'histoire économique et financière de la France, 1996.
7. A typical example of this autonomy can be seen in the establishment of the Ottoman Public Debt, in 1881, as a result of a collaboration between the Imperial Ottoman Bank and the Deutsche Bank, the Wiener Credit-Anstalt and the German government itself. Weakened by the presence in their own countries of a great number of Ottoman debt bondholders, Paris and London had been incapable of providing the bank with the necessary support for the realization of its plans, and the bank had then turned to Berlin and Vienna, playing to a large extent the card of rising German influence in the Ottoman Empire to consolidate its position (Autheman, op. cit., pp. 87–9). In a rather similar way, during the initial phases of the Baghdad Railway project that opposed Berlin to Paris, the Imperial Ottoman Bank did not hesitate to side with the German contractors, much to the bewilderment of French ambassador Constans, whose political convictions and diplomatic priorities made it impossible to understand a move that was, after all, motivated by a 'financial sympathy' for the most reliable and viable project (Jacques Thobie, *Intérêts et impérialisme français dans l'Empire Ottoman (1895–1914)*, Paris: Sorbonne, 1977, pp. 547–56).
8. In the words of Christopher Clay: 'The European bankers, or at least those of the B[anque] I[mpériale] O[ttomane], whilst certainly making extremely good profits out of their dealings with the Porte, cannot be held to have tempted or encouraged the latter to go on borrowing for the sake of those profits', Christopher Clay, 'The financial collapse of the Ottoman state, 1863–1875', paper presented at the *Sixth International Conference of Economic and Social History of the Ottoman Empire and Turkey (1326–1960)*, 1–4 July 1992, Aix-en-Provence, p. 32.
9. The proportion of advances to the government to total advances increased regularly from 20–30 per cent in the 1860s to 80–90 per cent after the bankruptcy of 1875, and started to decrease only after 1886 when the Ottoman Empire was able, after the creation of the Public Debt Administration in 1881, to resort once again to foreign loans.
10. One cannot overlook or discard as mere rhetoric the statement made during the first general assembly of shareholders by the representative of the committee: 'The domestic wealth and resources of Turkey cannot be evaluated too highly; they open a vast field to regular enterprise and the

bank will have the duty and objective of taking up and increasing these resources together with national prosperity', Adrien Biliotti, *La Banque Impériale Ottomane*, Paris: Henri Jouve, 1909, p. 319.

11. This vision of the bank's support being conditional on the guarantee that the Ottoman government was *really* intending to carry out reform projects – implicitly evoking the strong possibility of the contrary – is obvious in the following passage from a letter of Casimir Salvador, one of the founding concessionnaires, to the Marquis de Plouec, administrator of the Bank: 'If ordinary expenditures are met by ordinary revenues ... if [the government] does not engage in ruinous extraordinary expenditures, if you believe that this path of order and regularity we have been told of for so long is real, serious, continuous, ... it is necessary – and the bank has been created for that purpose – to offer [the government] a rapid and wide support for its projects of renovation', *Archives Nationales*, 272 AP 15, 21 January 1867, quoted by Christopher Clay, op. cit., p. 4.
12. 'La Banque sera administrée à Constantinople par une Direction de deux à trois membres et par un Conseil de trois membres. L'une et l'autre seront nommés par un Comité choisi par les fondateurs de Londres et de Paris. Le comité aura tout pouvoir, conformément aux Statuts, de guider, contrôler et surveiller les opérations de la Banque' (Article 7); 'Le Gouvernement Impérial exercera son contrôle sur la Banque par le moyen d'un Haut Commissaire (Nazir) choisi par lui, qui aura la faculté de prendre connaissance des opérations de cette Institution sans pouvoir s'ingérer dans son administration, et qui veillera à la fidèle exécution des Statuts' (Article 3), *OBA*, Legal Affairs Files, Certified copy of the 4 February 1863, agreement, February 1307/1892.
13. *OBA*, Legal Affairs Files, Amendments to the 1863 convention, 17 February 1875.
14. 'Nous nous permettons de faire respectueusement remarquer à Votre Excellence que le Gouvernement Impérial suit une politique bien aventureuse en ne secondant pas les efforts constants de la Banque pour maintenir son crédit sur les marchés européens et que c'est précisément au moment où il examine s'il ne lui serait pas possible de procéder à une opération financière très importante qu'il fait dévier de leur destination des fonds destinés à assurer le service d'un de ses Emprunts', *OBA*, CD-CPCA 08, f° 75, Letter from Director-General J. Deffès to Retad Pasha, Minister of Finance, 18 May 1904.
15. 'Notre politique – et en cela nous sommes unanimes – doit tendre à retirer du nouveau régime les avantages légitimes auxquels nous avons droit et à assurer à notre Etablissement son rôle de Banque d'Etat, qui lui est du reste attribué par son Firman de Concession.

    Pour l'instant et en attendant le moment où nous pourrons utilement intervenir dans l'élaboration des réformes financières, nous devons prêter tout notre loyal concours au Gouvernement et l'aider à faire face aux difficultés actuelles, ainsi que les Comités de la Banque l'ont eux-mêmes jugé nécessaire. Mais devons-nous accepter des concours financiers? Je ne le pense pas et je considère que ce serait une faute politique que de donner, aux Allemands surtout, le droit de se faire valoir auprès du nouveau régime', *OBA*, CD-CPCA 11, ff. 344–8, copy of the letter by Deffès to M. de Cerjat from the Paris Committee.
16. 'Un des premiers effets du rétablissement de la Constitution Ottomane a

été de faire ressortir la nécessité d'établir, pour la reconstitution des finances de l'Empire, un budget régulier.

Votre Excellence sait quel est le rôle très important que l'Art. 7 de l'acte de concession de la Banque Impériale Ottomane et le Règlement déterminant ses rapports avec la Ministère des Finances lui assignent dans l'élaboration du Budget et dans les services de Trésorerie de l'Empire.

Le régime auquel s'est substitué le régime constitutionnel n'avait pas cru devoir recourir à la collaboration de la Banque Impériale Ottomane, parce qu'il jugeait inutile l'établissement d'un budget dans les formes prévues par la Constitution de 1876.

Les diverses tentatives faites par la Banque pour l'étude et la publication d'un budget n'eurent aucun succès et nous rappellerons qu'un projet en fut même établi par nous il y a plusieurs années, mais qu'il ne reçut aucune sanction pratique.

Les circonstances ont changé. Le peuple ottoman comprend que les réformes auxquelles il aspire ne pourront être réalisées si elles n'ont pour base la réorganisation des finances de l'Empire.

Le programme du Ministère et la presse qui reflète les aspirations du pays, placent en première ligne l'élaboration d'un budget sérieux.

Fidèle à sa tradition d'entier dévouement aux intérêts et à la prospérité de l'Empire, sûre de pouvoir apporter au Gouvernement Impérial un concours puissant pour la réorganisation de ses finances et remplir, pour le plus grand bien du pays, le rôle qui lui est assigné par son acte de concession, la Banque Impériale Ottomane vient déclarer à votre Excellence qu'elle met à la disposition du Gouvernement Impérial Ottoman son travail, ses conseils et son expérience et qu'elle est prête à remplir dans la Commission du Budget la mission que lui attribue l'Art. 7 de l'acte de 1875', *OBA*, Copy of the letter by J. Deffès and Al. Pangiris to Ziya Pasha, Minister of Finance, 21 August 1908.

CHAPTER FOUR

Western Capital and the Bulgarian Banking System: Late Nineteenth Century–Second World War

Alexandre Kostov

The influx of foreign capital[1] in Bulgaria took various forms in the late nineteenth and early twentieth century. As in the other Balkan countries, most of the foreign capital came to Bulgaria in the form of state loans; direct investments in railway building made as early as in the pre-1878 period were of secondary importance. A little later – and on a smaller scale – western banks began making investments in Bulgarian banking and industry. The present study aims at exploring the emergence and operations of banks established with foreign capital as well as the role which these banks played in Bulgaria's banking system[2] and economic development from the end of the nineteenth century to the Second World War.

After several centuries of Ottoman rule, in 1878 Bulgaria regained its sovereignty. At that point, one of the nation's most urgent economic tasks was to create an up-to-date banking system which would speed up its economic development. It was in the early 1900s that the first phase in the process of the creation of modern banking in Bulgaria came to its end. During that period the two biggest state-owned banks, the National Bank of Bulgaria (NBB) and the Bulgarian Agricultural Bank, were established; in the following decades, these two banks were to form the backbone of Bulgaria's banking system. In the 1880s and 1890s several joint-stock banks were established; however, due to the lack of national capital, private banking developed at a slow pace and played a relatively minor role in the Bulgarian economy. It is worth noting that bigger private banks were first established in provincial cities. Thus, the Danube city of Russe became an important banking centre: in 1881 the Girdap Bank was established there, followed, in 1895, by the Banque Commerciale Bulgare.[3]

The activity of the Ottoman Bank

The interest that western banks showed in Bulgarian banking in the 1880s and 1890s was quite limited. The Ottoman Bank/Banque Impériale Ottomane (BIO) seems to have been the only foreign bank that played a relatively important role in the Bulgarian economy. During these two decades, the Ottoman Bank opened branches in Plovdiv, Sofia, Russe and Burgas.[4] Their activity was mostly limited to financing the grain trade and foreign currency exchange. There is evidence that the Ottoman Bank invested in certain credit and industrial companies as well. Its operations in Bulgaria were quite successful which is the reason why the bank did not close its branches in Bulgaria even during the crisis of 1895. Somewhat later in 1899, however, the BIO was compelled to close its Bulgarian branches: this was largely due to the series of poor harvests and the decline of grain export at the turn of the century, which decreased the bank's profits.

The British historian Christopher Clay[5] argues that it was the Bulgarian authorities' bad attitude that accounted for the closure of the BIO's branches in Bulgaria. In our opinion, Clay's assertion needs further clarification. Thus, in 1898, the London and Paris committees of the BIO gave their consent to the bank's participation in the establishment of the Banque de Commerce et d'Industrie Bulgare. This project failed to materialize; nevertheless, the very fact that negotiations were conducted testifies to the existence of good relations between the BIO, on the one hand, and some influential figures in the then ruling National Party of Bulgaria, on the other.[6]

The rapid pulling out of the credits given by the BIO caused serious difficulties for the monetary system in Bulgaria due to the limited resources of the NBB which could not cover traders' needs.[7]

The founding of the first foreign banks

Prior to the 1900s several more attempts at establishing banks with foreign capital were made; however, nearly all of them were unsuccessful.[8] It was only in 1898 that the Hungarian Pester Ungarische Commerzialbank established the Banque de Commerce in Sofia with share capital of 250 thousand leva, which in 1901 was increased to 1 million leva.[9]

There was a massive influx of western capital in Bulgarian banking in the mid-1910s. This was largely due to the increased competition among the Great Powers each of which strove to establish economic domination in the region. By that time the big western banks had already issued several loans to the Bulgarian state; as a result, their respective governments gave them support in the struggle to obtain stronger positions in Bulgaria's banking system. The economic boom in Bulgaria, which led to the opening of numerous factories and increased industrial production and foreign trade, also favoured the influx of foreign capital in the country.

Over a short period of time, between 1905 and 1906, three big commercial banks with foreign participation were established in Sofia.[10] In October 1905 a German group of banks (Diskonto Gesellschaft, S. Bleichröder, Norddeutsche Bank) established the Banque de Crédit. The German banks owned 83 per cent of its share capital which amounted to 3 million leva.[11] In December of the same year the Banque Générale Bulgare was established with a share capital of 4 million leva. The French Ministry of Foreign Affairs played an important role in its establishment: the Quai d'Orsay recommended to Paribas (the Banque de Paris et des Pays-Bas) (which was the Bulgarian state's main creditor at that time) that they should establish a bank in Bulgaria with the purpose of defending French interests in the country. The Parisian bank took over 60 per cent of the share capital of the Banque Générale Bulgare while another 30 per cent was taken over by its partner, the Pester Ungarische Commerzialbank, which merged the existing Banque de Commerce into the newly established venture.[12] In January 1906 the Banque Balkanique was established; its share capital was 3 million leva. The main shareholder was the Wiener Bankverein with 40 per cent of the capital, while another 43 per cent was taken over by the Banque de l'Union Parisienne (BUP), the Anglo-Österreichische Bank and the Crédit Anversois.[13]

A comparative study of western investment in the banking of all the Balkan countries would show that the competition among the Great Powers should not be exaggerated. Although linked with their respective governments, the big western banks preserved their relative independence; this could best be seen from their choice of partners in the Balkans. Thus, in 1906, the group associated in the Banque Balkanique established the Rumanian Commercial Bank in Bucharest while Paribas and the Pester Ungarische Commerzialbank took part, in 1905, in the establishment of another bank in Bucharest, the Marmorosch Blank & Cie.[14] These, as well as some other facts (e.g. the participation of the Diskonto Gesellschaft and S. Bleichröder in the Rumanian General Bank in Bucharest) show that after 1906 Bulgaria became part of a network of Balkan affiliates of powerful western banking groups.

In the first years following their establishment the functions of the Banque Balkanique, the Banque Générale Bulgare and the Banque de Crédit were mostly limited to issue of credits to traders and industrialists.

They relied on deposits and credits from their shareholders rather than their own share capital and reserves. Due to the lack of local deposits the main amount of capital used in the credit operations of the three banks came from their founding banks, which charged a 2–3 per cent rate of interest on their capital, that is a rate of interest that was 1 per cent higher than the average one in Western Europe. In a short period of time the three banks obtained stable positions in the Bulgarian capital market; this they achieved thanks to their stability as well as the lower rates of interest they charged on the credits they offered – their rate of interest was usually 8–9 per cent while the Bulgarian commercial banks charged 12–13 per cent.[15] Furthermore, the establishment of the three banks contributed to the transformation of Bulgaria's capital, Sofia, into an important financial centre. In addition, they opened quite a few branches in provincial cities. The biggest of the three, the Banque Balkanique, conducted other operations, too, for example, the export and transportation of grain.[16] Both the Banque Balkanique and the Banque Générale Bulgare participated in the establishment of trading and industrial companies. Foreign banks were also interested in mortgage credit which will be discussed later in the text.

Before the Balkan Wars, several smaller banks with foreign capital were established as well. Thus, the German Commerz- und Diskonto Bank participated in the establishment of the Banque Danubienne (Russe);[17] the Ungarische Bank- und Handels AG (Budapest) opened its affiliate in Sofia under the name Bulgarische Bank- und Handels AG.[18]

These examples show that in the early twentieth century several commercial banks were established in Bulgaria; their founders were banking institutions from France, Germany, Austria-Hungary and Belgium. Certain financial circles in Britain too showed some interest in Bulgarian banking; however, they did not establish a bank in Bulgaria.

Table 4.1 Share of the foreign banks* in Bulgaria's private banking sector, 1911–13 (million leva)

Year	Capital & reserves	%	Deposits & credits	%	Portfolio & advances	%
1911	15.2	39.45	51.5	54.78	63.7	51.67
1912	15.4	37.11	60.4	63.98	72.8	49.26
1913	15.7	36.01	80.6	54.03	72.2	47.94

* Banque Balkanique, Banque Générale Bulgare and Banque de Crédit

Source: *Bankov pregled*, 1914, pp. 226–9.

Thus, in 1908, in connection with the investment of British capital in the Bulgarian textile industry, some British businessmen advanced the idea of a future English-Bulgarian Bank; this project, however, failed to get the support of the British government and banks and did not materialize.[19]

The role that foreign banks played in the Bulgarian economy is best illustrated through the financial results of the Banque Balkanique, the Banque Générale Bulgare and the Banque de Crédit, as compared to the results of the remainder of other commercial banks in the country (see Table 4.1).

Interest in mortgage credit

In 1910–12 western capital showed a noticeable interest in mortgage credit in Bulgaria which, in turn, led to the establishment of specialized bank institutes. It is true that some western banks had been conducting this type of operation since the moment they were established. Following the crisis of 1907 in America they collected most of the loans they had issued in Bulgaria with the purpose of transferring this money abroad. On the whole, mortgaging was at an early stage of its development in the country. The most important roles belonged to the Bulgarian Agricultural Bank which began issuing loans to farmers and the NBB, which issued its loans to traders and industrialists. In 1909 these two banks, together with two insurance companies, issued mortgage loans to the amount of 69.4 million leva. Among the private banks, the Banque Balkanique issued loans amounting to 4.56 million leva which was 4.5 times as much as the sum total of the mortgage loans issued by all the other private banks.[20]

The Banque Balkanique's interest in issuing mortgage loans was demonstrated in the establishment of Crédit Foncier Bulgare (1910),[21] which took over its mortgage operations. In 1911 the Banque Générale Bulgare also opened a subsidiary company, the Banque Générale Hypothécaire du Royaume de Bulgarie, whose main field of operation was the issue of mortgage loans.[22] These two banks, however, were not really successful due to conflicts with the Bulgarian government regarding their rights of issuing mortgage bonds.

In 1912 the two western banking groups decided to collaborate through the newly founded Crédit Foncier Franco-Bulgare, which was established under French law with headquarters in Paris and a branch in Sofia. This bank took over the assets and liabilities of both the Crédit Foncier Bulgare and the Banque Générale Hypothécaire du Royaume de Bulgarie.[23] In 1912 one more bank was established; this was the Banque

Commerciale et Foncière des Balkans[24] the bulk of whose share capital was French and whose main field of operation was to be mortgage credit. A small Belgian company, Credit Hypothécaire Agricole et Urbain d'Egypte, opened a branch in Sofia too. More interesting in this case is the opinion of its management: 'Mortgage operations in Bulgaria looked very promising and profitable, and the existing conditions in the country made them look economically feasible.'[25] However, because of the Balkan Wars the activity of the foreign mortgage banks in Bulgaria was not so successful.

The superiority of Austro-Hungarian banks during the war

The First World War laid its seal on the functioning of foreign capital in Bulgarian banking. In October 1915 Bulgaria entered the war siding with the Central Powers. This limited to a great extent the participation of French banks which were forced to withdraw from the country. The war allies of Bulgaria profited from this situation. In banking, particularly active were Austro-Hungarian banks achieving, albeit temporarily, dominant positions in existing banks. Thus the Pester Ungarische Commerzialbank together with the Allgemeine Bodencreditanstalt established full dominance in the Banque Générale Bulgare through the increase of its share capital in April 1917 from 5 to 8 million leva. In the same year the Wiener Bankverein jointly with other Austro-Hungarian banks[26] took over the new shares in the increase of the capital of the Banque Balkanique from 6 to 10 million leva. Another Austro-Hungarian group led by the Allgemeine Depositenbank founded in the beginning of 1918 the Banque de Crédit Austro-Bulgare with share capital of 25 million leva of which 10 million was paid up. The share capital of the Bulgarische Bank- und Handels AG was also increased from 1 to 5 million leva and it was renamed the Banque Hongroise-Bulgare.[27]

The growth of foreign banking during the postwar decade

After the end of the First World War the Bulgarian economy, and in particular banking fell into deep crisis. Heavy reparations were imposed on the country due to its defeat in the war. Devaluation of the Bulgarian currency started immediately after the war and gained in intensity. The NBB could no longer serve the economy's needs as it was directing its funds mainly to the state. This unstable situation in the credit system determined the role of western banks as intermediaries in attracting spare capital from Western Europe.

French banks were particularly active, usually cooperating with Belgian groups to invest in Bulgarian banking. Their penetration was facilitated by the dominant position of France in this region. On the other hand, the dismemberment of the Hapsburg Monarchy caused the partial retreat of Austrian and Hungarian banks from Bulgaria.[28]

A massive influx of foreign capital into Bulgarian banking occurred in the period 1919–22, which was the most difficult time for the country's economy. Operations at the three biggest banks, the Banque Balkanique, Banque Générale Bulgare and the Banque de Crédit, continued after the war, whereas some smaller banks with foreign participation ceased to exist. As already stated, due to the favourable political situation French capital not only restored its positions in the first two above-mentioned banks but also was able to increase its influence in this sector. Paribas played an important role in stabilizing the Banque Générale Bulgare,[29] while the Banque de l'Union Parisienne together with the Société Générale de Belgique won a leading position in the Banque Balkanique. In 1920 another French-Belgian group created the *commandite* company 'Angel Kujumdgiiski, which was reorganized as a joint-stock company three years later under the name Banque Franco-Belge de Bulgarie.

In some cases Bulgarian bankers took the initiative in attracting western (mainly French) capital. This was motivated by their need for financial as well as political support from western countries.[30] So in the postwar period two of the greatest Bulgarian banks attracted French participation. French banks took part in the reorganization of the Banque Bulgare pour le Commerce International in 1920–21; as a result the share of foreign groups became bigger than that of Bulgarian participants. The bank was renamed Banque Franco-Bulgare pour le Commerce International.[31] Paribas took part in the capital increase of the Banque Bulgare de Commerce in 1921. It formally remained a 'Bulgarian' bank but the French share was one-third.[32]

It is also worth mentioning the formation of the Banque Commerciale Italo-Bulgare. Supported by its main shareholder the Banca Commerciale Italiana (Milan) it soon became one of the most important private banks in Bulgaria. It was a part of the network of affiliates of the Milan bank in South-east Europe.[33]

In 1922 branches of the Deutsche Bank and the Banque de Crédit de Prague were also registered as joint-stock companies. The Czech bank's branch[34] financed mainly industrial enterprises created by itself – the biggest one was the sugar mill in Gorna Orjahovica (northern Bulgaria) opened in 1913. Some minor participation of foreign capital was present in the Banque Internationale de Bulgarie[35] and the small Anglo-Bulgarian 'Viticulture Bank'.

During the 1920s foreign banks definitively imposed their domination on lending to Bulgarian industry and trade. Their stability attracted more and more deposits from the Bulgarian population. They were facilitated by the weakened financial resources of the NBB and the orientation of the Agricultural Bank, cooperative and popular banks towards financing agriculture only. The credit activities of foreign affiliates were based mainly on short-term credits and deposits of their patron banks. The amount of these sums was greater than local deposits in the first postwar years and later – in the second half of the 1920s – the proportion was 42.5/47.5.[36]

The interest rates in Bulgaria before the First World War as well as after it were higher than in developed countries in Western Europe. These rates increased considerably in 1919–23 due to high inflation. After the war foreign banks in Sofia replaced the NBB's role as the main influence on interest rates. The interest on their deposits was 8–9 per cent and on their credits 18–20 per cent yearly. These high interest rates were caused by measures taken by the banks against eventual dramatic devaluation of the lev. They were preserved even after the stabilizing of the Bulgarian currency, which had started by the beginning of 1924. It was not until 1926 that interest rates were reduced to 10–13 per cent. So the reproaches of a number of Bulgarian economists were reasonable to some extent – large profits of foreign banks were due to their dominant position in the banking sector, which allowed them to dictate interest rates.[37] It is worth noting, however, that Bulgarian banks were both reluctant and unable to give credits with interest rates lower than those of western affiliates.

In 1926–27 foreign banks increased their lending in foreign currency credits whose interest rates were considerably lower than those in leva. This practice brought advantages to borrowers but on the other hand contained some risk of reduction or even withdrawal of credits by foreign banks in Sofia or by the patron banks in Western Europe. Such events were frequent especially after the beginning of the Great Depression.

Another important aspect of foreign banks' activity was their direct participation in the capital of trade, industrial and insurance companies. Almost all big banks controlled a number of such companies and their crediting was the bank's main activity. The only exception was the Banque de Crédit which mainly financed trade operations. The biggest Bulgarian enterprises were linked to foreign banks. For instance, the most powerful bank, Banque Franco-Belge, controlled the large industrial and trade company United Tobacco Factories (Cartel), the textile company Berov & Horinek and a number of others. It also created three subsidiary banks outside Sofia: Banque de Plovdiv, Banque Bulgare du Nord (Russe) and Banque Bulgaro-Belge (Burgas) which completed its branch network in the country.[38]

The influx of foreign capital into Bulgarian banking encouraged a process of consolidation. There are data from 1928 showing that 43.7 per cent of the capital and reserves were concentrated in ten out of 128 existing private banks in Bulgaria. These ten banks also dealt with 71.7 per cent of deposits and current credits and 66.8 per cent of investments as well. In seven of them foreign participation was predominant whereas the others were 'Bulgarian' banks with a majority of local capital. The biggest bank was the Banque Bulgare de Commerce (see Table 4.2).

The process of concentration of Bulgarian banking continued on the eve and at the beginning of the Great Depression. To a greater extent it concerned the foreign banks. In 1929 the Banque Franco-Belge and the Banque Balkanique merged. The new Banque Franco-Belge et Balkanique became the largest private bank in Bulgaria with share capital of 150 million leva. Following the merger of the Deutsche Bank and the Diskonto Gesellschaft in Germany their Bulgarian affiliates merged as well. Thus the Banque de Crédit merged with the branch of the Deutsche Bank in Sofia. Also, in 1929 the French shareholders lost positions in the Banque Franco-Bulgare pour le Commerce International,[39] which in its turn merged with two other Bulgarian banks at the beginning of the following year to form the Union des Banques Bulgares in which the amount of foreign capital was much smaller. Thus in 1930 there were six large banks in Bulgaria of which four had foreign majority participation while in the others, the Banque Bulgare de Commerce and the Union des Banques Bulgares, Bulgarian capital dominated.

The new interest in mortgage credit

In 1927 the NBB stopped its mortgage activity. In the following year the Banque Hypothécaire Bulgare was founded in accordance with an agreement between the Bulgarian state and the banks which had, in the same year, arranged the state loan to Bulgaria. The western group[40] took over 60 per cent of the share capital (10 million Swiss francs) of the mortgage bank. In 1930 the new bank contracted a bond loan abroad in the amount of 3 million francs. The activity of the Banque Hypothécaire Bulgare was limited to giving loans for housing construction, while the Agricultural Bank 'reserved' for itself the agricultural long-term crediting. In 1929–30 the Crédit Foncier Franco-Bulgare, which previously had fallen into lethargy, restored its activity for a short while.[41]

Table 4.2 Largest commercial banks in Bulgaria, deposits and investments, 1928 and 1929 (million leva)

Bank	Deposits & credits				Portfolio & advances			
	1928	%	1929	%	1928	%	1929	%
Franco-Belge*	588	12.5	855	17.0	534	12.4	904	18.7
Balkanique	413	8.8	—	—	408	9.4	—	—
Italo-Bulgare	898	19.1	1203	23.8	854	19.8	1131	23.4
Générale	320	6.8	384	7.6	330	7.7	385	7.9
de Crédit**	473	10.1	960	19.1	424	9.8	857	17.7
Deutsche Bank	247	5.2	—	—	93	2.2	—	—
Commerce International	485	10.3	458	9.1	442	10.3	428	8.8
Bulgare de Commerce	623	13.2	518	10.3	593	13.8	496	10.3
Crédit National	374	7.9	375	7.4	281	6.5	283	5.8
Bulgare	287	6.1	290	5.7	350	8.1	356	7.4
Total	4708	100	5043	100	4309	100	4840	100

Notes:
* In 1929 the Banque Franco-Belge merged with the Banque Balkanique
** In 1929 the Banque de Crédit merged with the branch of the Deutsche Bank

Source: *Bulletin de la Banque Nationale Bulgare* 8, 1930, p. 197.

The retreat of western capital in the 1930s

The Depression limited the credit activity of foreign banks because of decreased volume of trade. As banks' short-term assets reached maturity they could not be reclaimed owing to the crisis and were, in effect, transformed into long-term assets. Both investments and loans of the banks decreased due to withdrawal of deposits and freeze on crediting from the western patron banks.

Depression affected most of the enterprises linked to foreign banks, so they had to be financially reorganized with the support of the participating banks. Credits owed by enterprises were paid through the emission of new shares or the conversion of debt into new shares in the name of the respective banks. For instance, United Tobacco Factories and the company Berov & Horinek, which were linked to the Banque Franco-Belge, were reorganized in a similar fashion.[42]

Since the beginning of the 1930s two major tendencies in Bulgaria's economic policy determined the development of the banking system and the participation of foreign capital in it: the increase of state intervention in the economy and the intensifying trade exchange with Germany.

In order to overcome the aftermath of the crisis Bulgarian governments took a number of measures intended to increase the role of the state in the banking system. In the first place, the powers of the NBB were enlarged in connection with the introduction of a clearing system in foreign trade operations and the law of deposits protection, which forbade their use in long-term investments. The NBB played an active role in a liquidation and amalgamation of banks. As a result, in 1934, the semi-state bank Banque de Crédit was founded, which united 19 small and bigger banks, the Union des Banques Bulgares included. The newly founded bank was soon to become one of the leading banking institutions in the country. During the 1930s the role of the Agricultural Bank also increased: in 1934 it absorbed the small Co-operative Bank and two years later it bought out the foreign shareholders in the Banque Hypothécaire Bulgare.[43]

In the 1930s economic relations with Germany intensified greatly. The German share in Bulgarian export nearly doubled in a few years – from 36 per cent in 1932 to 68 per cent in 1939. Imports followed a similar trend. Quite naturally the Banque de Crédit profited a lot from this situation and took a leading place among foreign banks in Bulgaria in the second half of the 1930s. On the other hand, the orientation of Bulgarian trade contributed to a great extent to a weakening of the position of French and Belgian groups. Additional causes of their withdrawal from the Bulgarian economy were the limitations introduced in the transfer of profits abroad. The patron banks almost stopped crediting their affiliates in Bulgaria,[44] which forced them to rely mainly on the resources of local deposits. Foreign banks limited their participation in industrial, trade and insurance companies. Yet in the second half of the 1930s the activity of the Banque Franco-Belge et Balkanique was quite successful. By limiting its activity in crisis years and closing six of its branches in the country, it reduced its participation to four companies only, which achieved good results in this period. For instance, the dividends allocated by United Tobacco Factories in 1936–38 were 7–10 per cent and by Berov & Horinek 5–6 per cent.[45]

In 1938 the Banque Franco-Belge et Balkanique absorbed the Banque Générale Bulgare which suffered difficulties in that period. Simultaneously, due to a conflict between its major shareholders (BUP and Banque Belge pour l'Etranger) and their subsequent withdrawal, it passed into control of a group including Paribas, Lazard Brothers & Co., Louis Dreyfus & Co. and the Stockholms Enskilda Bank. Its name was changed to Banque Franco-Bulgare.

So, on the eve of the Second World War three big foreign banks continued their activity in Bulgaria: the Banque de Crédit, the Banque Franco-Bulgare and the Banque Commerciale Italo-Bulgare. Their share in assets of the commercial banks fell from 46 per cent in 1929 to 34 per cent in 1938.[46]

The further development of the foreign banks in Bulgaria was determined by the political events during and after the Second World War. The definitive retreat of western capital from Bulgarian banking was accomplished by the end of 1947 after the nationalization of the whole private sector by the communist regime.

Conclusions

The activity of western capital in Bulgarian banking at the end of the nineteenth century and in the first four decades of the twentieth century can best be understood against the backdrop of Bulgarian economic development in this period. Undoubtedly, the opening of affiliates of the largest European banks played an important role in the modernization of the country's credit system. New methods of work were introduced and popularized. These stimulated both state and local private banks to modernize their organization and work. The imported capital increased the credit capacity in the country during important moments of its economic development – at the beginning of the twentieth century and in the 1920s. Foreign banks favourably influenced the management and the results of the large industrial enterprises as well as the foreign trade relations of Bulgaria. They contributed to closer links between the country and the world economy, with all attendant positive and negative effects. At the same time, the activities of foreign banks show that they very often felt like guests and in many cases unwelcome. During some critical periods they chose to leave the country. Their positive impact on the Bulgarian economy could have been even more favourable had it not been for their selectiveness in choosing investments aimed primarily towards enterprises related to them. Of course, it would be setting too high standards to expect that foreign capital could have been the main motor of progress in an economy, however underdeveloped it was.

Notes

1. We use the term 'western' as a synonym of 'foreign' to avoid the discussion on the origin of Central-European banking capital which is not necessary here.
2. Another form of participation of western capital in Bulgarian banking were the bond loans contracted by the state banks, the National Bank of Bulgaria and the Agricultural Bank, in Western Europe between 1889 and 1909. It has remained outside our attention.
3. We have adopted the French names of the Bulgarian banks.
4. A. Autheman, *La Banque Impériale Ottomane*, Paris, 1996, pp. 134, 274.
5. C. Clay, 'The Imperial Ottoman Bank in the late nineteenth century: a multinational "national" bank?', in G. Jones (ed.) *Banks as Multinationals*, London and New York: Routledge, 1990, p. 155.
6. *Bulgarian Historical Archives* (*BHA*) 597–1–38, 1–2. Letter of A. Durastel (BIO) to Iv. Grozev, Iv. Ev. Geshov, St. Danev, D. Yablansky, Sofia 12/24 August 1898.
7. G.T. Danailov, 'Nezavisimostta I čuzdite banki u nas' (Independence and the foreign banks in our country), *Bankov pregled*, 8, 1908, pp. 232–3.
8. In 1892 the establishment of a Bulgarian-Belgian Bank was authorized by a royal decree with stock capital of 5 million leva, but this bank was never founded. See *State Gazette* No. 270/ 8.12.1892; A. Kostov, 'The Belgian Capital in the Balkans, 1878–1914', unpublished dissertation, Sofia, 1989, p. 28.
9. A. Mitrović, 'Mreža austrougarskih I nemačkih banaka na Balkanu pred prvi svetski rat' (The network of Austro-Hungarian and German banks in the Balkans on the eve of the First World War), *Jugoslvenski istorijski časopis* (Belgrade), 23 (3–4), 1988, p. 56.
10. In 1905, mostly with German capital, the Bulgarian Lottery Bank was established. Its stock capital was 850 thousand leva. Its founders were the Norddeutsche Bank, the Banque de Salonique and a few Hamburg companies. See R. Daskaloff, *Das auslaendische Kapital in Bulgarien*, Berlin, 1912, pp. 149–50.
11. In 1910 its stock capital was increased to 4 million leva. See Daskaloff, op. cit., pp. 135–6.

12. Ibid., pp. 135–6 and S. Damianov, *Frenskoto ikonomičesko pronikvane v Bălgarija*, 1878–1914 (French economic penetration in Bulgaria, 1878–1914), Sofia, 1971, pp. 182–3.
13. In 1908, the stock capital of the Banque Balkanique was increased to 4 million leva; thus the BUP's share was increased. See Daskaloff, op. cit., pp. 137–8; Damianov, op. cit., pp. 185–6; E. Bussière, 'The interests of the Banque de l' Union Parisienne in Czechoslovakia, Hungary and the Balkans, 1919–1930', in P.L. Cottrell and A. Teichova (eds) *International Business and Central Europe, 1918–1939*, Leicester: Leicester University Press, 1983, p. 407.
14. J. Riesser, *The German Great Banks and their Concentration with Connection of the Economic Development of Germany*, Washington: Government Printing House, 1911 (reprint 1977 by Arno Press), pp. 432–61; Mitrovič, op. cit., pp. 51–68; E. Bussière, *Paribas, l'Europe et le monde, 1887–1992*, Paris, 1992, p. 55.
15. D. Yordanov, 'Pet godini na čuzdite banki v Bălgarija' (Five years of the foreign banks in Bulgaria), *Bankov pregled*, 1911, pp. 206–10.
16. This bank took over the export activities of one of the largest grain export companies 'Neufeld & Cie' (Berlin-Russe).
17. *Bankov pregled*, 1912, p. 3.
18. Ibid., p. 197.
19. Representatives of the British government argued that this project was not economically feasible because of the insignificant volume of the Bulgarian–British trade at that time. See *Bankov pregled*, 1908, pp. 21, 87.
20. See St. Bočev, *Ipotekarnijat kredit u nas* (Mortgage credit in our country), Sofia, 1911, pp. 3–12.
21. *State Archives (SA)* – Sofia 3k-7-205.
22. *SA* – Sofia 3k-6-733.
23. *SA* – Sofia 3k-7-207; Damianov, op. cit., pp. 187–8.
24. Ibid., pp. 189–90.
25. See A. Kostov, 'The Belgian Capital in the Balkans, 1878–1914', unpublished dissertation, Sofia, 1989, p. 33.
26. Österreichische Creditanstalt, Ungarische Allgemeine Creditbank and Bank Rothschild.
27. Österreichische Länderbank, Ungarische Escompte- und Wechselbank and Vaterländische Bank. See D. Yordanov, *Vojnata i yovite a Kcioyezni dzužestva* (The war and the new joint-stock companies), Sofia, 1919, pp. 248; A. Mitrovič, 'Pester Ungarische Commerzialbank na Balkanu do 1918 godine' (Pester Ungarische Commerzialbank in the Balkans until 1918), *Zbornik Matice sprske za istoriju*, 34, 1986, pp. 66–7.
28. So in 1921 the Banque de Crédit Austro-Bulgare was liquidated.
29. Important changes occurred in the Banque Générale Bulgare in 1925–26 when its capital increased from 12 to 50 million leva and it absorbed the Banque Hongroise-Bulgare.This decreased the position of Paribas in favour of the Hungarian group led by the Pester Ungarische Commerzialbank. The main shareholder in the Banque Hongroise-Bulgare before 1925 was the British-Hungarian Bank (Budapest).
30. Many of the leading bankers in Bulgaria feared the legislative measures of the ruling Agrarian Party aimed at punishing people responsible for national catastrophe during the wars of 1912–18.
31. The Group of Caisse Commerciale et Industrielle de Paris, Crédit Foncier

du Brésil et d'Amérique du Sud and later Crédit Français and Banque Franco-Roumaine (Bucharest) held 12 million of the 22 million leva share capital of the bank. *SA* – Sofia, 3k-6-1955; N. Usunov, *Die fremden Kapitalien in Bulgarien*, Berlin, 1927, pp. 76–7.

32. Later in 1925 the share of Paribas rose to 38 per cent of the newly 60 million capital of the bank.
33. G. Toniolo, *One Hundred Years, 1894–1994. A Short History of the Banka Commerciale Italiana*, Fiesole, 1994, pp. 63–4.
34. In 1930, it was renamed Banque Anglo-Tchechoslovaque et de Crédit de Prague.
35. This bank was founded under the initiative of the Agrarian Party government, which intended through it to encourage exports. The main shareholders were the NBB and the Agricultural Bank. A few Swiss nd German participants had a smaller share in the capital.
36. *Bulletin de la Banque Nationale Bulgare,* 3–4, 1930, pp. 76–7.
37. See D.I. Simidčiev, *Cuzdite kapitali v naseto narodno stopanstvo* (Foreign capital in our economy), Sofia, 1930, pp. 48–53.
38. See Z. Natan and L. Berov, *Monopolističeskijat kapitalisam v Bălgarija* (Monopolist capitalism in Bulgaria), Sofia, 1958, pp. 196–203; As. Čakalov, *Formi, razmer i dejnost na čuzdija kapital v Bălgarija, 1878–1944* (Form, extent and activity of foreign capital 1878–1944), Sofia, 1962, pp. 65–6.
39. *SA* – Sofia 3k-6-1955.
40. The group included the Bancamerica Blair Corp. (New York), the Chase Securities Corp. (New York), Lazard Brothers & Co. (London), the Amsterdamsche Bank (Amsterdam), the Schweizerische Bankgesellschaft (Zürich), the BUP, the Banca Commerciale Italiana, the Banque Belge pour l'Etranger and the Hypotecni Banca Ceska (Prague).
41. See Čakalov, op. cit., pp. 60–61; M. Rusenov, *Istorija na finansovata I kreditnata sistema v Bălgarija* (History of Bulgaria's financial and credit system), vol. 2, Varna, 1983, pp. 741–3.
42. See A. Hristoforov, 'Akcionernite banki prez perioda na krizata' (The joint-stock banks during the crisis period), *Spisanie na Sajuza na Populjarnite Banki* 1, 1937, p. 35.
43. See M. Karamihailov, *Kreditnoto delo v Balgarija I stopanskata kriza* (The credit system in Bulgaria and the economic crisis), Sofia, 1939, pp. 71–82.
44. In 1934, for financial and political reasons, Paribas severed its relations with the Banque Bulgare de Commerce although it still kept its shares in this bank.
45. *Rapport du Conseil d'administration de la Banque Franco-Bulgare pour 1938,* Sofia, 1939, p. 5.
46. *Bulletin de la Banque Nationale Bulgare*, 9, 1939, p. 7.

CHAPTER FIVE

Foreign Banks in Serbia, 1882–1914[1]

Andrej Mitrović

In Serbia, more precisely in its capital Belgrade, where not only the major but the most complete transformation of the country was occurring, six banks were founded in the years prior to the First World War with complete or predominant foreign capital.[2] Only four of them are usually mentioned, the other two seldom and with less emphasis. One of the latter two was a Serbian bank with the parent bank in Zagreb, while the other was formally founded, but never put into operation.

Establishment, founders and power

The four most frequently mentioned banks were the most significant in Serbia, where a network of as many as one hundred banks (43 in Belgrade in 1911) was rather fragmented.[3] The oldest was the Serbian Credit Bank (Banque de Crédit Serbe). It was founded in 1882 and started to operate in 1883. In 1888 the Bank Andrejević (Banque Andréevitch et Cie) was founded as the second foreign bank in Serbia. After more than two decades, two other banks were founded in the summer of 1910 within just a week or two – first a branch of the Prague Credit Bank (Pražska Úverni banka),[4] then the French-Serbian Bank (Banque Franco-Serbe, hereinafter BFS).[5] The remaining two banks were founded subsequently: in 1911 the Danubian Joint-Stock Trade Company,[6] while in early autumn 1912 the authorities granted permission for the establishment of the Serbian-English Bank[7] (it was probably never put into operation due to three consecutive wars in 1912, 1913 and 1914). The Serbian Credit Bank was the first one to branch out in the provinces. It first opened an office in Šabac, the biggest town of an affluent agricultural region and export centre near the Austro-Hungarian border; in 1910 Bank Andrejević opened a branch in Niš, an important traffic hub.[8] When the Serbian border moved southward during the wars in 1912 and 1913, the BFS acquired branches in Skopje and Bitola from their former and its then owner the Imperial Ottoman Bank (Banque Impériale Ottomane – BIO).[9]

The bank network was by no means negligible for a country which had just started to develop in conformity with European models. In 1910 it encompassed an area of 48 300 km^2 with nearly 2.9 million inhabitants, and in 1913 acquired an additional 39 000 km^2 (areas even less developed than its former territory) with 1.6 million inhabitants. The population of its capital between 1910 and 1914 exceeded 90 000. In the former territory the middle class successfully championed progressive changes, while peasantry accounted for 85 per cent of the population, with rare literate persons among them.[10]

The four banks stressed earlier were absolutely dominant with respect of the capital at their disposal. During the last year before the First World War a modern periodical *Ekonomist* (published in Belgrade since May 1912) classified all Serbian banks into four groups according to invested capital: up to 250 000, up to 500 000, up to 1 000 000 and banks with over 1 000 000 dinars as the strongest group.[11] There were six banks in the strongest group, all from Belgrade. This means that the Serbian Credit Bank, with its 1 200 000 French francs at the time of establishment, was as strong as the strongest Serbian banks 30 years later. It was the leading monetary institution in the country perhaps until the beginning of the twentieth century, when it surrendered its leading position to the Bank Andrejević, which became by far the predominant bank from the beginning of 1910 with nominal 4 million and invested 1 million francs. However, this lasted for a very short period; the branch of the Prague Credit Bank was founded that summer with 5 million francs, while only a few weeks later the BFS with 12 million nominal and 4 million invested francs took the undisputed leading position. The Danubian Joint-Stock Trade Company had nominal 2 million and invested 600,000 francs. The emergence of foreign banks increased the possibility for loans and investments in industry and trade, as well as in public works, introduced business security and planning opportunities for small and larger businesses, and contributed to a revival of economic processes.[12] The Serbian–English Bank, which never began operation, was planned to start with a capital of 5 million francs.[13]

However, the true strength of these banks was that they were backed by powerful financial institutions as their founders, which made sure that their 'daughter banks' in Serbia obtained necessary resources for their operation easily and quickly. The Serbian Credit Bank was founded through cooperation between the Comptoir d'Escompte from Paris and the Länderbank from Vienna. The Vienna co-owner soon acquired nearly a three-quarter stake in the bank's capital, but the French stake remained at around a quarter, while a number of shares were in the ownership of Serbian investors.[14] The Bank Andrejević became foreign in 1888, when it was taken over by the Hungarian Commercial Bank of

Pest. The latter opened its representative office in Belgrade back in 1883, and in April 1908 included in this business a renowned German bank, Berliner Handelsgesellschaft, thus increasing the bank's capital to 4 million (with 60 per cent Hungarian and 40 per cent German stake), while at the beginning of 1910 the Bank Andrejević was reorganized into a joint-stock company.[15] The BFS founders were among the strongest French monetary institutions: the Banque de l'Union Parisienne (BUP), the Banque Impériale Ottomane (BIO) with its Brussels 'daughter bank' the Société Financière d'Orient, and the renowned banking institution N.J. et S. Bardac.[16] It was a truly powerful concern of international proportions. The Danubian Joint-Stock Trade Company was the creation of the Budapest branch of the Serbian Bank from Zagreb, with sound operation and providing strong backing to its Belgrade branch.[17]

It follows that four out of the five most significant financial institutions in Serbia had their roots in two Central-European empires – German and Habsburg – with Austrian, Hungarian and Czech capital, in addition to Serbian from the Banovina of Croatia (part of Hungary). The remaining bank of the Big Five was founded and operated with French capital, but was an extremely strong bank with a predominant role. This situation arose from the geopolitical location of Serbia, from its borderline position toward the Danubian empire, as well as from its place in the Middle East and Balkan zone, with dominant French and over time – from about 1905 – increasingly active German capital.

The extent of interest in founding banks

Foreign capital had shown considerable interest in the opening of banks in Serbia. These ideas were also encouraged by the Serbian state. A characteristic example is the report of the German embassy in Paris of May 1910 on the establishment of a French bank in Belgrade, which quotes the comment of the Serbian envoy on this event before the German diplomats: 'Je mehr Konkurenz, um so besser für die Interessen des Landes [Serbia].'[18]

As far as we know the first and the most frequent ideas referred to a French-Serbian bank. An extensive elaborated project was made as early as spring 1872.[19] It was later followed by various proposals of French economic and diplomatic representatives in Serbia and Serbian businessmen, as well as some representatives of banks from third countries. The Banque Française pour le Commerce et l'Industrie[20] and the Société Générale pour favoriser le Commerce et l'Industrie,[21] both of Paris, joined (in 1911 and 1913 respectively) the founders of the bank established in summer 1910 as their business friends. The Société

Générale intended to cooperate with capital from Austria and Hungary and thus create business opportunities for itself in the Balkans, starting with Serbia, so the French representative in Belgrade pointed to the Serbian Credit Bank as a suitable *point de départ* for such cooperation.[22] At least since the middle of the first decade of the twentieth century the German foreign policy service had kept repeating that it was necessary to establish a German bank in Belgrade and the idea was ardently supported by some Serbian businessmen and prominent figures in the Serbian government.[23] To carry out these intentions, there were also some deliberations about cooperation with the French. In autumn 1913 it seemed that this effort would succeed when, at the urging of the Ministry of Foreign Affairs, the Darmstädter Bank für Handel und Industrie (hereinafter Bank für Handel und Industrie) started negotiations with the Economic Bank in Belgrade, though ultimately without result.[24]

There was also much talk about English banks over a longer period, starting at least in 1883,[25] and the news of imminent opening started to multiply just prior to the outbreak of the First World War. The name of the strong J.C. Morgan and Co. was mentioned as one of the interested founders. It is interesting that the adopted project was signed by a certain Karl Neff, who called himself the 'Bankier aus Hannover', although it seems, as Serbian sources suggest, that solely English capital was involved.[26] For the opening of its bank the Hungarian Banking and Trade Company tried to ensure the participation of the Paris-based Société Générale and Société Financière Franco-Suisse from Geneva.[27] Before it made an agreement with the Berliner Handelsgesellschaft, the Hungarian Commercial Bank of Pest wanted to reinforce the Bank Andrejević – with or without the German partner – by attracting the BIO (Banque Impériale Ottomane) or Banque de Paris et de Pays-Bas (Paribas).[28] The latest issue to be raised by the end of 1910 was an Italian-Serbian bank (the application referred to the bank under the French name of Banque Italo-Serbe), but Serbian authorities did not accept the proposal, submitted in 1911 by Mario Modiano from Thessaloniki.[29] In early 1914 the Banque de Salonique demanded restoration of the work of its branches from the time of the Turkish administration in Bitola and Skopje, as well as the business unit in Kumanovo.[30] By the beginning of 1914 a proposal came from Ljubljana for the establishment of a 'big Yugoslav bank' with the nominal capital of 8–10 million francs, to be carried out by the transformation of the Belgrade Export Bank and creation of a consortium consisting of a wider circle of Slavonic banks from Austria-Hungary (one each from Ljubljana and Trieste, two from Zagreb with Croatian names in addition to the Serbian Bank, four Czech from Prague and one from Brno).[31]

This shows the extent of interest in financial matters in Serbia, which is additionally supported by other facts. In several instances the Wiener Bankverein investigated the opportunity of opening a branch office in Belgrade.[32] In spring 1912 there was some talk about a Belgian–Austro-Hungarian financial consortium. This was an attempt by the Hungarian Commercial Bank of Pest to counter French capital in Serbia by reinforcing the Bank Andrejević's shaky position through the joint effort of the Bank für Handel und Industrie, the Österreichische Creditanstalt and the banking house Sal. Oppenheimer, and ensuring the cooperation of financial friends from Paris, Antwerp and Geneva.[33] In spring 1913 the news that aroused interest concerned the intention of a strong English-American trust to set up a bank in Serbia with a capital of 30 million French francs, a transport company with 30 million, a real-estate company with 20 million and, finally, an industrial and mining company with 15 million francs.[34] Since 1908 the establishment of the Banque Hypothécaire et Agricole had been contemplated, and the Crédit Français invested much effort in 1913 in providing a concession for the former. Then, there were ideas about the joint intention of English and French financial institutions.[35] This interest is confirmed by other factors as well. For example, in January 1911 in connection with the loan to the city of Belgrade 16 bids were submitted by 18 banks of which only two were truly Serbian. In addition, none of these banks was within the BIO circle, where some were extremely interested in this project.[36] There were also attempts to set up strong enterprises, such as the Italian-Serbian trade company Giuseppe Kosovich, Karmelli e Co in January 1914,[37] and the establishment of an English public works company by the Railway and Works Company Limited in February 1914.[38]

Superiority of French capital

Soon after its establishment the BFS assumed the central position in the economic and hence modern development of Serbia. This should be understood in the following context: Czech capital at that time became significant in the sugar and cement industries, as well as in export of cereals; Hungarian and Austrian capital already had their traditional footholds, and in 1913 strengthened their position by creating the Serbian Mining and Smelting Joint-Stock Company (SARTID);[39] German financiers, even without a separate bank, already held the sugar factory in Belgrade and a slaughtering plant in Velika Plana, while German participation in Serbia's foreign trade in these years became significant; three German firms were awarded contracts for execution of railway works (Lenz und Ko, on the Bitola–Skopje route, probably in cooperation with the Deutsche Bank; J. Berger-Tiefbau built the Bitola–Debar stretch;[40] the Syndikat für serbische Bahnbauten, which included the Bachstein-Prohl enterprise and the Bank für Handel und Industrie built the Uvac–Užice track).[41] Finally, F. Krupp und Ko obtained a significant order for cannons (payment from the French loan)[42] although Schneider et Cie was by far the biggest artillery supplier for Serbia. Belgian and particularly English capital were invested in some Serbian mines,[43] while Belgians owned the Belgrade electric power plant and electric streetcar transport.[44]

The BFS – itself a 'daughter bank' – very soon extended the network of subsidiary enterprises in the area of large-scale public works and industry. In cooperation with the Société française d'Entreprises de Dragages et de Travaux Publics and the renowned banking house Louis Dreyfus et Cie, in 1912 it established the Société franco-Serbe d'Entreprises Industrielles et de Travaux Publics (4 million French francs, but soon 10 million Francs; undertaking the execution of the contract of 4 April 1913 and new contracts of 26 May and 8 December 1913 and 9 February 1914, it obtained concession for the construction of ten railway routes in total length approximately 800 km). With the Serbian Trade Bank from Belgrade it founded in 1913 the Société de Cimetries et Charbonnages Franco-Serbes (600,000 French francs).[45] In early 1914, with the State Class Lottery as the representative of an interested Serbian group (25 per cent stake in capital), it founded the Société Franco-Serbe en vue de la Construction d'Hôtels dans les nouvelles Provinces with an intention to build in Skopje (a total of 150 rooms), Bitola, Štip, Veles, Ohrid, Priština, Prizren and Novi Pazar.[46] Parallel with this, the BFS was in the interest group of the Banque de l'Union Parisienne, not only because the latter was one of its founders, but as the bank which took control of the BIO.[47] In addition, it acquired wider influence in the Serbian economy through its founders including, besides L. Dreyfus, the Banque Mirabaud, owner of the Société française des Mines de Bor. (The capital of this company soon rose to 6.8 million francs, value of installations was assessed at 12.4 million, annual output 7 600 tons of high-quality copper ore, net annual income *c.* 4 million francs.)[48] The BUP was also in the same interest group as the French military industry giant Schneider et Cie.[49]

The French interest in the small country of Serbia emerged relatively early and gradually increased. It dates back to the late 1830s, following stabilization of the small vassal principality of Serbia, and may be credited to the curiosity of Ami Boué and his interest in the geology of the Serbian soil.[50] It is worth noting that this scholar had shown interest in the entire Balkan region, thus demonstrating that the French were considering different countries only in a wider geopolitical context.

The outlines of economic interest became finally quite clear by the mid-nineteenth century. In its issue dated 7 September 1885 *Journal de Débats* offered an extensive review of early Serbian railway construction plans.[51] The term 'French-Serbian society' – referring probably to a joint economic organization contemplated but not founded at that time – can be found in a letter of a Serb from Constantinople in late November 1860.[52] We have mentioned that in spring 1872 a comprehensive proposal was drafted for the founding of a French-Serbian bank, with the aim of encouraging and supporting French business.[53] French engineer Kuss was the author of the first study for the building of a railway in 1865,[54] while the Belgrade government signed a Convention for the construction of the first Serbian railway with the Société de l'Union Générale on 3 February 1881.[55] Pronounced interest of French financiers is confirmed by an analytical memorandum *Les chemins de fer serbes*, prepared on 3 June 1889 for the Minister of Foreign Affairs.[56] The same proved true on the occasion of the establishment of the first foreign financial institution in Belgrade, the Serbian Credit Bank: the Comptoir National d'Escompte was given a prominent place, while the Österreichische Länderbank, its partner in this venture, was the creation of the Société de l'Union Générale (1880); when l'Union Générale went bankrupt in 1882, its Vienna creation, and in particular the Serbian Credit Bank, fell under the permanent influence of the Paris Société Générale.[58] Although the Comptoir National d'Escompte soon got into trouble, the French capital stayed in the Serbian Credit Bank.[58] After Serbia was proclaimed a kingdom (1882), an international consortium was founded to provide credit under the leadership of the Comptoir National d'Escompte. The consortium encompassed the Berliner Handelsgesellschaft and a group of German banks, as well as the Österreichische Länderbank.[59] Resources originating from Paris banks also played a role in Serbian loans extended in the 1880s. From the late 1880s and, in particular, during the 1890s, the French interests grew stronger and were expressed in an expanded scope of business deals and a growing invested sum.

Natural and geographic setting

Ambassador Maurice Bompard's memorandum, dated 21 September 1917 and made for Alexander Ribot, Minister of Foreign Affairs, places the Serbian issue within the then traditional French vision of the Balkan East and of the Balkan peninsula as an economic whole, however stressing the Asian part as the more significant.[60] It reflected a view resulting from highly developed businesses, established back in the sixteenth century and expanded over time throughout the Turkish Empire. It can be seen from French diplomatic documents even in the years preceding the First World War. Namely, when the texts refer to Balkan states, they use terms such as 'Europe, Afrique, Orient' or 'Levant'. The June 1889 memorandum reviews the Serbian issue in respect of 'les capitaux français en Orient'.[61] Accordingly, the main representative of the French finances in Serbia was indeed the BIO, while the first French monetary institution devoted to Serbia was named Société Financière d'Orient (founded in 1897 as a formally Belgian society).

Yet at the beginning of the twentieth century the dual character of that stand became apparent. The changing circumstances in the Balkans, profoundly and visibly different from those prevailing in the Near East, called for the recognition of new realities. Thus Bompard's memorandum refers to investments 'dans la fortune française en Turquie et dans les Etats balcaniques' and includes Serbian issues at the same time in the integrity of the dual area and in its Balkan part.[62] The Balkans started to be recognized as a separate unity, with six independent states, by contrast to the still rather large territory of the Ottoman Empire.

1. According to the data provided by Bompard, on the eve of the war in summer 1914 the French financiers invested in the Near East–Balkan area the amount of 5 746 236 881 French francs.[63] Out of this, 2 891 251 750 referred to the Ottoman Empire, and 2 854 985 131 to all Balkan states. Serbia received 814 546 000 francs, accounting for 14.18 per cent of the total investments and 28.53 per cent of investments into Balkan states. The percentage of investments in Serbia to those in the Ottoman Empire was 28.17 per cent.

   By the amount of *total French investments*, Serbia ranked second among the Balkan states. Greece took the lead with just slightly higher investments of 825 802 578 French francs, accounting for 14.37 per cent of the total and 28.92 per cent of investments into the Balkan states. The next in line after Serbia were Romania with 751 649 180 francs (13.08 per cent and 26.33 per cent respectively) and Bulgaria with 457 216 000 francs (7.96 per cent and 16.01 per cent). The French interest in Montenegro was 4 million francs (0.07 per cent and 0.14 per cent), and in Albania 1 771 373 francs (0.03 per cent and 0.06 per cent).
2. *Public loans* were the biggest item in French interests.[64] Throughout the two-part region they reached the amount of 4 474 988 150 francs, of which 2 246 334 150 were invested in Turkey and 2 228 644 000 in the Balkans. The total amount of loans to Serbia was 770 754 000 francs.

The total amount invested in *monetary institutions* was 257 256 000 francs, with 138 250 000 in Turkey and 119 006 000 in the Balkans. The figure for Serbia is 18 625 000 francs.

Railway construction attracted 531 044 600 francs – 262 144 600 in Turkey and 268 900 000 in the Balkans. Investments in Serbian railways were 5 362 000 francs.

Routes (marine), *quays*, *ports* and *lighthouses* absorbed 96 001 000 francs, with the biggest share invested in Turkey (72 506 500 and 24 494 500 in the Balkans, of which Serbia accounted for 250 000 francs).

Investments in *hydraulics*, *gas* and *electricity* (total 99 630 358 francs) did not encompass Serbia.

Investments in *mines* and *petroleum* reached the amount of 121 571 373 francs, with Turkey accounting for 37 525 000 and Balkan states for a much higher share – 84 046 373. Serbia accounted for 8 875 000 francs.

A total of 165 754 400 francs was invested in *industry*, *trade* and *agrarian enterprises*, with the Turkish part amounting to 92 447 900 francs and the Balkan to 73 297 100, of which 10 680 000 went to Serbia. However, no investments were made in the petroleum business, while agrarian business did not attract French investors.

3. From the proceeds of a French loan (770 754 000 francs) Serbia financed public works and armament.[65] All other French investments in Serbia totalled 43 720 000 francs, but this figure should be assessed bearing in mind that most of the loans were used for railway construction. A German representative in the Autonomous Monopoly Administration, probably in spring 1918, summed up the Serbian pre-war debt (assessed to be 900 million francs on 1 January 1915) to non-French creditors in the following way: 'only 158 000 000 FFr is in our [German] possession and in the possession of our allies [Austrians and Hungarians], neutrals [probably the Swiss] and Serbs.'[66] In any case, Serbia had by far the largest total loan amount lent by the French of all Balkan states. Romania followed with an amount lower by 118 754 000 francs, while Greece (338 004 000 less than Serbia) and Bulgaria (409 604 000 less) were way behind. A 4-million franc loan was the only French investment in Montenegro, while Albania did not have any French loans.

   By investments in *monetary institutions*, Greece had the most with 75 million francs. Serbia took 57 357 000 francs less. However, investments in Serbian monetary institutions exceeded those in Bulgaria (17 756 000) by 869 000 francs and Romania (7 625 000) by 11 million francs.

Investments in *railway construction* were the highest in Greece (204 121 000 francs), exceeding by as much as 199 759 000 the investments in Serbian railways (5 362 000 francs). Relevant investments in Bulgaria (53 300 000 francs) were also manifoldly higher than those in Serbia. Romanian railways were financed with 6 million francs and Albanian with 117 000 francs.

The French invested 250 000 francs in *road construction* in Serbia. Since it was landlocked, no comparison can be made with Greece and Bulgaria (the French did not invest in Romania).

Investments in *oil* have certainly had a considerable share of investments in Romania (47 667 000 francs), while in Serbia the French invested in *mining* (8 875 000 francs) –15 975 000 francs less than they had invested in Greece (24 850 000 francs). However, Bulgaria with investments of 2 550 000 francs in these areas trailed Serbia by 6 325 000 francs. Investments in Albania totalled 800 000 francs.

In different *enterprises* in Serbia French financiers invested 10 680 000 francs or 17 877 500 less than in Greece (28 557 500 francs) and 12 470 000 less than in Romania (23 150 000 francs). Investments in Bulgaria (10 910 000 francs) were slightly above those in Serbia, while in Albania they were low (104 373 francs).

Compared with Greece, Romania and Bulgaria, Serbia held the second position by total investments and investments in monetary institutions, third by investments in mining, and fourth by investments in roads and enterprises.

Promoter of French interest

In the summary of a document dated 30 October 1917 the establishments mentioned as the main promoters of French interests in Serbia include the banks Banque Franco-Serbe and Société financière d'Orient, then Société Franco-Serbe d'Enterprises Industrielles et de Travaux Publics and Société française d'Enterprises and, finally, Bor, Neresnica, Radinka and Studena mines.[67] However, there was indeed one main promoter of French interests. The Serbian sources mention 'the Ottoman group' as the main French partner.[68] Bompard designates the Banque Franco-Serbe as 'la société' which 'avait crée pour syndiquer les interêts français' but which faced competition from 'la Régie générale des chemins de fer et de travaux publics, la Société française d'enterprises et d'autres rivaux encore'.[69]

During three and a half decades, from 1880 to 1914, there was hardly any major French bank that did not show more or less interest, for longer or shorter periods, in business in Serbia. Yet from the beginning of the twentieth century it became increasingly obvious that in Serbia the BIO was the most important foreign and hence the most significant French financial factor.[70] Indeed, it was a British-French bank, but at the time considered here the French interest in its capital prevailed, which became particularly evident after the BIO was taken over by the recently founded BUP, which remained under the strong influence of its founders among the 'haute finance' in Paris – strong and reputable private protestant banks.[71] Otherwise, the BIO operated in Serbia continuously from the beginning of the 1890s and at first maintained the closest cooperation with German (Berliner Handelsgesellschaft) and Austrian (Österreichische Länderbank) capital. The three banks were involved in 1895 in the settlement of Serbian government finances, ensuring solvency through the Autonomous Monopoly Administration (l'Administration autonome des Monopoles du Royaume de Serbie).[72] Furthermore, the BIO developed its predominant role by strengthening the position in public loans, pushing out from this line of business first its Austrian partner (in 1905) and then the German one (after 1909). Parallel with this, it was increasingly successful in incorporating other strong French banks in the consortium, and was thus able to extend higher loans. It fortified its leading position by loans amounting to 150 million francs in 1909 and, in particular, 250 million francs in 1913.[73]

The BIO started relatively late in developing economic institutions in Serbia. Actually, in early autumn 1892 it agreed to establish 'une réprésentation directe a Belgrade, par example par l'ouverture d'une sucersale'[74] and it was perhaps this idea that ultimately resulted in the establishment of the Société financière d'Orient. The BIO firmly backed the idea of a French bank in Belgrade only at the urging of the BUP and played the key role in the establishment of the BFS as a French society with a head office in Paris and a branch office in Belgrade. Through its 'daughter bank' it soon created the Société Franco-Serbe d'Enterprises Industrielles et de Travaux Publics, and then also the Société des Cimenteries et Charbonnages Franco-Serbe.[75] This was a predominant interest group, with its respectable and expanding network of subsidiaries in Serbia. Its business was managed by the 'Comité', which was formally led by the Société financière d'Orient, as the establishment created to do business with Serbia. Members of the 'Comité' – following a pattern with obvious practical meaning – included the BIO as the direct managerial bank, the BUP as the effective decision-maker, the BFS, as the executive in the field and N.J. et S. Bardac as the associated bank.[76] The visible centre was the BIO, with operative assistance of the Société financière d'Orient, which directly influenced the operation of the BFS. The decision-making BUP was managed by the founders, who were also the leading owners of the BIO and whose private banks could also undertake special roles (the Banque Louis Dreyfus et Cie was one of the founders of the Société Franco-Serbe d'Enterprises Industrielles et de Travaux Publics, while the Banque Mirabaud, with business connections with the BFS[77] was the owner of the Compagnie française des Mines de Bor). This network controlled all government loans in Serbia, major public works (above all an extremely extensive programme of railway construction) and exploitation of the copper mines, extremely rich in European proportions. As in the Balkans and the Ottoman Empire, the BIO acted in Serbia as the leading bank, while the decisive influence and the true managerial power remained with the BUP, although Russia was the target of its main and largest transactions. On the eve of the First World War Serbia was obviously in the extensive zone of exceptional economic 'eastern interests' (Russia, Balkans, Near East) of French financial capital.

Significance of French investments

The investments referred to here developed, increased and accelerated, reaching significant proportions sometime in 1910, and exceptional proportions in the second half of 1913 and the first half of 1914. War interrupted this course and what the final effect might have been remains a mystery.

What had been achieved was unquestionably remarkable.

Judging from the French point of view. Bompard volunteers this assessment: 'En Serbie dans les années qui ont précédé la guerre, la France a fait un sérieux effort d'organisation financière. La Banque franco-serbe ... donnait les meilleures espérances.' This source mentions nine most significant French addresses in the Near East and Balkans including also, along with the BUP and the BIO, the Banque Franco-Serbe (plus only the Banque de Salonique from the Balkans).[78] Conspicuously, in the analysis of effects in the period since the mid-nineteenth century, made in the BIO towards the late summer of 1918, along with a detailed presentation of operations in the Ottoman Empire and after a brief remark that the activity 'c'est étendue à toute la pénisule balkanique', on a page and a half followed 'interessée au developpement economique et aux finances de la Serbie', as the only presentation of activities in a Balkan state.[79] The history of the BIO, written on the first pages of the archive register, refers only – besides extensive presentation of its business in Turkey – to its business in Serbia.[80] Let us note that almost all French financial giants became over time increasingly involved in Serbian loans, and some in other deals as well. Unquestionably, for French capital with worldwide ambitions, Serbia offered modest but – as it subsequently became obvious – increasingly interesting opportunities.

For Serbia, still predominantly agrarian country, the engagement of French capital was exceptionally and manifoldly significant. It could procure necessary resources on the Paris financial market at relatively favourable terms, in adequate amount and without any particular difficulties. Trying to maintain its solvency, Serbia could, owing to French investments, attempt to introduce modern concepts in its economy, above all planning and launching an extensive railway construction programme and in addition ensuring the high quality results offered by French civil engineering. At the same time, with the same resources, it could engage in ventures with German builders and in trade with German arms manufacturers. Finally, French assistance was valuable in the development of the Bor mine, including adequate high-quality copper metallurgy and special technology for gold separation. Also, armament from renowned French manufacturers was provided for the army, which mobilized over 700 000 troops in 1914 and 1915. All these data evidence a very significant role for French capital in maintaining Serbia's independence under the political, economic and, finally, military pressure of the Habsburg Monarchy, particularly between 1905 and 1914.

Connection with the modern era

Foreign capital initially assisted in development, but its interest later strongly expanded because the Serbian economy proved to be very sound. A clear indication was the foreign trade balance, which was continuously positive in the years preceding the First World War, above all in the trade with big states. Another characteristic sign was that Serbia set up its trade representative offices from Hamburg (Elba estuary and transoceanic port) to Cairo, including also Munich, Athens, Malta and Alexandria. This trend was also confirmed through the expansion in the number of honorary consuls, chosen from among the citizens of European countries, including Portugal. Where banking is concerned, Serbian state statistics for 1910 record a total of 173 banks, savings organizations and money cooperatives, with a total capital of 53 234 727 paid in and savings deposits amounting to 54 506 637 dinars (these figures also encompass foreign banks founded up to the end of 1910). The dinar was stable and state finances sound after they were settled in 1895 through the intervention of international finances (Ottoman Bank and Berliner Handelsgesellschaft). This is when the State Monopoly Administration was founded, whose revenues primarily served for foreign debt servicing. It was a very successful venture, with steadily growing profit. This made it possible to have enough money for debt servicing and for contracting new loans.

Sound economy attracted more foreign capital, which continued to expand. In this way Serbia, and indeed the entire Balkans of that time, was additionally linked with the modern world in three ways. First, it was connected economically, through increasing volumes of foreign trade and presence of financiers. They operated on a worldwide scale and brought with them 'economic cosmopolitanism' into the remote South-east European area. Serbian ministers used to stress that only with these new influences did bankers in their country realize the need for financial discipline and mastery of modern financial operations.

Second, this was the beginning of a process that substantially affected society, introducing features from more advanced communities, first through the establishment of social strata with particularly safe and high incomes, thus promoting a new middle class. Additional impetus came from the arrival of professionals – bankers and engineers – who made direct impact through new culture. New classes of modern city dwellers were more prone to adopt the models of developed Europe than their predecessors in earlier decades. Modernization changed the social environment and Europeanized living conditions and lifestyles.

Finally, capital provided a particular means to enter the international political scene. Diplomatic and consular representatives of foreign states actively fostered capital and exports of their states with the Serbian government and, when necessary, did so rather resolutely. Capital brought along economic rivalry between big powers, in addition to mounting political competition. This made the situation complex. First, animosity between two blocs of powers increased, and could be in general terms described as confrontation between France and Russia, on the one hand, and Germany and Austria-Hungary on the other (extremely pronounced in connection with the establishment of the BFS), while Great Britain and Italy acted independently. Therefore, in a written note, the British embassy demanded that the Serbian government respect British economic interests in the area of public works – contrary to the increasingly strong position of a French construction company at that time. French and German representatives attentively observed the economic intentions and moves of the other party, and there were many instances when they protested to the Serbian government against preferences granted to the rival party. Second, since the beginning of the twentieth century the Belgrade government had feared the economic penetration of the neighbouring Habsburg Monarchy and hence considered the growing interest of Slavic capital (Czech and Serbian from Zagreb) as a possible threat to Serbia's independence. Therefore, it considered French capital as a means to protect itself from the neighbouring great power. At the same time, it encouraged German investments as a possible means to control excessive French influence, but it also saw them as a means to ensure the support of Berlin in Vienna – an increasingly important capital for Serbia's position. Third, Hungarian and Austrian capital did not openly compete, but it was apparent that they did not act jointly, though they came from the same state, but side by side, making sure to provide a counterbalance. For example, soon after an Austrian bank was opened in the 1880s, a Hungarian bank was opened as well. In the years prior to the First World War when a Vienna bank investigated the opportunity of opening its branch in Serbia, a Budapest bank immediately inquired about similar possibilities. Fourth, another characteristic feature was the relation between the German and Hungarian capital. Their cooperation in the Bank Andrejević was neither fruitful nor long. When planning its operations in Serbia, Budapest, at least in several instances, counted on cooperation with German rivals – Paris banks. They also tried to drive German economic interests out of Serbia by setting up a strong international bank consortium, also involving French capital. However, the Reich government learned about this intention and prevented its realization by a harsh *démarche* to Vienna.

Continuous interest of capital from all developed European countries in operations in Serbia provided the latter with a triple connection with the modern world: first, through integration into modern economy and its processes, then by introducing and developing modernizing changes in society and, finally, through involvement in conflicting relations between the Great Powers, including internal conflicts in Austria-Hungary due to economic and political rivalry between the German, Hungarian and diverse Slavic population.

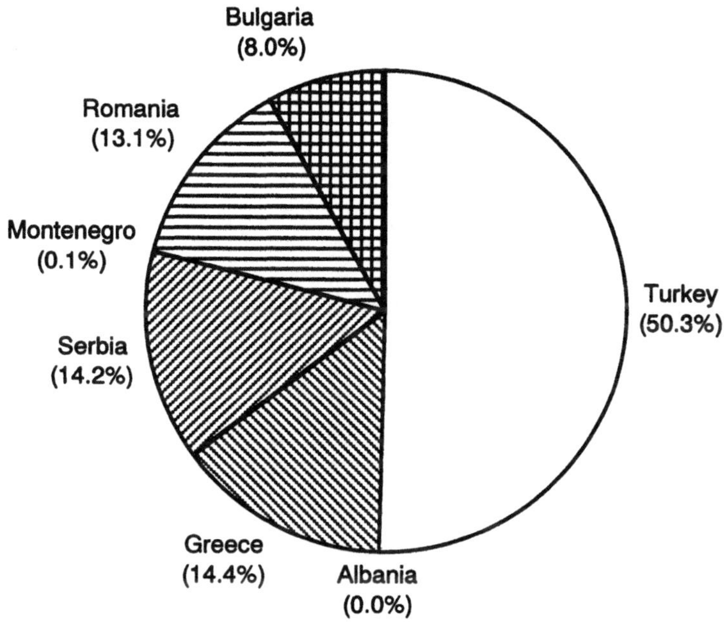

5.1 French investments in Balkan countries, 1917

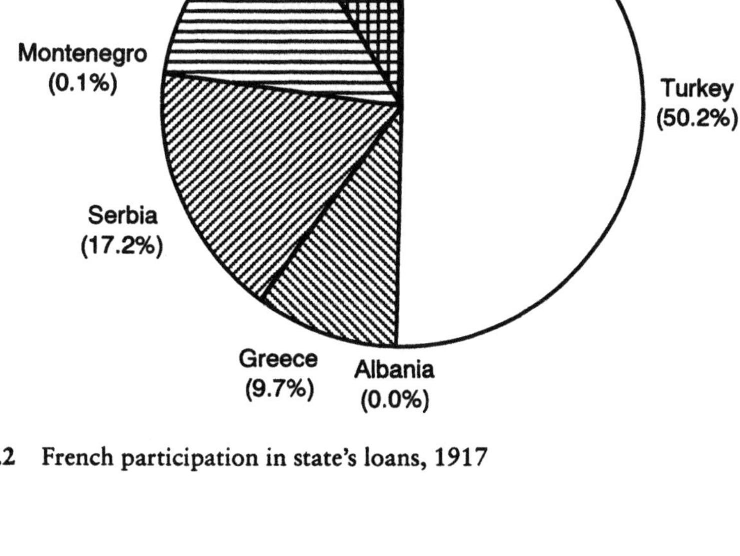

5.2 French participation in state's loans, 1917

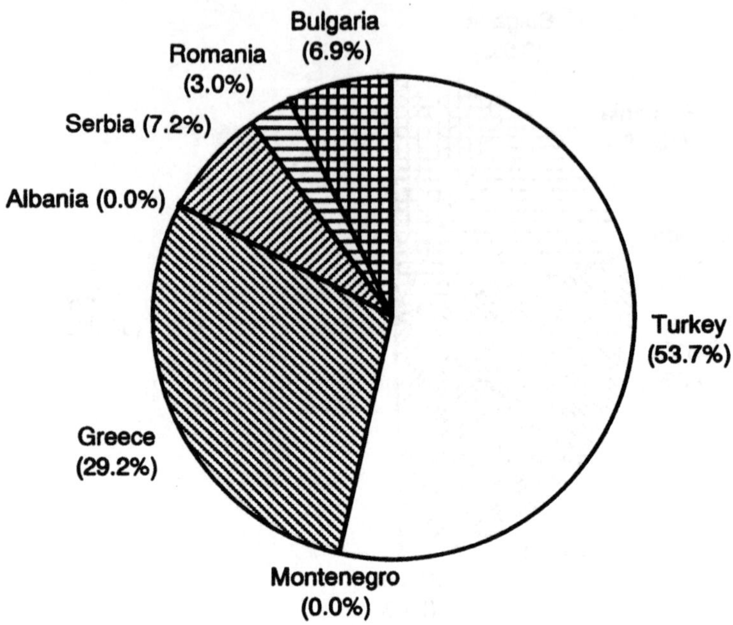

5.3 French participation in bank capital, 1917

Notes

1. The aim of this paper is to set the groundwork for subsequent elaboration of the place and role of major foreign capital in Serbia since its independence until World War I (1878–1914), which is a task whose character and volume call for a monograph. Namely, a study that should encompass problems of economic development, the entirety of the modernizing process and implications of political issues. The author has already presented the initial findings on two occasions: first in the paper 'The foreign banks in Serbia (1882–1914)', submitted at the international conference Modern Banking in the Balkans. Role of West European Capital Nineteenth and Twentieth Century, Athens, 24 January 1997, and then in the text 'Les intérêts français en Serbie à la veille de la première guerre mondiale', *Godišnjak za društvenu istoriju*, II (3), 1995, published in March 1997, pp. 365–78.
2. General studies: Fritz Fischer, *Krieg der Illusionen*, Düsseldorf, 1969; Bernard Michel, *Banques et banquiers en Autriche au début du 20e siècle*, Paris, 1976; Jean Bouvier and René Girault, *L'impérialisme français d'avant 1914. Recueil de textes*, Paris, 1976; see also Karel Herman, 'Novoslovanstvi a česka buržoasie', *Kapitoly z dejin vzajemnych vztahu narodu ČSR a SSSR*, Prague: sbornik praci, 1958, pp. 235–312. For the topics directly referring to Serbia: Stanislav Kukla, *Razvitak kreditne organizacije u Srbiji do svetskog rata. Ekonomsko-istorijska strudija* (Development of the credit organization in Serbia until the First World War.

An economic-historic study), Zagreb, 1924; Dimitrije Djordjević, *Carinski rat Austro-Ugarske i Srbije 1906–1911* (The Customs War between Austria-Hungary and Serbia 1906–1911), Belgrade, 1962; Ljiljana Aleksić-Pejković, *Odnosi Srbije sa Francuskom i Engleskom 1903–1914* (Serbia's relations with France and England 1903–1914), Belgrade, 1965; Danica Milić, *Strani kapital u rudarstvu Srbije do 1918*, (Foreign capital in Serbian mining until 1918), Belgrade, 1970. The following book should also be taken into consideration: David F. Good, *Der wirtschaftliche Aufstieg des Habsburgerreiches 1750–1914*, Vienna, 1986.

3. The author has formerly published separate closer studies (with detailed specification of sources and references): 'Berliner Handelsgesellschaft u Srbiji' (Berliner Handelsgesellschaf in Serbia), *Zbornik Filozofskog fakulteta u Beogradu*, XVI, 1985, pp. 167–97; 'Pester Ungarsiche Commerzialbank na Balkanu do 1918' (Pester Ungarische Commerzialbank in the Balkans until 1918), *Zbornik Matice srpske za istoriju*, 34, 1986, pp. 43–80; 'Mreža austrougarskih i nemačkih banaka na Balkanu pred prvi svetski rat' (The network of Austro-Hungarian and German banks in the Balkans on the eve of World War I), *Jugoslovenski istorijski časopis*, 23, (3–4), 1988, pp. 51–75.
4. The *Archives of Serbia*, Belgrade (hereinafter *AS*, Fund of the Ministry of National Economy – MNP), Banke, No. 2550, 3048, 4268, 9498. See *Politika*, 3 March 1910. In the decade preceding the First World War, the Živnostenská Banka and the Sporobank also played some role. Kukla, op. cit., points to subsequent role played by the Živnostenská Banka in the capital of the Serbian Credit Bank, as confirmed by Serbian, Austrian and French sources.
5. *Archives Nationales*-Paris (*AN*), 207 AQ, 424.
6. N. Stanarević, 'Beogradske banke u 1911' (Belgrade banks in 1911) *Ekonomist*, I–II, 1912, 21; separate publication under the same title, Belgrade, 1912, pp. 4–5.
7. 'Englesko-srpska banka' (English-Serbian Bank) *Srpske novine*, 3/ 10. 1913; *AS* MNP, Banke, No. 3794, 6132 and 6546. Immediately prior to World War I a bank named Otadžbina (Fatherland) was founded with Hungarian capital (probably from the Hungarian Banking Commercial and Trade Company), Danica Milić, 'Učešće Jevreja u bankarstvu Srbije do Prvog svetskog rata' (The role of Jews in Serbian banking until World War I), *Zbornik Jevrejskog istorijskog muzeja u Beogradu*, 6, 1992, pp. 168–82, particularly p. 181.
8. Mitrović, 'Pester Ungarsiche Commerzialbank', op. cit., p. 52.
9. *Archives économiques et financières*-Paris (*AEF*), B 31.272, Belgrade 8.03.1914; *AS* MNP, Banke 1913, No. 889.
10. *Statistički godišnjak* (Statistical yearbook), 13, 1909–10; Holm Sundhausen, *Historische Statistik Serbiens 1834–1914*, Munich, 1989.
11. Stanarević, op. cit., p. 22 (separate edition, pp. 6–7).
12. See note 3.
13. See note 7. Also, 'Une Banque anglo-serbe', *Financial News*, 22 October 1913.
14. *Archives diplomatiques du Ministère des Affaires étrangères*-Paris (*AMAE*), NS, Serbie, vol. 26, 4.12.1910; *AEF*-Paris, 9.12.1913; Michel, op. cit, pp. 249 and 263; A Pirerger, *100 Jahre der Österreichischen Länderbank 1880–1980*, Vienna, 1980, pp. 43–4; Good, op. cit., p. 182.

15. Mitrović, 'Pester Ungarische Commerzialbank...', op. cit., pp. 50–56; see also from the same 'Berliner Handelsgesellschaft', op. cit., pp. 182–4.
16. *AN*, F/23/ 154: Banque Impériale Ottomane, Mémoire, 2.09.1918.
17. AMAE, NS, Serbie, vol. 26, No. 21, Belgrade 20.02.1912.
18. *Politisches Archiv des Auswärtigen Amtes*-Bonn (*PA AA*), Serbie 7, Bd.20.
19. *AN*, 207/AQ/424, Jules Corso et Cie, Marseille, 29.05.1872.
20. Raymond Poidevin, 'Les intérêts financiers français et allemands en Serbie de 1895 à 1914', in *Revue historique*, 232, 1964, pp. 49–66, especially p. 62. See *AS*, Ministry of Foreign Affairs, Political Department (MID, PO), 1910, I/8, a letter of this bank from Paris, dated 21 January 1910.
21. *AEF*, B 31.727, Belgrade 9.02.1913.
22. The French reports frequently mention this bank as theirs: No. 136, Belgrade 4.12.1910 (*AEF*, B 31.292, as well as note 20); see also note 4. A concise French view of the foundations, compiled probably according to the status in 1913: *AEF*, B 39.078, Banque de Crédit Serbe, siège Sociale à Belgrade, succursale à Schabatz, s.d. The Austro-Hungarian consul advised from Belgrade on 12 July 1911 that this bank 'operates' with approximately 5.5 million francs, of which some 3 million refer to Austrian capital (*Haus-Hof und Staatsarchiv* (*HHStA*), AR, F.23, K.70, No 64/h.p.).
23. The first characteristic mention of the initiative from the Serbian side dates from the time when the Customs War between Serbia and Austria-Hungary was at its peak. The German ambassador reported that during a routine discussion of economic circumstances Pašić mentioned Serbia's desire to have a bank founded in Belgrade with German capital to promote trade between two countries. See Mitrović, 'Berliner Handelsgesellschaft', op. cit.
24. Poidevin, op. cit., pp. 63–5; Aleksić-Pejković, op. cit., pp. 306–309; Mitrović, 'Mreža austrougarskih i nemačkih banaka', op. cit. from the same author, 'Pester Ungarische Commerzialbank', op. cit., pp. 61–2. See 'Les Allemands en Serbie', *Vie Financière*, 27 November 1913.
25. *Archives of the Serbian Academy of Sciences and Arts*, Belgrade, a letter of Aleksandar Jović addressed to Čedomilj Mijatović, 5/17 November 1883.
26. *AS*, MNP, Banke 1913, No. 3794, 6152, 6546, 11.010.
27. Plans with consortiums and 'daughter banks' encountered in reports of embassies and consulates, with the letters of the banks, are also an indication of tensions transfered into Serbia through finances.
28. *PA AA*, Serbien 7, Bd 19, Berlin 6.4.1908.
29. *AS*, MNP, Banke 1913 and 1914, No. 828, 2175, 11.498. It is interesting that the German embassy in Belgrade reported on 22 July 1909 that rumours about the establishment of an Italian bank were not true, *Bundesarchiv* (*BA*), Abteilung Potsdam, AA, Nr. 6511, report under No. 289/XIV.
30. *AS*, MNP, Banke 1914, T No. 4410, 7576.
31. *AS*, Embassy in Paris, 1914, File I, various documents.
32. *HHStA*, AR, F.23, K.70, Nr. 119 /h.p, Belgrade 1911. Various documents in the same series.
33. *BA* Abt. Potsdam, Finanzministerium, Nr. 2523, Belgrade, 20.05.1912.
34. *AS*, MNP, without number, Belgrade 16/29.03.1912. Austrian documents refer to the same issue, *HHStA*, F.34, K.70, Z. 33/h.p., Belgrade 21.04.1912.

35. *AMAE*, NS, Serbie, vol. 27, No. 64, Belgrade 9 March 1913; *AEF*, B 31.272, letter to the Ministry of Finances dated 8 October 1913.
36. *HHStA*, AR, F.23, K.58, Nr. 7/h.p., Belgrade 30.01.1911. However, Louis Dreyfus et Cie had applied.
37. 'Italijansko-srpsko trgovačko društvo' (Italian-Serbian Trade Company), *Srpske novine*, 30 January 1914.
38. *AS*, MID, PO, 1914, F.III.
39. Jovan Stojković, 'Srpsko akcionarsko topioničarsko industrijsko društvo 1913–1945' (Serbian Smelting and Industrial Joint-Stock Company 1913–1945), master's thesis submitted in 1994 to the Center for Interdisciplinary Studies, Belgrade University.
40. *PA AA*, Apt. I, Serbien 23, Bd. 3; in a series of reports see, for example, those in March 1914. Also a group *HHStA*, AF, F.23, K.65, Nr. 229–C, Belgrade 25.10.1913.
41. *BA* Abt. Koblenz, E 85, Nr. 88, for example material for June–August 1914.
42. *AMAE*, Serbie Armée et armement, Serbie vol. 8 and 9, No. 418 dated 27 September 1913, etc. C. Beaud, 'Les Schneider marchands de canons 1870–1914', *Histoire, économie et société*, 1995, pp. 107–30, particularly p. 121.
43. Milić, op. cit., pp. 127–53, 346–65.
44. *AEF*, B 39.078, Tramways et éclairage de Belgrade, siège Bruxelles.
45. *AEF*, B 31.272, Paris 11.02.1913; *AMAE*, Intérêts français 30.10.1917, published in A. Mitrović, 'Les intérêts français' op. cit., pp. 373–5. The Austrian consul reported that for the foreign capital in Serbia – with the exception of Austro-Hungarian, and above all 'dem französischen Geld' – 'Tür und Tor geöffnet', group *HHStA*, AR, F.34, K.70, Nr 47 /h.p. Belgrade 1.08.1913.
46. *AEF*, B 31.272, No. 80, Belgrade 28.03.1914.
47. See note 16.
48. *AMAE*, NS, Serbie, vol. 19, 'Les resources minérales de la Serbie', in Bureau d'Etudes de l'information diplomatique, No. 490; *AEF*, B 39.078, *Compagnie française des mines de Bor*; Milić, op. cit., pp. 289–308.
49. See note 42; C. Beaud, 'De l'expansion internationale à la multinationale Schneider en Russie (1896–1914)', *Histoire économique et société*, 1985, pp. 575, 601.
50. A. Boué, *La Turquie d'Europe*, I–IV, Paris, 1940.
51. Petar Milenković, Istorija gradjenja železnica i železnička politika kod nas 1850–1935 (Railway construction history and our railway policy 1850–1935), Belgrade, 1936, pp. 12–13.
52. *The Belgrade Historic Archives*, Ilija Kolarac Legacy Fund, Box 6, No. 391.
53. See note 18.
54. Milenković, op. cit., pp. 16–20.
55. Ibid., pp. 186–214.
56. *AMAE*, Serbie, vol. 2, Paris 3.06.1889.
57. Michel, op. cit., p. 249; Pireerger, op. cit., pp. 43–4; Good, op. cit., p. 182.
58. See reports: *AMAE*, NS, Serbie, vol. 26, 4.12.1910; *AEF*, B 31.242, 9.02.1913. These interests have not been recorded in the document dated 30 October 1917.

59. Carl Fürstenberg, *Die Lebengeschichte eines deutschen Bankiers, niedergeschrieben von Hans Fürstenberg*, Düsseldorf, 1968, p. 159.
60. *AMAE*, Europe 1918–1940, Yougoslavie, vol. 121, Paris 21.09.1917. This view was widespread among all developed western states, including economic circles. For example, the renowned German firm Siemens in a document *Verfügung Nr. 308*, to guide some of its departments 'in welcher Weise die Verfolgung der Geschäfte im Orient und in Ungarn im Zukunft gehandhabt werden sollen', takes 'Balkanstaaten' as the first group encompassing Romania, Serbia, Bulgaria and Greece, while Turkey and Egypt are included in the second group. Hungary, according to the primary definition, is separated, *Siemens-Archiv*, Munich, Li 117, 5.12.1907.
61. See note 56.
62. See note 60.
63. Ibid. Bompard's table was published in: Mitrović, 'Les intérêts français en Serbie', op. cit., p. 378.
64. A. Mitrović, op. cit.
65. The most recent study of the loans in that period: Dragana Gnjatović, *Stari državni dugovi. Prilog ekonomskoj i političkoj istoriji Srbije i Jugoslavije 1862–1941* (Old government debts. A contribution to the economic and political history of Serbia and Yugoslavia 1862–1941), Belgrade, 1991. Earlier references remain relevant: M. Nedeljković, *Istorija srpskih državnih dugova* (History of Serbian government debts), Belgrade, 1909; M. Todorović, 'Plasman stranog kapitala u Srbiji' (Foreign capital investments in Serbia), *Ekonomist*, II, 1913, pp. 212–14; Milan Simitch, *La dette publique de la Serbie de l'origine à la guerre de 1914*, Paris, 1925. About French loans Milan Erčić, 'Naši predratni i ratni dugovi Francuskoj' (Our pre-war and war debts to France), *Ekonomist*, January–February 1929, pp. 188–202; Milan Stojadinović, 'Ratni dug prema Francuskoj' (Pre-war debt to France), *Politika*, 25 February 1929; from the same author 'Naši predratni i ratni dugovi Francuskoj', *Bankarstvo*, April 1929, pp. 149–53; *Affaire concernant le paiement de divers emprunts Serbes émis en France*, Publications de la Cour permanente de justice internationale, Serbie C, No. 16–III, Leyden 1929. Loans in the context of general political circumstances: Aleksić-Pejković, op. cit.
66. *BA*, Abt. Koblenz, R 85, Nr. 6990, quoted in the report of the German consul in Belgrade, K. Nr. 66, Belgrade, 15 May 1918.
67. *AMAE*, NS, Serbie, vol. 19, Intérêts français en Serbie, 30.10.1917, handwritten mark D 132–3. Published in Mitrović, 'Les intérêts français en Serbie', op. cit., pp. 373–7. Poidevin, op. cit., pp. 61–3, incompasses the following in the 'French initiatives': Administration of Funds, BFS, the syndicate founded in Paris in May 1911 to administer Serbian loan bonds invested in Paris and, finally, a loan granted in 1913.
68. See material from 1908 to 1914 in *AS*, Embassy in Paris Fund, confidential, and Government Loans Fund in 1909, 1910, 1911.
69. See note 60.
70. G. Pougli-Bey, 'La Banque Impériale Ottomane', *Annales des sciences politiques*, 24, 1910, pp. 346–89; Jacques Thobie, *Intérêts et impérialisme français dans l'Empire Ottoman (1895–1914)*, Paris, 1977; André Autheman, *La Banque Impériale Ottomane*, Paris, 1996. In serbian literature: Milan Dimitrijević, 'Carsko-otomanska Banka' (Imperial Ottoman

Bank), *Ekonomist*, I, 1913, pp. 278–80; Mitrović, 'Mreža austrougarskih i nemačkih banaka na Balkanu', op. cit., pp. 70–74.

71. Hubert Bonin, *La Banque et les banquiers en France du Moyen Age à nos jours*, Paris, 1992, pp. 49–61; Karl Erich Born, *Geld und Banken in 19. und 20. Jahrhundert*, Stuttgart, 1977, pp. 151, 424; J.A. Lesourd and Cl. Gérard, *Nouvelle histoire économique*, I, Paris, 1976, p.196. See *Dictionnaire d'histoire économique de 1800 à nos jours*, Paris, 1987, pp. 36, 41, 162.
72. See note 59.
73. See note 20, R. Poidevin's work.
74. *AMAE*, NS, Serbie, vol. 3, Procès verbal d'une réunion tenue à Karlsruhe 25.09.1892.
75. Mitrović, 'Mreža austrougarskih i nemaèkih banaka', op. cit., pp. 70–74.
76. *AS*, Government loan 1913, conf. No. 6. letter of Société financière d'Orient, Paris 6.06.1911.
77. *AMAE*, Guerre 1914–1918, Serbie, vol. 370, Paris, 17. and 22.03.1915.
78. See note 60.
79. See note 16.
80. *AN*/ 207/ AQ, Autheman, op. cit.

CHAPTER SIX

The Greek Banking System and its Deregulation: History, Structure and Organization in a European Context

George Pagoulatos

This paper examines the historical evolution and structure of the Greek banking system, focusing on institutional arrangements which defined its standing at the time of reform. With a bias towards sectoral specificity we delineate the 'institutional memory' of the banking sector as conditioned by its exact development path. We place the Greek banking system in a European and South-European comparative context in order to highlight similarities with other 'adjusting' financial systems. We finally provide an outline of postwar credit policies, and a more detailed account of the evolution of banking deregulation from the second half of the 1980s until its completion in the early 1990s.

A site of antinomies, the Greek banking sector was most responsive to the imperatives of modernization and liberalization, yet at the same time a most unflinching carrier of Greek étatisme; instrumental in promoting state retreat from the economy, yet a generator of serious impediments to its realization; protagonist of technocratic voluntarism and at the same time subject to some of the heaviest structural constraints. An introductory look at the institutional structure, scope and operational logic of the Greek banking system lays the groundwork for understanding why.

The Greek banking system: evolution, structure and organization

History and development

The contemporary Greek banking system evolved in parallel with the modern independent Greek state. The country's first credit institution, the National Financial Bank, was created in 1828 but was soon dissolved. In 1841 the National Bank of Greece (henceforth National Bank or NBG) was established as the country's first private bank. Albeit deficit ridden, the Greek Treasury took strong interest, buying about one-fifth of the NBG's initial share capital.[1] The NBG provided commercial credit and mortgage loans. Most importantly, it issued banknotes, which in 1920 became its exclusive privilege until 1928, when it was obliged to transfer the issuing privilege to the newly founded Bank of Greece (BoG, the country's central bank).[2] The NBG soon established itself as central pillar not only of the banking sector but of the country's economic system. Surviving consecutive economic crises, from the nineteenth century it undertook the financing of major development projects and very often provided support to the frail government Treasury.[3] Its economic might, combined with the state's constant indebtedness, occasionally brought the NBG into conflict with government, and in 1914 the NBG governor was forced to resign, replaced by a political ally of the government.[4] That was the beginning of a tradition of government control over the NBG's administrations, which continued throughout the postwar period to this day.

The Ionian Bank, which also issued banknotes,[5] was the country's second bank, which followed in 1864. Between 1841 and 1900 40 credit institutions were founded, out of which only four (National Bank, Ionian Bank, Bank of Athens and Industrial Bank) survived until the end of the nineteenth century.[6] New banks were added at the beginning of the twentieth century, most notably the Popular Bank in 1905, and the Commercial Bank in 1907. In an unregulated and highly competitive environment a number of smaller banks also operated on a local level.[7] Through the introduction of new banking techniques and successful mergers the NBG and the Bank of Athens consolidated their market positions.[8]

As far as that rudimentary early banking system was concerned, the principle of non-state interventionism had carried the day all through the First World War, with only two exceptions: the establishment by the state of various agricultural credit funds, and the Postal Savings Bank in 1909. But in the years following the First World War, and in accordance with European standards, state presence became more visible.

In 1919 the National Fund for Deposits and Loans was founded to provide loans to public corporations. In the late 1920s institutionally imposed specialization settled in as functions previously carried by the NBG were assigned to specialized institutions. In 1927 the National Mortgage Bank was founded to provide housing credit. Then in 1928 the Bank of Greece was established to act as the country's central bank in issuing and controlling currency, and to that effect the first legal framework for banking was established in 1931. Almost conjointly, in 1929, the Agricultural Bank of Greece (ABG) was founded to finance and support agricultural production. The 1920s shaped what evolved into the contemporary Greek banking system, with 48 new banks being established between 1900 and 1930, out of which 40 were founded between 1921 and 1930.[9]

The 1929 economic crash gravely affected a Greek economy heavily dependent on foreign credit inflow. State bankruptcy was declared in 1932. The banking system reacted to the shock through bankruptcies and mergers, and by 1938 the number of banks operating in Greece had fallen to 31.[10] At the same time, and as the great interwar depression eroded the dominance of laissez-faire liberalism, a growing number of technocrats surrounding the newly founded Bank of Greece atuned to the ascending ideas supporting a more active degree of state planning in the economy.[11] This was meant to confront the structural weaknesses of Greek capital and the financial system, characterized by massive capital flight, a predominance of family-run industrial firms relying on cheap labour and antiquated equipment, and a failure to channel funds into what were regarded as 'productive' sectors, that is manufacturing and long-term agricultural credit.[12] From the late 1920s and during the 1930s industrialization intensified.[13] The growing financial requirements of industrial activity, which had been reflected in the expansion of credit institutions from the 1920s, would become far more visible and demanding in the postwar years.

The period after the Second World War marked the structuring of the Greek banking system through increasing state intervention. The war's devastating effects and the five-year civil war that followed necessitated urgent economic reconstruction and the state called for the banking system to contribute. The development of government institutions to finance investment upon criteria unconstrained by profit considerations was deemed a necessity. The industrialization process for a 'late-late' industrializer such as Greece appeared to require the application of institutional instruments typically employed by later industrializers (e.g. Germany and France) such as investment banks and a strong centralized steering and allocative economic capacity in the hands of the state.[14] Thus in the 1950s two state development corporations were established. The first, the Economic Development Financing Organization (EDFO), in 1954 succeeded the state committee charged with the task of managing the inflowing aid from the Marshall plan, undertaking all claims from reconstruction loans to the private sector. Then in 1959 the Industrial Development Organization (IDO) was created to provide funding for the new industrial projects, and quickly adopted a 'hands-off' economic philosophy, abstaining from active participation in the investment risks.[15] The EDFO and the IDO merged in 1964 to form a new long-term financing institution, the Hellenic Industrial Development Bank (ETBA), which evolved into the main Greek investment bank. In the course of the years numerous subsidiaries of the ETBA and the ABG were created.

The government's affirmed presence in the postwar economy and its grip on the banking system was confirmed in 1953 when the NBG was forced to merge with the second largest bank, the Bank of Athens; the NBG's administration was replaced by the chairman of the Bank of Athens. This highly controversial merger was unilaterally imposed on the National Bank by government law without prior recourse to the bank's General Assembly of Shareholders. The government's professed aim, grounded on a developmental rationale which favoured strong large-size credit institutions, was to confront the NBG's large deficit for the year 1952.[16] In the years that followed, however, the NBG recovered its prominent status.

In 1957 the Ionian Bank merged with the Popular Bank to create the Ionian-Popular Bank, which was taken over by the Commercial Bank. In the 1960s both the NBG and the Commercial Bank, in cooperation with foreign credit institutions, established investment subsidiaries – the Hellenic Investment and Industrial Development Bank (ETEBA) and the Investment Bank respectively – specializing in long-term finance and capital participation in industrial firms.[17] Further, throughout the 1950s and 1960s both the NBG and the Commercial Bank expanded into the industrial and insurance sectors. Influenced by the German banking 'philosophy', Greek postwar monetary authorities viewed commercial banks as engaging in long-term financing of industrial undertakings, maintaining permanent interests in business concerns and actively participating in their management and development.[18] Consequently, the two largest commercial bank groups ended up affecting 'the whole investment-decision mechanism in Greece, including government investment'.[19]

The establishment of the Third Republic by Constantine Karamanlis in 1974, after the collapse of a seven-year military dictatorship, initiated a new period of state intervention and public sector expansion. As a seminal step towards strengthening the fragile republican polity in the triple sense of emitting a signal of government determination, appealing to politically progressive social strata, and concentrating economic power in state hands, Karamanlis nationalized a few large companies whose powerful owners had cooperated with the colonels. Highly consequential among those initiatives of the conservative Nea Democratia (ND) government was the nationalization in 1976 of the Commercial Bank group – also comprising the Ionian Bank and other significant subsidiaries. The private majority ownership and management was accused of illicit business activity, and the governing boards of the two banks were replaced after the government doubled the equity capital and acquired the majority.[20] Thus the nationalizations of the period of transition to democracy shaped the structure of the modern Greek banking system, in that Greece echoed the Portuguese experience of the 1974–75 period, where nearly the entire and until then privately owned banking system – including Portugal's central bank – was nationalized.

Under the socialist PASOK government of the 1980s, and particularly in the first half of the decade, the public sector expanded dramatically. While no significant change of ownership occurred in the banking system, the scope of state control grew as numerous industrial firms, mainly overindebted enterprises, were acquired by state-controlled banks (SCBs). The sheer scope of total state control that resulted, linking, in a network of interdependencies, public enterprises with SCBs and their controlled subsidiaries, has prompted some economists to speak of 'state corporatism'.[21] These policies were both politically motivated and enhanced by a neo-Keynesian economic doctrine which viewed the state sector as central as ever in directing and implementing structural interventions in the economy for the promotion of development.[22] That phase invites particular attention.

The short story of SCB industrial subsidiaries and the IRO

Some of the postwar credit policies favouring manufacture had important direct implications for the asset structure of banks. Most notable among them was the 1957–imposed obligation of commercial banks to devote 10 per cent (raised to 15 per cent in 1959) of their deposits for the finance of capital formation in industry, extended in the form of medium-term loans or invested in securities issued by industrial concerns.[23] That created the basis for many contemporary equity participations of SCBs in the industrial sector.

A new wave of SCB equity participations came in the 1980s. By 1980 a large number of private industrial firms had become overindebted and were ready to collapse due to extensive reliance on foreign and domestic credit, combined with the economic recession of the 1970s.[24] In order to save employment the PASOK government in 1983 created the Industrial Reconstruction Organization (IRO),[25] a state holding firm which took over an initial 44 ailing firms with the aim of overhauling them after imposing a capital increase, often against their owners' will.[26] However, and though their debts had been written off, due to poor management and subjection to patronage these IRO firms began reporting new losses which the state budget or SCBs were forced to finance in order to avoid closing them down.

The IRO affair had notable implications for SCBs, which were forced by government to accept the conversion of their debt claims against IRO firms into equity participations. Through debt capitalization a further number of ailing firms became subsidiaries of their former SCB creditors, often against the will of SCB administrations.[27] As the new SCB industrial subsidiaries were subject to very lax budget constraints and the various abuses of political control, also having easy credit access, they gradually amassed large debts and evolved into grave portfolio burdens, probably the chief structural problem of the SCB sector by the end of the 1980s.[28]

Structural features of the Greek credit and financial system

The state of the market by the late 1980s: concentration, oligopoly and state control High concentration and oligopoly structure have persistently characterized the Greek banking system.[29] Since the last century a handful of large institutions have dominated the Greek market, the NBG usually controlling almost half of total commercial bank assets. Indicatively, after the Second World War, the NBG and Commercial Bank duopoly handled around 90 per cent of the country's savings.[30] While this oligopoly character helps explain the stability and endurance of the commercial banking system through consecutive economic crises,[31] it also holds its share of responsibility for some of its most important long-standing structural weaknesses.

The extensive scope of direct or indirect state control has been the other defining feature of the Greek banking system. The traditional group of the three largest SCBs (NBG, Commercial Bank and ABG) held, in 1991, 65 per cent of total commercial bank assets, 69 per cent of total commercial bank deposits and 67 per cent of total commercial bank loans.[32] The NBG alone, in 1991, controlled 37 per cent of total loans and 51 per cent of all deposits.[33] All this made the scope of state control over the Greek banking sector one of the largest on an EC/EU and OECD scale.[34]

State control has been complete and direct in all specialized credit institutions. The two largest commercial banks, the NBG[35] and the Commercial Bank, have been indirectly state-controlled through the ownership of their share capital majority by a number of welfare funds whose management has been government-appointed; under a 1953 law and until July 1992 these pension and insurance funds were obligatorily represented by the Finance Minister. However, even after the 1992 banking legal reform, welfare funds refrained from exercising their autonomy, and in 1994 the pre-1992 regime was formally reinstated. The NBG and the Commercial Bank have owned majority stakes in a number of other smaller banks. In 1990 only two traditional private Greek banks operated, the Credit Bank and the Ergobank, though by 1994 five new small Greek private commercial banks had been added.

Hellenocentrism and the 'dual economy' Apart from being state-dominated, the Greek banking system has also been highly hellenocentric, that is dominated by Greek credit institutions. Typically of Southern Europe, foreign banks were only allowed to establish branches in the 1960s; for many years they refrained from competing with domestic commercial banks in fear that monetary authorities, pressured by Greek banks, could restrict their activities.[36]

They thus directed their attention to a small number of foreign enterprises operating in Greece.[37]

In the mid-1970s there were 12 foreign banks operating in Greece, controlling approximately 7 per cent of total commercial bank activity.[38] Quite indicative of the inherently low presence of international players in the Greek banking market is the fact that by the beginning of the 1990s, and despite market liberalization, there was little noticeable change. In 1991 a total of 18 foreign commercial banks controlled a mere 13 per cent of total commercial bank assets (and 10 per cent of total assets, that is, including specialized credit institutions), 10 per cent of total commercial bank deposits (and 8 per cent of the total of deposits) and 11 per cent of total commercial bank loans (and 7 per cent of the total of loans).[39]

A limited number of private banks, both Greek and foreign, were added in the late 1980s and early 1990s. Usually small and specialized, private banks positioned themselves as 'niche players' in the market, concentrating their activity almost exclusively in profitable market segments, by, for example, refusing to accept small deposits or finance non-dynamic enterprises, activities that SCBs have still been forced, though to a diminishing degree, to perform.[40] Consequently, also reflecting different employment policies, foreign banks clearly performed better in almost every qualitative aspect, with a productivity estimated at almost double and a return on equity more than four times the average of SCBs by the beginning of the 1990s.[41] The picture overall confirmed the notion of 'dual economy' which has been used to describe other national banking sectors in the EC/EU as well: while international banking activity is concentrated in the wholesale end of the market occupied by large corporate customers and open to competitive international pressures (and in the Greek case predominantly exercised by private and foreign banks), the majority of retail banking remains confined in the national boundaries operating under government regulation and protectionism (and, in the Greek case, prerogative of large SCBs).[42]

The Greek banking system in a European comparative context Within an EC/EU context Greece has been part of the lower speed group of European banking systems comprising France and the South-European block (Italy, Spain and Portugal).[43] South-European financial systems have traditionally constituted a strong case of credit-based systems: governments administered prices and the quantity of credit available to most sectors of the economy either through controlling the ownership of a large percentage of the banking system or by being able to determine the national system of credit controls and regulations. France and Japan have been other typical representatives of credit dirigisme. In a different typology, credit-based systems correspond to what is known as an 'overdraft economy', that is one in which firms and deficit units do not borrow from the residual or non-existent capital markets but depend fully for their liquidity on bank credit.[44] Credit-based systems are juxtaposed to (a) the capital market or market-based systems, where market competition determines the allocation of resources and the monitoring of companies (as in the US and Britain), and (b) the negotiated credit systems, where financial institutions dominate a credit-based system but government does not control the financial system directly, it only provides *ad hoc* special assistance when necessary in an otherwise negotiated relationship between major social partners (e.g. Germany and Sweden in the 1980s).[45] Both credit-based and negotiated credit systems can be regarded as institution-based systems, given the dominant position of bank institutions in industrial affairs.

Thus the underdevelopment of the Greek capital market historically has been associated with the dominance of commercial banks and the excessive proportion of deposits over other means of financial savings.[46] The weakness of the capital market has been causally related to structural features of Greek capital and business development. A traditional reliance on relatively easy access to bank credit and the predominance of small-scale, domestic-oriented and family-run business undertakings at the expense of large corporate firms both underlay the persistently limited offer of new securities.

By the mid-1980s over 90 per cent of the private sector's financial savings passing from the official Greek financial system were kept in the form of bank deposits, and about 70 per cent were deposited with commercial banks.[47] However, with the capital market's rapid growth from 1990, most new savings were directed away from bank deposits towards securities; the vast majority (over 95 per cent) corresponded to government paper and bonds issued by specialized SCBs, and not shares.[48] While in 1985 equity capitalization (shares only) represented a scant 2 per cent of GDP, with total market capitalization (shares and bonds) amounting to just 7.3 per cent of GDP, by 1993 the percentage had risen to 15.1 per cent and 59.2 per cent respectively.[49]

In institution-based banking systems, banks have been major and stable shareholders in firms dependent on them for their finance. While in 'market-based systems' banks have been discouraged or prohibited not only from controlling industrial companies but also from owning shares in them on their own account, 'institution-based systems' (in countries such as Japan, Germany and the South-European countries including Greece) have nurtured close interrelationships between banking and industry. Thus, for example, the NBG's holdings of non-financial firms in 1990 exceeded 100 per cent of its capital, and its participation in the equity of a few firms exceeded 15 per cent of its capital – which exceeded the limits set by the Second EC Banking Directive.[50] As a result of banking penetration in industry combined with the growing obsoleteness of the more traditional sectors during the 1980s, banking reform in Greece has also involved shedding off equity participations of banks in several loss-making industrial subsidiaries, privatizing them or closing them down, as already mentioned.

South-European banking systems have been traditionally the least developed in the EC, heavily taxed and regulated, protected from external competition, and the least open in the EC in terms of average foreign assets and liabilities.[51] Contributing to their relative underdevelopment, South-European banking systems have employed technology of low capital intensity and/or low productivity. As a reliable indicator of efficiency, by the end of 1986 they presented the lowest assets/employee ratio of all EC countries: US$m 0.70 for Spain, 0.59 for Italy, 0.34 for Portugal, and 0.28, the lowest, for Greece.[52] By 1992 their relative position remained unaltered, while their ratio of loans over assets (indicator of the banks' low contribution to the development process) remained considerably below the EU average.[53]

Extensive state control defined the banking systems of South-European economies. Market oligopoly and concentration has been high in Greece as well as Portugal (with the largest five banks controlling some 83 per cent and 78 per cent of total market share respectively in 1988), contrary to Italy and Spain (55 per cent and 46 per cent respectively) where the banking systems – reflecting national path dependencies – have been considerably decentralized and segmented.[54]

As a consequence of concentration combined with extensive public ownership, interest rate liberalization in some cases failed directly to produce its competitive effects, as will be seen later in our account of Greek credit deregulation. In Greece interest rates were practically set by cartel agreement in the immediate post-deregulation phase, remaining at high levels in order to accommodate the main state-controlled commercial banks; only after 1994–95 could it be claimed that credit institutions had really begun to compete with each other. As a point of remarkable similarity between Greece and Portugal, older, state-controlled banks were placed at a disadvantage compared to newcomers as a result of the various accumulated restrictions on their portfolios under the pre-deregulation regime, as well as due to their often being forced to finance other public enterprises without much prospect of repayment.[55]

By the late 1980s and early 1990s South-European governments had begun to retreat from controlling the ownership and administration of banks. The most radical privatizer has been Portugal: Banco Totta e Açores, Banco Português Atlantico, Banco Espiritu Santo, CPP, BPSM, and others were successfully privatized in the early 1990s. Italy was not immune to the trend: Banca Commerciale Italiana, Credito Italiano, IMI, Banco di Napoli, Istituto Bancario San Paolo di Torino, all entered a process of full or part privatization in the 1990s. In Greece the policy of bank privatizations was far more reluctant, initiated by the 1990 ND government and followed even more reluctantly by the post-1993 PASOK governments; by early 1997, however, only two small banks had been fully privatized (Bank of Piraeus and Bank of Athens), one partly privatized (Bank of Attica) and a few more were on the cards (Bank of Crete, Bank of Central Greece, Bank of Macedonia-Thrace).[56]

Structural weaknesses of the Greek credit system and the dual connection

A range of institutional arrangements constituted the system of financial 'repression' structural deregulation was called to uproot: a complex array of credit controls and regulations (credit rationing), and the fixing of interest rates; investment ratios and obligatory special reserve requirements[57] for public deficit financing; line of business regulations and international capital controls; institutional specialization dictated by administrative frameworks.[58] These constraints, from a financial sector's viewpoint, obstructed sectoral and broader economic efficiency, as will be now argued.

The extensive state interventionism and administrative determination of the credit system was mainly justified by two distinct objectives, both associated with economic policy approaches that prevailed throughout the postwar period. The first objective, which we shall call the credit system/development policy connection, was to use credit rationing in order to promote development. Thus, bank finance was channelled into what were considered 'productive' activities (industry and agriculture) and was restricted from 'unproductive' ones (trade, import trade in particular, and housing). Credit rationing was gradually phased out by deregulation. Related to the first objective was the second one, which we shall call the credit system/fiscal policy connection. The objective there was to use the credit system for supporting fiscal policy through ensuring cheap government finance. This strategy reached its apogee in the 1980s and beginning of the 1990s under the asphyxiating pressure of a soaring public sector requirement and public debt.

The credit system/development policy connection The distinction between 'productive' and 'unproductive' sectors, and the adoption of credit rationing as means for influencing the allocation of available resources, found forceful support in the mainstream economic literature and international policy practice of the 1950s and 1960s.[59]

However, despite its short-term efficiency, credit rationing ended up generating perverse effects in the middle and long run. The attempt to direct bank funds into manufacture through restrictions on lending to trade turned manufacturing enterprises into financiers of trade, consolidating an extensive underground credit sector. At the same time, long-term lending to manufacture failed to improve substantially as credit institutions were able to circumvent regulations and satisfy their preference for short-term claims.[60] The ease of access of manufacturing firms to bank credit, instead of expanding industrial investment, induced firms to compete not for better prices and quality but for the length of term of the commercial credits these firms would extend to their clients. The monopoly or oligopoly conditions that prevailed in many industrial branches further discouraged firms from undertaking investment.

Credit controls led Greek banks to concentrate their attention on avoiding formal violations of regulations, often in full cooperation with their clients, instead of assuming the initiative in evaluating the prospects and real financial needs of their clients. The lack of adaptability of credit to the specific conditions of each industry or firm contributed to the excessive indebtedness and credit risks of industrial enterprises; high indebtedness was in many cases the crucial factor that inhibited the increase in size of industrial firms and the development of a competitive manufacturing sector. Credit regulations impaired the banking system's adjustment – in terms of operational methods and portfolio policies – to changing economic conditions. Regulations and restrictions generated an unnecessary and largely arbitrary differentiation among the various financial intermediaries which aggravated the financial system's oligopoly character and inhibited its modernization. In such ways, the postwar regime of administered credit contributed to what were later perceived as 'distortions' of the financial system and a general failure effectively to conduct financial resources back into production.[61]

The credit system/fiscal policy connection The credit system function of ensuring cheap government finance is also historically intertwined with the postwar dirigiste approach. Given the structural incapacity of the private sector in developing countries to undertake economic development, the build up of a national infrastructure remained the state's primary task. As the traditional absence of an adequate capital market rendered commercial banks the main stores of savings, a mechanism had to be implemented through which those deposits would be diverted to financing development. The reluctance of commercial banks to support private productive investment through long-term loans or equity participations necessitated state regulatory intervention to ensure that a considerable percentage of these resources were channelled into long-term development loans, government securities, or non- or low-interest bearing deposits with the central bank, to be utilized for financing development and government investment projects.[62] That was more or less the original rationale.

Consequently, in the postwar years commercial banks operated as an instrument for government control over monetary policy. Monetary interventionism included a detailed regulatory framework circumscribing the earmarking of funds for cheap government finance. Additionally, since the beginning of the 1970s and until 1987, and despite mounting inflation, nominal interest rates were fixed below inflation rates and market level under the pretext of financing development but with the real aim of alleviating the servicing of public debt.[63]

However, the easy and cheap government access to finance was leading to public spending which would have been avoided if government had to rely on the real cost of capital.[64] Between the 1960s and the end of the 1970s, not only total public expenditure as percentage of GDP grew steadily, but, particularly in the 1970s, public sector consumer spending expanded while gross fixed capital investment exhibited a negative rate of increase.[65]

The 1980s finalized the complete distortion of the credit system/government finance connection. Between 1981 and 1986 total credit to the private sector tripled (which is considered a normal development) but finance to the public sector sextupled (a less normal development) as public deficits rose.[66] Between 1981 and 1989 interest payments had quadrupled as GDP percentage, reaching a distressing 12.5 per cent of GDP in 1989.[67] So, while until the late 1970s public sector borrowing was mainly aimed at financing investment, by the end of the 1980s the trend had been radically altered and the composition of public expenditure was adjusted at the expense of public investment in order to make room for the rising share of interest payments.[68]

The high PSBR had a visible impact on the capital and money market. Traditionally, until the early 1980s, public deficits were being financed either through the obligatory purchase of Treasury bills by the banking sector upon negative interest rates or through BoG advances.

After 1984 government securities were increasingly purchased by non-bank private investors. However, given the PSBR rise in absolute numbers, government reliance on the banking sector for deficit financing remained consistently heavy.

The interdependence through the 1980s of the credit and financial system's structural weaknesses generated a self-feeding cyclical reproductive process. The fixing of interest rates until 1987 at below-inflation levels made it unnecessary for state and private sector enterprises to seek to raise capitals in the market. The lack of attractive offers in the capital market practically deprived depositors of any serious investment alternative outside the bank deposits system. The consequent growth of bank liquidity directed savings towards consumption, enhanced the policy of 'cheap money', and undermined capital market development. At the same time, easy government access to cheap bank finance encouraged public deficits to be maintained at persistently high levels.[69] As a result of government control over the credit system and interest rates, the banking system operated as a virtual second state budget, actually undertaking the burden of debt servicing, financing development social and economic goals, not to mention the accruing political objectives.

The political economy dimension: the banking system as a political instrument, and the Bank of Crete

Apart from reflecting each government's development priorities, the distribution of favourable credit throughout the pre-deregulation era served as an instrument of protectionist policy for selected sectors and recipient groups.[70] More often than not, the postwar doctrine of state-assisted or state-directed development cohabited comfortably with political clientelistic patterns of resource distribution typical of a South-European context. The SCB system was the source and instrument through which credit was granted to friendly entrepreneurs; subsidies were extended to small businesses prompting their political 'indebtedness'; copious funds at negative rates were distributed to agricultural cooperatives; small but 'targeted' grants were spread all over the country to selected municipalities, cultural centres, local projects of all kind, usually through the helpful intermediation of a local patron (government minister, MP, or local 'baron').[71]

To all the above should be added the alleged operation of SCBs in recent times as illicit sources of political funding. It has been alleged that a portion of SCB funds (about 10–15 per cent), after being channelled to private firms as loans, was then fed back to the political system in the form of business donations to political parties and the governing party in particular.[72] The demand for such lateral funding has been enhanced since the 1980s by the rapid development of mass party structures by PASOK and ND, the consequent cost of party mobilization, and the liberalization of radio and television since the late 1980s which multiplied political advertising expenses. The triple round of consecutive elections in 1989–90 led parties to financial exhaustion and excessive debts. All these factors, combined with the relative inadequacy of official finance from the state budget, intensified the dependence of ND and PASOK on business funding and compelled them to utilize, among others, the SCB system as an instrument for obtaining that funding. As a BoG ex-governor meaningfully summarized, 'the traditional temptation of all governments [is] to control the country's political life and businessmen through loans from state-controlled banks'.[73]

A paradigm case of the political role of banking capital has been the Bank of Crete issue, which invites mention for serving as a focal point in the entire banking politics and privatization debate. Traditionally small and privately owned, the Bank of Crete was acquired in the first half of the 1980s by businessman George Koskotas, entering a course of dynamic modernization. However, in 1988 and against various obstacles raised by certain government actors, BoG controls revealed a long chain of illegal activities of the Bank of Crete, and in October 1988 the appointment of a BoG commissioner was imposed. It was soon proved that Koskotas's short-lived imperium (including a press group and a football club) was built on extensive fraud, embezzlement and forgery.[74] The scandal was a serious blow to the credibility of the political system which through clientelistic patterns of a mutually accommodative nature had nurtured the Koskotas phenomenon, offering political backing in exchange for financial and publicity services.

The Koskotas scandal had a further significant impact at the level of symbols and perceptions, enhancing suspicion towards aggressive private entrepreneurship and privately owned banking in particular. That had notable implications for banking reform politics as it offered a potent example to those arguing in support of retaining state control over the banking system or imposing strict requirements for the establishment of private banks and enhancing the BoG's supervisory authority.[75] That line of argument was further enforced by the fact that the three – publicized – most important breaches of banking system legislation in recent time, namely those of Commercial Bank in 1976, the Bank of Central Greece in 1984 and the Bank of Crete in 1988, were all committed under private ownership. However, a justified anti-private bias reflected only one part of the picture. What rendered the Bank of Crete's collapse a scandal of epic proportions was not the element of private treacherousness itself as that of government (and more broadly political) accommodation and collusion.

Organizational weaknesses of the SCB sector and the implications of government control

The long tradition of structural subjection of SCBs to government control fostered operational attitudes which were more politically conscious than market-driven or profit-oriented. Government intervention in the administrative function of SCBs has been constant and unrestrained. With a 1990 law[76] formally excluding commercial SCBs from the public sector, the main bulk of hierarchical administrative control was lifted. Formally, commercial SCBs were left free to formulate and implement their entire range of policies. In reality, however, as long as SCB administrations continued to be government-appointed, interventions persisted almost unabated with regard to all issues of interest to government actors: from higher SCB investment in Treasury bills (until their abolition), to supporting the drachma from speculatory attacks; from credit policies to personnel recruitment and promotions, even to procurement policies.

To partly offset the negative impact of state-imposed obligations upon SCB efficiency and competitiveness, governments in earlier times would typically extend direct or indirect subsidies, usually through unofficial and oblique means, such as low-interest BoG finance, subsidized interest rates or special SCB commissions from the sale of Treasury bills.[77] A traditional long-standing practice was the extension of a regular annual subsidy from the BoG to the SCBs, proportionate to their size, as a direct support on their balance sheet. Governments would also intervene, mainly in the earlier postwar decades, through favourable legislation and regulatory clauses endowing SCBs with various minor or less minor privileges, some of which even survived deregulation.

Thus, the relationship between government and the SCB sector prior to deregulation could be described as mutually parasitic as much as symbiotic; at various instances each benefited from the other and each had to rely on the other. However, the heavy structural predicaments faced by almost all SCBs compared to the considerably higher competitiveness of the privately owned banking sector suggested that SCBs were net losers from their forced engagement with government.

Some additional factors collaborated to that effect. SCBs have been distinguished for the entrenched power of their trade unions. Over the decades, SCB employee organizations, and mostly that of the NBG, encouraged by their dominant oligopolistic market position, accumulated a range of privileges.[78] In the post-junta years, after the nationalization of the Commercial Bank group and particularly in the 1980s, SCB trade unions consolidated their power. The unions obtained public employee status for SCB employees, ensuring regulations which made it virtually impossible for staff to be dismissed. Welfare advantages of SCB employees, as opposed to those of private banks, were not based on productivity, a fact which, combined with the overstaffing of SCBs,[79] explained why labour costs per employee were higher in the SCB sector than in the private one despite the latter's higher wages.[80]

The SCB sector was probably the most open, modernizing and efficient part of the entire wider public sector. However, by the middle and end of the 1980s SCBs displayed important organizational weaknesses such as lack of adequate qualified personnel, low incentives for productivity and poor career prospects for employees. Worse was the case of specialized SCBs, formally subjected to government hierarchy. That framework resulted in tight control by the supervising ministries, lack of flexibility in vital decision-making, time-consuming implementation processes, considerable difficulties in recruiting qualified personnel, incapacity to formulate and implement long-term strategic decisions, and strong reluctance to assume entrepreneurial initiatives.[81] In the entire SCB sector, highly centralized and personalistic administration discouraged serious professionalism on behalf of employees, rendering the management inflexible and bringing about corporatistic attitudes and suspicion towards change. All in all, in the words of a Commercial Bank CEO, SCBs displayed an 'alarming qualitative and technological distance from international professional standards'.[82]

Credit policies and the deregulation of the Greek banking system

The evolution of financial reform: the European framework

Financial deregulation and liberalization represented Greece's adjustment to a specific political economy conjuncture generated by converging international forces and propitious domestic factors. These highly interrelated forces can be factored into three categories, namely (a) market/economic, (b) legal/institutional, and (c) political/ideological.

Economic pressures, either general or sector-specific, were related to the expanding realm of market forces. General pressures resulted from the growing convergence of western economic policies towards monetary discipline, fiscal austerity and free market competition, and the requirements of adjustment such convergence posed for less competitive national economies. Sector-specific pressures were the most decisive: they involved the rapidly evolving financial liberalization, the course towards a Single European financial market, and the urgent need to keep track of change in order to remain competitive under conditions of globalization. The legal/institutional pressures pertained to the obligation to comply with EC competition rules, banking legislation and convergence targets within given deadlines. Legal/institutional factors played a crucial role in increasing the salience and urgency of economic pressures by objectifying them into a 'positive' European legislative reform programme. Finally, political/ideological pressures arose with the ascendancy of neo-liberal ideas and policies in Europe against the political decline of domestic economic statism.

Three main developments could be claimed to have contributed to bringing about banking competition in Greece and the EC in general. First, the significant decline since 1980 of interest rate controls and regulations or interest rate cartel agreements in the EC countries; second, the development of short-term money, bond and equity markets; and, third, the deregulation of fees and commissions on financial services.[83]

While Germany, the UK, the Netherlands and Denmark had the least restrictive controls on interest rates and capital flows in the EC, Spain, Portugal and Greece, along with Belgium, were the most regulated. The gradual process of interest rate deregulation in Southern Europe was initiated mostly in the second half of the 1980s, beginning with sectors relevant mainly for large corporate investors, and culminating with the elimination of lending rate ceilings and deposit rate minima. The exact deregulation process depended on the existing regime of controls. Thus, in Greece, by the time liberalization began, there existed more than ninety different categories of interest rates, targeted to specific economic sectors and subsectors (and corresponding voter groups). The piecemeal process of the upward unification of those special interest rates began slowly after 1983–84, serving the Greek central bank's gradual shift of monetary policy from negative to positive and rising real interest rates (by 1992 real short-term interest rates in Greece were well above the EU average). Since the Greek government and the Bank of Greece had decided to employ monetary policy as the chief anti-inflationary weapon (imitating to a considerable extent the Italian experience), the general strategy was first to equalize interest rates upwards, then to set minima, and then finally to liberalize. Overall, South-European countries (along with Ireland) were the last in the EU to complete interest rate deregulation: Italy in June 1990, Spain and Portugal in December 1992, and finally Greece in March 1993, two months after Ireland.[84]

Throughout Southern Europe the slow pace of liberalization was associated with those countries' crucial preoccupation with their high levels of public debt, whose servicing was bound to become more costly with the rise of real interest rates and the abolition of obligatory investment requirements of banks in government paper. Typically of semi-industrialized countries subject to financial repression, state-controlled banks in South-European economies acted as forced buyers of public debt and also as implicit tax collectors.[85] In Greece a 1982 reform of the Bank of Greece charter placed a limit on the Bank's credit advances to government, which were completely prohibited after 1994. The obligation of banks to invest some 40 per cent of their new deposits in Greek Treasury bills began to be gradually reduced as late as 1991 until it was completely eliminated in May 1993 in compliance with the Maastricht Treaty provisions.

The freedom of capital movements was a central desideratum of European financial integration. South-European countries were the last to abolish capital controls, which had been extensively employed as means for exchange rate stability. Again, in this case, Italy preceded in the liberalization and the others followed. Italy was within the core of eight EC member countries which met the 1 July 1990 deadline for the elimination of all remaining capital controls.[86] The deadline extended to the end of 1992 for Spain and Ireland, and 1 July 1994 for Portugal and Greece; all made it well in time.

The effects of financial liberalization were, among others, evident in the wide range of new financial institutions that emerged. Progress was most visible in the least developed financial sectors. By 1994 in Greece there were 120 mutual funds (from two in 1988), 15 portfolio investment companies (from six in 1987), a number of merchant banks, 12 leasing companies (from three in 1987), 18 foreign exchange companies, and around 60 securities companies (instead of approximately 30 stockbrokers in 1986), indicating the rapid development of specialized financial services. But let us take a closer look at the evolution of banking deregulation and liberalization.

Credit and monetary policies, and the evolution of banking deregulation

Postwar credit policies and the Currency Committee[87] In line with other European countries, the 1946 establishment of the Currency Committee had given a clear signal of the reality of the new postwar policy which was to be characterized by the excessive concentration of government control over the economic and financial system. The creation of the Currency Committee also reflected the view (championed mainly by the country's major postwar economist and post-1955 Governor of the Bank of Greece, Xenophon Zolotas) that in developing countries a formal framework for economic policy coordination between the central bank and the government was necessary in order to harmonize monetary with fiscal policy and jointly formulate the necessary policy mixes for the promotion of short- and long-term economic objectives.[88] As in most OECD countries of the postwar period, an array of regulations were established including interest rate controls, securities market regulations, quantitative investment restrictions on credit institutions, line-of-business restrictions, restrictions on foreign entry of banks, and foreign exchange and capital account controls. The Currency Committee supplanted the BoG in undertaking all monetary, credit and foreign exchange policy responsibilities as well as the task of formulating the legal framework concerning financial transactions. The Currency Committee consisted of the ministers of coordination (chair), finance, agriculture, commerce and industry, and the BoG governor;[89] decision-making was based on majority vote. The Currency Committee had the power to determine the volume of bank credit, the sectors or activities entitled to it, the exact percentages or even absolute amounts of expenditures entitled to bank finance, the specific interest rates charged on each type of bank loan, the terms of the loans and the security to be demanded by the banks for each type of credit, and the exact procedures to be followed for the approval and provision of the various types of loan. Enforcement of these provisions and regulations, a breach of which could result in severe penalties, was assigned to the Banking Supervision Division (which later evolved into an important department of the BoG's internal mechanism), acting as agent of the Currency Committee.

The regime of heavy credit controls and regulations that emerged in 1946 was largely inevitable given the immediate postwar circumstances. Bank assets were depleted, no new savings were flowing in, and hyperinflation remained persistent until 1951. At the same time the country was left in ruins, and the task of reconstruction required new investment (which had been frozen for nearly a decade), extensive replacement of antiquated or destroyed capital stock, and massive inflow of funds. The banking system's lending capacity was scarce, and the financing of the economy had to rely chiefly on economic assistance from the USA and the issue of new money. Under those conditions the power of monetary authorities over the banking system increased and the influence of credit institutions shrunk as the Currency Committee controlled their sources of finance. The combination of general quantitative credit controls with qualitative ones was the means through which the monetary authorities aimed not only to control the commercial banks' capacity to extend credit, but also to influence its composition.[90]

In the late 1940s a system of rationing was introduced on long-term bank credit to various sectors financed out of US assistance funds, and compulsory reserve requirements were imposed at fixed levels. In 1950 the deposits of public entities were transferred by law to the BoG, which assumed the authority to either invest them as deposits with financial intermediaries or use them for direct lending under the rules set by the Currency Committee. The central unifying logic behind all these measures remained to channel the inadequate amount of available funds to sectors and activities deemed as 'productive'. To that aim lending to individual firms in excess of a certain amount was subject to the Currency Committee's prior approval. Such prior approval was required for commercial bank loans to export trade and handicrafts, and the banks were given the opportunity to withdraw the credit funds extended to these sectors from the BoG up to their total amount. Industrial credit funds for capital equipment were subject to the same regime but only half of the total amount was allowed to be drawn from the BoG. On the other hand, industrial working capital as well as the 'unproductive' import and domestic trade sectors could be financed only out of the commercial banks' own funds, and was therefore practically hindered by the banks' low percentage, until 1956, of private deposits.[91] Finance to any other sector or activity in the period throughout the 1950s was prohibited without case-by-case advance approval by the Currency Committee.

A first indication of the tenacity of credit controls was that they remained unaffected by the economic liberalization process launched in 1953 with the devaluation of the drachma, the abolition of a wide range of government controls and regulations, and the restoration of freedom of imports. The predominance of foreign aid and new money as sources of finance, given the low level of bank deposits, still provided a convincing pretext for the continuing government control over credit policies. However, the ensuing stabilization of the drachma and the economy, and the restoration of a high rate of inflow of private savings into the banking system after 1956 deprived credit control policies of their immediate postwar justification. As the credit control regime continued unabated it became clear that it was now viewed as more than just a temporary measure. In fact, the monetary authorities within a decade since the Currency Committee was established had become convinced of the value of quantitative and qualitative controls for achieving monetary stability, as well as for affecting national expenditure, in particular the size and structure of investment, and thus influencing the rate and pattern of economic development.[92]

The drastic rise in the inflow of private savings after 1956 reduced the commercial banks' dependence on the BoG for funding, and gradually restored the power of the large commercial banks in deciding themselves upon the credit they would extend. Consequently, some quantitative credit restrictions were relaxed and the requirement for prior approval of the monetary authorities to commercial bank loans was eased, and gradually abolished. However, overall liberalization of bank transactions was far from restored. While favourable credit policies (such as a BoG subsidy to commercial bank interest rates) were aimed at the sectors considered as 'productive' (agriculture, export trade, manufacturing, mining, later on tourism), important credit restrictions continued to apply for financing import trade, dwellings and the sale of consumer goods. At the same time, after 1957 commercial banks had been encouraged or obliged to contribute to the government's investment programme by investing a percentage of their funds in government securities or bonds issued by public enterprises such as the Public Power Corporation.[93]

Around the mid-1960s the discretionary power of banks was enhanced by peripheral reforms such as their authorization to control whether the terms of credit were being implemented, and the abolition of most qualitative credit controls to industry and export trade.

In the early phase of the 1967 junta regime expansionary credit policies were introduced in order to stimulate economic activity. Both commercial banks and special credit institutions were given increased access to BoG funds, and a number of qualitative credit controls and regulations were relaxed and simplified. Interest rate differentiation, however, was maintained as a means of favouring the financing of certain sectors, to which the construction of tourist facilities and dwellings was added, and the use of the system of credit controls and regulations as the main policy instrument remained unchallenged. After the first two years of the junta, and as the economy expanded, the initial trend towards simplification was reversed and monetary authorities brought into effect an even more complex system of special discount rates, credit controls and regulations.[94] Preferential terms were established for the financing of manufacturing and several other activities as specific as shipping, trucking companies, cotton spinning mills, motion-picture companies and others. It could be said of the dictatorship period, particularly of its first years, that the pre-existing tendency of using credit policy as a means for wooing specific client economic groups was intensified.[95] After 1972, and as economic overexpansion was threatening price stability, restrictive measures were introduced including two new types of primary reserve requirements and the contraction of credit to dwellings and consumption.[96]

The period of transition to democracy Democracy was established in 1974 amid galloping inflation and deepening recession. Consequently a number of credit restrictions were relaxed, particularly with regard to manufacturing, shipping, tourism and export trade. However, as these measures accelerated money growth, restrictive monetary and credit policies were called in to control overall credit expansion, and moderate selective credit controls and regulations were employed. Thus reliance on the postwar regulatory system as an instrument for influencing the allocation of resources continued with new strength after the 1974 restoration of democracy. As Halikias has argued, the maintenance of the system of credit controls and regulations, albeit the varying reliance of monetary authorities on it, was an inevitable result of the arbitrary fixing of interest rates on the basis of priority treatment of certain sectors instead of according to banking criteria of yield, security and liquidity.[97] During 1974 and 1975 the direction of bank funds to industrial and export activity became the declared principal aim of credit policy, and financing to those sectors was freed from the general limit to credit expansion.[98] Between 1976 and 1978, however, money and credit supply was rising hand in hand with fiscal deficits and inflation, and the BoG Governor in his annual reports was cautioning on the side effects of credit expansion to the industrial sector in the form of credit leakages to imports and 'other speculatory activities'.[99] The BoG tried to confront violations through intensifying control over credit institutions.[100] By 1979 anti-inflationary policy and the serious curtailment of public deficits had become the principal expressed government objectives, encouraged by a slight retreat of inflation at the end of 1978 and supported by restrictive credit and monetary policies which placed increased emphasis on the employment of interest rate policy.[101] However, the 1979 second oil shock gravely disappointed expectations for an economic stabilization as almost all economic figures deteriorated, inflation mounting.

The 1980 Governor's Report and a momentous shift of direction

Remarkably, and while a new wave of restrictive measures and credit controls was expected by the central bank, the Governor's Report of April announced a momentous shift of direction. The intention of the monetary authorities, Governor Xenophon Zolotas stated, was gradually to move towards a 'new system, based on liberalized interest rates and the abolition of special credit rules, controls, restrictions and regulations'.[102] The new regime would rely strictly on banking criteria for the allocation of credit, and monetary and credit controls would be general. These conditions would be expected to stimulate credit institutions to compete with each other, raise the productivity and efficiency of the banking system and force it to adjust to the market's changing requirements.[103] While the pronouncement represented a radical break with the entire postwar credit policy doctrine, 'gradualism' was the keyword.

This official announcement of a shift in the BoG Governor's Report of April 1980 was clearly a direct response to the novel conditions that had emerged from Greece's admission in May 1979 to the European Communities,[104] and what was broadly perceived as an emerging general future pressure to 'catch up' with European competition. Apart from that, the 1979 Accession Treaty of Greece to the European Communities provided no direct formal obligations for credit system liberalization except for the gradual abolition of certain restrictions concerning foreign currency and specific capital movements.[105] But the EC momentum was unambiguously leading to liberalization. The trend was bolstered by the reports of two domestic banking expert committees in 1980, chaired by the Underminister of Coordination Ioannis Palaiokrassas and the BoG Deputy Governor Harissopoulos respectively. Both committees coincided in their defence of the banking sector's interests, and proposed the extension of interest rate subsidies to various sectors directly from the state budget instead of the banking system; the non-employment of credit policy as a means for supporting economic development; the recourse of government to the capital and money markets; the weakening of banking oligopoly conditions through the separation of bank operations from other undertakings; the granting of independence to non-financial subsidiaries of banks; the establishment of new financial intermediaries (for example, real-estate companies, mutual funds, consumer credit cooperatives, credit and financial companies, investment banks), as well as a secondary capital market; the termination of BoG subsidies to commercial banks.[106]

The further deterioration of almost all macroeconomic indicators in 1980–81, and the prospect of a PASOK landslide in October 1981, postponed any further move of the government-controlled monetary authorities along the lines of structural reform. On the contrary, to BoG despair and under strong government pressure in view of the 1981 election, earmarked deposit amounts were set higher, so were credit ceilings, and the whole commercial bank mechanism was geared to significant credit expansion towards all existing and newly favoured recipient categories. At the same time, in 1980 public sector borrowing from the credit system was absorbing 93.4 per cent of all private deposits.[107] As the sole deregulation measure, and in the hope of encouraging foreign exchange inflow and ensuring competitiveness of domestic interest rates from frequent and abrupt changes in foreign money markets, in 1980 the monetary authorities liberalized interest rates in foreign currency deposits.[108]

Credit policies under the socialist PASOK The October 1981 rise of PASOK to power signalled a forceful as ever neo-Keynesian bias in macroeconomic management. The professed aim of economic stabilization was coupled and soon overrun by a demand stimulus which was hailed both as a strategy of recovery and an instrument for income redistribution. The new BoG Governor, politically minded technocrat Gerasimos Arsenis, along with denouncing the frequent submission of the credit system to powerful private interests in the past, was also keen to send the uneasy financial and business community a reassuring message of central bank continuity by reaffirming the monetary authorities' determination to achieve a – gradual – transition to a new 'rational' system of general and simplified credit rules.[109] The BoG commitment to a moderate version of 'rationalization' continued unabated throughout the first half of the 1980s, and criticism of the system of credit controls and regulations was uttered in several BoG Governor Reports. The 1982 Report castigated the large differentiation of interest rates as often being the 'result of pressures on behalf of organized interest groups',[110] and the 1983 Report made reference to the credit leakages and serious distortions resulting from the complex regulatory *status quo*.[111] Along the same lines was the 1984 Report, which affirmed the BoG's intention to proceed to a 'simple and easily applicable system of general credit rules, which would grant ample space for initiative to the banks'.[112]

Considerable overall credit expansion characterized the remaining months and first year (1981–82) of PASOK government. Significantly higher amounts of commercial bank deposits (from 7 per cent to 10 per cent) were earmarked for financing handicraft industry and small–medium scale manufacturing enterprises (SMEs) and more favourable terms were set for the granting of state guarantees to SME loans; also special funds were 'temporarily' extended to overindebted firms of the private sector (which would later come under the IRO).[113] At the same time important institutional reforms were put forward as part of the new government's programme, including the 1982 abolition of the Currency Committee and the strengthening of the role of the BoG through the legislation of a ceiling to its permitted outstanding credit to government. After 1983–84 the process of interest rate equalization began through the upward adjustment of a whole range of special lending rates.[114] Most importantly, in 1983 interest rates for government lending from the BoG were raised and so were rates of Treasury bills, which opened the way for government recourse to the money market.[115]

The slight economic recovery after the end of 1983 encouraged the implementation in 1984 of certain small-scale measures of monetary and credit policy rationalization. A number of operations were allowed to take place without prior BoG approval: more freedom was granted to the banks for settling debts, general rules were set for the activity of agricultural finance organizations, certain categories of commercial bank loans in foreign currency were permitted, and procedures were simplified in other areas. BoG responsibility for the credit expansion of the Agricultural Bank and the National Mortgage Bank was limited to the fixing of a total upper limit, and the responsibility for the allocation of credit was transferred to the two banks. With the participation of the drachma in the European Currency Unit (ECU), the ECU was recognized as foreign currency and time deposits in convertible drachma were permitted to foreign citizens, which paved the way for making the drachma negotiable in European money markets.

As the June 1985 elections approached, once again credit facilities were significantly eased: housing, agricultural, consumer and small-scale enterprise loans were set at more favourable conditions and credit ceilings were raised or doubled. Banks were allowed to issue letters of guarantee, under certain provisions, without the prior *ad hoc* approval of the monetary authorities.[116] Overdue debts of artisan enterprises were settled up to a significant amount per company, being converted into a new loan. Consequently, and combined with the significant fiscal expansion and rapid pre-electoral rise of public sector hirings, in the aftermath of the 1985 poll economic indicators were once again on the downslide.

The 1985 election aftermath: banking deregulation on the official government agenda Typically, the election day aftermath was hailed as the opportunity for a fresh start. In autumn 1985 a new stabilization programme led by the then Economy Minister Simitis provided a relatively more propitious environment for the structural reform of the banking system. In addition, certain measures of financial liberalization were included as terms in the 1985 EC balance-of-payments support loan. Thus, in line with the European trend, the gradual abolition of special categories of preferential interest rates combined with an upward trend of the average nominal lending rate continued. The BoG's objective was to suppress liquidity through the exercise of indirect (raising the bank rate) rather than direct monetary controls, thus avoiding as much as possible resorting to quantitative credit controls which were perceived as hampering bank competition and modernization.[117] Moreover, transactions in Treasury bills between commercial banks were permitted under certain terms; special finance to ailing enterprises and fruit and vegetable processing companies was abolished; the ceiling on bank finance to commercial companies and professionals for the acquisition of fixed equipment was withdrawn; banks were allowed to set their commission freely on foreign currency transactions; certain foreign exchange operations were facilitated; the terms of Agricultural

Bank lending to private agricultural industries were equated to those of commercial banks; credit institutions were allowed to take time deposits of up to three months upon freely negotiable interest rates.

In 1986 an expert committee on banking reform was formed, chaired by the then Secretary General of the Economy Ministry Theodoros Karatzas. The highly publicized 1987 Karatzas Committee report, very much on the lines of the 1980 and 1981 Committee reports, gave a significant boost to the BoG's deregulation programme, which moved to the seminal step of liberalizing interest rates. The liberalization of lending rates began in June 1987 with the abolition of the maximum rate for short-term and other categories of bank credit representing some 55 per cent of total bank credit to the private sector. Instead, a minimum rate was set, and the banks were freed to negotiate over that. The minimum lending rate was abolished altogether with effect as from 1 January 1988. Then the first reduction (from 20 per cent to 18 per cent) was made in reserves on a certain category of bank credit, as a first step towards the gradual dismantlement of the entire reserve/rebate system, a complex scheme aiming at levelling out the banks' rate of return on different types of loan. From November 1987 long-term loans were liberalized and so were interest rates on time deposits and savings deposits on notice. This left the savings deposit rate and the two minimum lending rates (17 per cent for short-term bank credit and 16 per cent for medium- and long-term credit) as the only ones to be determined by the BoG. The 'despecialization' of specialized credit institutions (that is, their gradual equalization with commercial banks) continued at a faster pace, and a range of additional credit controls and regulations were eased or abolished. Moreover, since 1986 the BoG had been proceeding slowly but steadily towards liberalizing capital movements, a process that was finally concluded in 1994.

In March 1988 Prime Minister Papandreou, intent on holding early elections, abandoned the stabilization programme. In 1988 domestic credit expansion accelerated, boosted by the demand for credit created by the relative economic recovery. As a result of their liberalization, real lending interest rates increased substantially for the first time and remained over inflation levels, used by the BoG as a means for controlling liquidity and credit expansion and for supporting disinflation.

In the course of 1989, under conditions of consecutive national polls, coalition governments and extreme executive instability, macroeconomic conditions severely deteriorated. Encouraged by the perpetual electoral climate, credit expansion to the private sector was overshooting monetary targets, accelerating at a fast pace. This was a combined result of deregulation – which for the first time made funds freely available for sectors such as trade, imports and services – and inflationary expectations which enhanced demand for credit. As a result, the BoG (also forced to accommodate the government's swelling borrowing requirement) was obligated for the final months of 1989 to resort to a direct overall credit control and to restrict bank liquidity through increasing the commercial banks' compulsory investment requirement in Treasury bills.[118]

The implosion of the public borrowing requirement had the effect of slowing down some of the programmed reforms; bankers and businesses found it difficult to take full advantage of existing deregulation since the public sector was swallowing up an increasing share of available financial resources. Most notable among the measures of the 1988–89 period was the gradual reduction, during 1988, of the long-standing system of obligatory reserve/rebate ratios on bank loans, culminating in its complete abolition as from 1 January 1989, which released a total of nearly110 billion drachmas.[119] The abolition of the system paved the way for banks to differentiate their lending rates upon banking criteria. During 1988 and in the early months of 1989, further measures were taken towards the almost complete dismantling of the complex system of selective credit rules and regulations. After the gradual abolition of restrictions to credit for a range of specific categories (construction, trade, services, the easing of consumer credit) all firms acquired access to bank credit upon terms mostly freely determined by the banks. Moreover, interest rates on current accounts and sight deposits were allowed to be freely determined by the banks, and the interest rate on savings deposits with banks was liberalized, subject to a minimum of 15 per cent (June 1989).

The completion of banking liberalization in the 1990s The April 1990 election brought to power a neo-liberal-leaning, centre-right wing Nea Democratia government whose support for financial deregulation was a principal constituent of its programme. In accordance with the government's stabilization programme the BoG applied a severely restrictive monetary policy in 1990 and 1991. For three consecutive years to 1989 monetary and credit targets had been overshot, liquidity expanding due to both financial liberalization and the swelling public sector borrowing requirement. In 1990 the BoG's restrictive monetary policy, for the first time after many years, was closely adhered to. This was significantly facilitated by the 1990 stock exchange boom, which by responding to private sector capital needs alleviated demand previously exercised upon the credit system. At the same time, and despite the higher PSBR, increased absorption of government paper by the non-bank public decelerated the growth of bank credit to the public sector.[120] The increasing government recourse to the non-bank market for the absorption of its securities exercised upward pressure on interest rates, thus contributing to the central bank's restrictive monetary policy.

By 1990, when ND came to power, the bulk of deregulation had already been completed. Around 90 per cent of lending interest rates had been liberalized, leaving only the minimum savings deposit rate, lending rates to SMEs representing 7 per cent of total bank credit to the private sector, as well as rates of certain categories of housing loans. In addition, deposit interest rates with certain special credit institutions as well as special categories of loans were still being subsidized from the state budget. The principal remaining part of the regulatory regime concerned the obligatory bank investment in Treasury bills, the earmarking of bank funds for credit to public enterprises, and low interest loans to SMEs.[121] Emboldened by the propitious conditions of a new momentum of financial integration at the EC level and a liberalizing government at the domestic level, the BoG moved rapidly towards concluding its deregulation programme. The most important measures that took place in the first half of the 1990s, and through which the programme of financial deregulation was completed, included the complete deregulation of distinctions between state-controlled specialized credit institutions and commercial banks, the phasing out of all remaining credit and investment controls, including the final abolition of the obligatory investment requirement in Treasury bills (completely abolished by May 1993 in compliance with the Maastricht Treaty provisions[122]), and the phasing out of the earmarking of bank deposits for special SME finance (July 1993).

In conclusion

Our brief overview of postwar credit and monetary policies and the evolution of deregulation has highlighted their strong interdependency with economic policy and the political context. This has been most visible in the electoral cycles of the entire post-junta period, where apart from other macroeconomic indicators, a political/monetary cycle[123] also seems to make its mark: repeatedly monetary and credit policy loosen *en route* to a national election only to tighten again in the election day aftermath. The particular structural endowment of the Greek banking sector (extensive state control, oligopoly structure, relatively underdeveloped capital and money market) combined with persistent features of the Greek economy from the mid-1970s through the 1990s (a high public debt and inflation) defined the specific opportunity framework within which banking deregulation could evolve. However, given the strength of the EC pressure towards liberalization and adjustment, domestic factors carried a considerable influence on the timing and scope of reform but less so on its content or on the general policy direction.

This paper has examined the state of the Greek banking sector until and at the time of reform. Apart from delineating the sector's main actors, we traced the development and scope of state control over the banking system. An entrenched institutional framework of government control over the decades, we argued, legitimized by what we defined as 'the dual connection', accumulated various impediments on the banking sector and especially its SCB section. While in the postwar period those impediments were more or less offset by protectionist policies, conditions of EC competition rendered them increasingly counterproductive. The banks' growing detriment from state control and credit regulation, and the latter's alleged perverse effects on resource allocation offered the legitimizing discourse which – added to the most definitive external 'push' factors originating from financial globalization and the new European political economy – provided the internal 'pull' for banking deregulation.

Notes

1. See G. Dertilis, *The Banking Issue, 1871–1873*, Athens: National Bank Educational Foundation, 1980, pp. 6–7 (in Greek); E. Stassinopoulos, *The History of the National Bank of Greece*, Athens, 1966 (in Greek); M. Eulambio, *The National Bank of Greece: A History of the Financial and Economic Evolution of Greece*, Athens: Vlastos, 1924, pp. 2ff.
2. See M. Eulambio, op. cit., pp. 175–7; I. Valaoritis, *The History of the National Bank of Greece, 1842–1902*, Athens: National Bank Educational Foundation, 1902/1988, p. 234, *passim* (in Greek).
3. See, for example, Valaoritis, op. cit.
4. K. Kostis and V. Tsokopoulos, *The Banks in Greece, 1898–1928*, Athens, 1988, pp. 57–8 (in Greek).
5. See V. Mitsis, *The Issue Privilege of the Ionian Bank, 1839–1920*, Athens: Ionian Bank, 1987 (in Greek).
6. M. Dritsa, *Industry and Banks in Interwar Greece*, Athens: National Bank Educational Foundation, 1990, p. 234 (in Greek).
7. On that period see G. Dertilis, *Greek Economy, 1830–1910, and Industrial Revolution*, Athens: Sakkoulas, 1984, esp. pp. 54ff (in Greek).
8. Kostis and Tsokopoulos, op. cit., pp. 145ff.
9. Ibid., pp. 59ff; Dritsa, op. cit., p. 237.
10. C. Gortsos, *The Greek Banking System*, Athens: Hellenic Bank Association, 1992, pp. 9–12.
11. For an analysis of the Bank of Greece's institutional role and development, and an account of postwar economic and monetary policies, see G. Pagoulatos, 'Institutions and public policy making: the politics of

Greek banking deregulation and privatisation', D.Phil. thesis, University of Oxford, 1997.

12. See M. Mazower, *Greece and the Interwar Economic Crisis*, Oxford: Oxford University Press, 1991.
13. C. Hadziiossif, *The Old Moon: Industry in the Greek Economy, 1830–1940*, Athens: Themelio, 1993, pp. 279ff (in Greek) defines the post-1922 phase as marking the beginning of Greek industrial policy. For a discussion of late-late industrialization see N. Mouzelis, *Politics in the Semi-Periphery: Early Parliamentarism and Late Industrialisation in the Balkans and Latin America*, London: Macmillan, 1986.
14. Cf. A. Gerschenkron, *Economic Backwardness in Historical Perspective*, Cambridge, Mass.: Harvard University Press, 1966, pp. 7ff, *passim*.
15. D.J. Halikias, *Money and Credit in a Developing Economy: The Greek Case*, New York: New York University Press, 1978, pp. 245–6.
16. See S. Kostopoulos, *The Policy of Bank Merger*, Athens: Alfa, 1953, pp. 37ff (in Greek).
17. See M. Xanthakis, 'Investment banks: European and Greek experience', in T. Giannitsis (ed.) *Market Liberalisation and Transformations in the Greek Banking System*, Athens: ETBA-Papazissis, 1995, pp. 177ff (in Greek). On the 1960s perception of the role of investment banks and the importance of separating commercial from investment banking operations, see Bank of Greece, *Investment Banks – Placement Companies: Role and Importance in the Capital Market*, Athens: Bank of Greece, 1965, pp. 17–50 (in Greek).
18. The difference, however, with the German system was that it developed without state guidance and was not restricted, cf. A. Lukauskas, 'The political economy of financial restriction: the case of Spain', *Comparative Politics*, 27 (4), 1994, p. 69.
19. H.S. Ellis, *Industrial Capital in Greek Development*, Athens: Center of Planning and Economic Research, 1965, p. 93.
20. These nationalizations spurred a long legal controversy; on its constitutional aspects see A. Manesis, A. Manitakis and G. Papadimitriou, *The 'Andreadis Affair' and the Economic Constitution*, Athens: Sakkoulas, 1991 (in Greek).
21. L. Katseli, 'Economic integration in the enlarged European Community: structural adjustment of the Greek economy', in C. Bliss and J. Braga de Macedo (eds) *Unity with Diversity in the European Community: The Community's Southern Frontier*, Cambridge: Cambridge University Press, 1990.
22. On the economic rationale and policies of PASOK's 1981–85 first government period see G. Arsenis, *Political Statement*, Athens: Odysseas, 1987 (in Greek); E. Tsakalotos, *Alternative Economic Strategies: The Case of Greece*, Aldershot: Avebury, 1991.
23. Halikias, op. cit., p. 45.
24. But also due to weak creditor-SCB organization for serious project appraisal and supervision, Tsakalotos, op. cit., p. 233.
25. See Y. Caloghirou, 'Problematic structures in Greek industry', in T. Giannitsis (ed.) *Industrial and Technological Policy in Greece*, Athens: Themelio, 1993 (in Greek).
26. Many of the previous owners for years had been contesting their loss of equity control through judicial means, and the pending court decisions

added legal uncertainty which seriously obstructed later efforts (in the 1990s) to privatize the IRO firms.

27. *Karatzas Report on the Change and Modernization of the Banking System, Athens*, 1987, p. 35 (in Greek). See also G. Provopoulos, *Public Sector in the Greek Economy: Recent Trends and Financial Effects*, Athens, 1985, pp. 100ff (in Greek).
28. By 1989 IRO firms presented some 1.040 billion drachmas of accumulated debts, I. Tragakis, ND, Parliament Minutes, 3.12.91: 1895. In 1989 and 1990 alone, IRO absorbed bank loans amounting to 108billion and 139 billion drachmas respectively, European Commission, *Country Studies: Greece*, Brussels: Commission of the European Communities, 1992, p. 17. Of all SCBs, the NBG suffered the heaviest blow. After the IRO's creation the NBG was forced to convert into shares a total of 132 billion drachmas of claims against major IRO firms. As IRO firms continued making losses, the NBG was forced to commit additional funds, which by the end of 1989 represented about 30 per cent of the debt converted into shares, NBG, *Annual Report for 1989*, Athens: NBG, 1990, p. 48. Parallel was the case of other SCBs.
29. P. Alexakis and P. Petrakis, *Commercial and Development Banks*, Athens: Papazissis 1988, pp. 143ff (in Greek); J. Kostopoulos, 'Greek banking competitiveness compared to that of banking systems of EC member states', in Charissopoulos Committee, *Summaries of Papers*, Athens, 1981, pp. 91ff (in Greek); D. Psilos, *Capital Market in Greece*, Athens: Center of Economic Research, 1964, pp. 185ff; T. Galanis, *Banking Studies*, Athens: Papazissis, 1946, pp. 7, 12ff (in Greek).
30. Psilos, op. cit., p. 194.
31. Most notable among which were the 1848 halt of foreign credit due to the political upheaval in Europe, the 1893 bankruptcy of the Greek state, the 1929–32 financial crisis, the war and the immediate postwar hyperinflation period.
32. Gortsos, op. cit.
33. Such figures are very high for European standards, where normally the largest commercial banks, usually three or four, do not control more than 30–40 per cent of loans, Alexakis and Petrakis, op. cit., p. 144; D. Neven, 'Structural adjustment in European retail banking: some views from industrial organization', in J. Dermine (ed.) *European Banking in the 1990s*, Oxford: Blackwell, 1993, pp. 181ff.
34. G. Provopoulos, 'The Greek financial system: trends and perspectives', in G. Provopoulos (ed.) *The Greek Financial System*, Athens: IOBE, 1995, p. 17 (in Greek).
35. The largest, NBG, in 1990 ranked 138th among European banks in terms of total capitals, *The Banker*, October 1990; *Epilogi*, December 1991.
36. Halikias, op. cit., pp. 15–16; T. Giannitsis, *Foreign Banks in Greece: The Postwar Experience*, Athens: Gutenberg, 1982, pp. 178 (in Greek).
37. Giannitsis, *Foreign Banks in Greece*, op. cit., p. 178.
38. Halikias, op. cit., p. 15.
39. Figures rounded, end of 1991, C. Gortsos, op. cit.
40. Giannitsis, *Foreign Banks in Greece*, op. cit., pp. 175–9, D. Krontiras, 'Conflict of modernization and protection', *Hellenic Bank Association Bulletin*, March 1995, p. 30 (in Greek).

41. ICAP research data for 1993, published by *Kathimerini* 4 September 1994; P. Alexakis, 'Basic developments in the structure, operation and institutional framework of the Greek banking system', in T. Giannitsis (ed.) *Market Liberalisation and Transformations in the Greek Banking System*, Athens: Papazissis, 1995, p. 41 (in Greek); *Financial Times*, 27 February 1990.
42. OECD, *Economic Surveys: Greece 1995*, Paris: OECD, 1995, p. 41; L. Tsoukalis, *The New European Economy*, Oxford: Oxford University Press, 1993, pp. 121–2; J. Bisignano, 'Banking in the EEC: structure, competition and public policy', in G. Kaufman (ed.) *Bank Structure in Major Countries*, New York: Kluwer, 1990.
43. See G. Pagoulatos, 'Liberalizing Southern Europe: financial systems and their Europeanization', in K. Lavdas (ed.) *Junctures of Stateness: Politics and Policy Change in Southern Europe*, Aldershot: Ashgate (forthcoming).
44. J. Hicks, *The Crisis in Keynesian Economics*, Oxford: Blackwell, 1974, p. 51; C. de Boissieu, 'The "Overdraft Economy", the "Auto-Economy" and the rate of interest', in A. Barrère (ed.) *Money, Credit and Prices in Keynesian Perspective*, London: Macmillan, 1989.
45. J. Zysman, *Governments, Markets and Growth*, New York: Cornell University Press, 1983, pp. 16–18.
46. BoG, *Report of the Governor for the Year 1976*, Athens: Bank of Greece, 1977, p. 17; G. Kalamotousakis, 'Monetary and special credit restrictions of the Greek banking system. Interest rate and investment policy in Greece and the EEC member states. Currency Committee', in Charissopoulos Committee, *Summaries of Papers*, Athens, 1981, pp. 135ff; OECD, *Economic Surveys: Greece 1995*, op. cit., pp. 39ff.
47. Karatzas Report, op. cit., pp. 21, 61ff; Alexakis and Petrakis, op. cit., p. 144.
48. Alexakis, op. cit., pp. 24–5.
49. OECD, *Economic Surveys: Greece 1995*, op. cit., p. 55.
50. Ibid, p. 61.
51. H. Gibson and E. Tsakalotos, 'Economic theory and the limits to financial liberalization: domestic financial liberalization in Greece, Portugal and Spain', in H. Gibson and E. Tsakalotos (eds) *Economic Integration and Financial Liberalization: Prospects for Southern Europe*, London: St Antony's/ Macmillan, 1992.
52. European Banking Federation (FBE) *Annual Report 1987*, FBE, 1987.
53. European Banking Federation (FBE), *Annual Report 1993*, FBE, 1993.
54. M. de Cecco, 'The Italian banking system at a historic turning-point', *Review of Economic Conditions in Italy*, 1, January–June 1994; Neven, op. cit., p. 181; E. Gardener, 'Banking strategies and 1992', in A. Mullineux (ed.) *European Banking*, Oxford: Blackwell, 1992, p. 109.
55. Pagoulatos, 'Institutions and Public Policy Making', op. cit., pp. 113ff; A. Borges, 'Portuguese banking in the Single European Market', in J. Dermine (ed.) *European Banking in the 1990s*, Oxford: Blackwell, 1993, p. 340.
56. G. Pagoulatos, 'Governing in a constrained environment: policy-making in the Greek banking deregulation and privatisation reform', *West European Politics*, 19 (4), 1996, pp. 744–69; G. Pagoulatos and V. Wright, 'The politics of industrial privatization: Spain, Portugal and Greece in a

European perspective', in H. Gibson (ed.) *Economic Change in Southern Europe*, Baltimore, Md.: Johns Hopkins University Press (forthcoming).

57. Much higher than in other EC countries.
58. In its high degree of specialization and compartmentalization the Greek banking system resembled closely the French postwar banking system, C. de Boissieu, 'The French banking sector in the light of European financial integration', in J. Dermine (ed.) *European Banking in the 1990s*, Oxford: Blackwell, 1993, pp. 198ff.
59. Credit rationing was applied in the 1950s, 1960s and part of the 1970s in a wide range of developed and developing countries. Credit policy typically included instruments such as special reserve requirements, differential discount rates, eligibility requirements, central bank directives and instructions to the banks, interest rate ceilings, regulation and controls over real estate and consumer credit, along with other 'orthodox' monetary policy instruments such as bank rate policy and open market operations. In the Greek case, however, controls were more severe and particularistic than in most other countries see Halikias, op. cit., p. 209; A. Courakis, 'On the rationale and implications of constraints on the choices of deposit-taking financial intermediaries (with particular reference to seven European countries)', in D. Fair and L. de Juvigny (eds) *Government Policies and the Workings of Financial Systems in Industrialized Countries*, Dordrecht: Martinus Nijhoff, 1984; J.S.G. Wilson, *Banking Policy and Structure: A Comparative Analysis*, London: Croom Helm, 1986, pp. 398ff. See for various European countries, Institut d'Etudes Bancaires et Financières, *Institutions et Mécanismes Bancaires dans les Pays de la Communauté Economique Européenne*, Paris: Dunod, 1969; Institut d'Etudes Bancaires et Financières, *Systèmes Bancaires d'Europe Occidentale (hors C.E.E.)*, Paris: Dunod, 1970. For developing countries see C.K. Johri, *Monetary Policy in a Developing Economy*, Calcutta: World Press, 1965, pp. 59ff; J. Márquez, 'Financial institutions and economic development', in H.S. Ellis and H.C. Wallich (eds) *Economic Development for Latin America*, London: Macmillan, 1961, pp. 184ff. In France alone various government programmes introduced over the years had led by the 1980s to some 70 specialized interest rate regimes covering 44 per cent of national economy, W.D. Coleman, 'Reforming corporatism: the French banking policy community, 1941–90', *West European Politics*, 16 (2), 1993, p. 131. With regard to the utilization of the banking system to guide industrial development, notable were the similarities with postwar Spain, J-M. Maravall and J. Santamaria, 'Political change in Spain and the prospects for democracy', in G. O'Donnell, P. Schmitter and L. Whitehead (eds) *Transitions from Authoritarian Rule: Southern Europe*, Baltimore, Md.: Johns Hopkins University Press, 1986, pp. 75–6.
60. The aversion of bankers to long-term credit is well known. In Britain, for example, it was not until the mid-1970s that 'bankers shed their dislike of long-term loans and of being entangled in the affairs of their industrial customers', M. Moran, *The Politics of Banking. The Strange Case of Competition and Credit Control*, London: Macmillan, 1984, p. 12.
61. Analysis in these last three paragraphs draws on Halikias, op. cit., pp. 205–51; Kalamotousakis, op. cit., pp. 138–9; BoG, *Report of the*

Governor for the Year 1984, Athens: BoG, 1985, pp. 22–3; Karatzas Report, op. cit., p. 23; European Commission, op. cit., p. 31–2; OECD, *Economic Surveys: Greece 1995*, op. cit., p. 44ff.

62. The rationale behind these policies reached its apogee in the early 1960s, intensified by the discouraging observation of an upward trend of excess savings over investment between 1955 and 1961, H. Ellis, op. cit., p. 40. See for an authoritative defence, X. Zolotas, *The Role of the Banks in a Developing Country*, Athens: Bank of Greece, 1962; J. Pesmazoglu, *The Relation Between Monetary and Fiscal Policy*, Athens: Bank of Greece, 1965, esp. pp. 28ff, 53ff. Also H. Ellis, op. cit., esp. pp. 39–41, 313ff. The Greek mainstream approach to the role of banks in supporting development, led by the BoG sages, probably constituted a slightly stronger version of the conventional economic wisdom of its time which recognized the need of government borrowing for development but advocated that while commercial banks had an important role to play in economic development they should not finance it past a certain limit, N.S. Buchanan and H.S. Ellis, *Approaches to Economic Development*, New York: The Twentieth Century Fund, 1955, pp. 323–42.
63. See G. Kalamotousakis, op. cit., p. 138; Karatzas Report, op. cit., p. 21; I. Papadakis, 'Credit reform and fiscal rehabilitation', in G. Provopoulos (ed.) *The Greek Financial System*, Athens: IOBE, 1995, p. 38. Cf. BoG, *Report of the Governor for the Year 1976*, Athens: BoG, 1977, pp. 17–18, 22–4.
64. BoG, *Report of the Governor for theYear 1979*, Athens: BoG, 1980, pp. 19–20.
65. Provopoulos, *Public Sector*, op. cit., pp. 92–3. This was also due to the post-1973 anti-inflationary policy of suppressing investment programmes.
66. Centre of Planning and Economic Research (KEPE), *Reports for the 1988–1992 programme: Financial and Credit System*, Athens: KEPE, 1991, pp. 17–18.
67. OECD, *Economic Surveys: Greece 1989/90*, Paris: OECD, 1990, p. 39.
68. Ibid., pp. 41–2.
69. Kalamotousakis, op. cit., pp. 136; BoG, *Report of the Governor for the Year 1986*, Athens: BoG, 1987, pp. 35–9; Karatzas Report, op. cit., pp. 21ff; Centre of Planning and Economic Research, op. cit., pp. 22–3; European Commission, op. cit., 1992, pp. 31–3; Alexakis, op. cit., p. 50.
70. This approach echoes the economic theory of regulation, stipulating that politicians have an incentive to establish regulatory policies that redistribute rents toward groups offering them crucial political support, G. Stigler, 'The theory of economic regulation', *Bell Journal of Economics and Management Science*, 2 (1), 1971, pp. 3–21; S. Peltzman, 'Toward a more general theory of regulation', *Journal of Law and Economics*, 19 (2), 1976, pp. 211–40.
71. Cf. Spain under Franco, where 'directed credit programs quickly became the principal means of distributing private benefits to favored groups', Lukauskas, op. cit., p. 80.
72. Journalistic sources. Cf. Y. Zografos, 'Dr15bn for electoral advertising', *Economicos Tahydromos*, 21.10.1993 (in Greek); Y. Zografos, 'Party finances: persistence on intransparency', *Economicos Tahydromos*, 2.6.1994 (in Greek); N. Nikolaou, 'The parties and the contractors', *To*

Vima, 7.2.1993 (in Greek). See also A. Loverdos (ed.) 'The financing of political parties', special issue, *Parliamentary Review*, 15–16, 1993 (in Greek); E. Katsoulis, 'Problems of finance to political parties', *Epicentra*, 80, 1994 (in Greek).

73. Yannis Boutos, interview in *Eleftherotypia*, 7.5.1995 (in Greek).
74. The so-called 'Koskotas scandal', which precipitated PASOK's decline and loss of power, resulted in long-term imprisonment for Koskotas and his closest collaborators, and limited sentences to a few government officials.
75. See, for example, frequent references to the Bank of Crete scandal by many opposition MPs in the discussion of banking law 2076/92 in the Parliamentary Committee and Assembly (July 1992).
76. Development law 1892/90 of July 1990, introduced by Economy Minister George Souflias.
77. A. Kefalas, 'Reforms and state banks', *Economicos Tahydromos*, 22.6.1995.
78. See OECD, *Economic Surveys: Greece 1995*, op. cit., pp. 41–2.
79. Inefficient productivity structures of the Greek banking sector were reflected in the ratio of assets and deposits to employees, the lowest on an EC level, Banking Federation of the EU, *Annual Report*, FBE, 1993; J.Kostopoulos, op. cit., pp. 95ff.
80. OECD, *Economic Surveys: Greece*, op. cit., 1995, pp. 41–2.
81. Centre of Planning and Economic Research, op. cit., p. 26.
82. P. Poulis, 'Banking system modernization and modern management information systems', *Hellenic Bank Association Bulletin*, November 1994, p. 11 (in Greek).
83. Bisignano, op. cit.
84. Economic Research Europe, 'A study of the effectiveness and impact of Internal Market Integration on the banking and credit sector', unpublished report (in collaboration with Public and Corporate Economic Consultants & The Institute of European Finance), 1996, p. 37.
85. J. Braga de Macedo, 'Comment', in J. Dermine (ed.) *European Banking in the 1990s*, Oxford: Blackwell, 1993, p. 346.
86. Tsoukalis, op. cit., pp. 119ff.
87. This particular section draws heavily on Halikias, op. cit.
88. See, for example, X. Zolotas, *Monetary Stability and Economic Development*, Athens: Bank of Greece, 1958 (in Greek), X. Zolotas, *Monetary Equilibrium and Economic Development*, Athens: Bank of Greece, 1964, pp. 9–11 and *passim* (in Greek).
89. Between 1946 and 1951 the Currency Committee also included as members one representative of the British and one of the US government.
90. Halikias, op. cit., pp. 32ff.
91. Ibid., pp. 35–8.
92. Ibid., p. 37.
93. Ibid., pp. 46–7.
94. Ibid., pp. 57–8; see also G. Soldatos, 'The postwar Greek economy: politics and economics', *Suedosteuropa*, 40 (5), 1991, pp. 232ff; G. Jouganatos, *The Development of the Greek Economy, 1950–1991*, Westport Conn., Greenwood, 1992, pp. 61ff.
95. This political manipulation of credit is strikingly similar to that observed in the case of the Franco regime in Spain, see Lukauskas, op. cit.

96. Halikias, op. cit., pp. 63–5.
97. Ibid., p. 70.
98. BoG, *Governor Reports for 1974 and 1975.*
99. BoG, *Governor Report for 1976*, pp. 16–17 and *1977*, pp. 22ff.
100. BoG, *Governor Report for 1976*, pp. 21–2.
101. BoG, *Governor Report for 1978*, pp. 25ff.
102. BoG, *Governor Report for 1979*, p. 22.
103. Ibid., pp. 21–2.
104. To be enacted from 1 January 1981, when Greece became the tenth member of the EEC.
105. Articles 50–55 of the Accession Treaty of Greece to the European Communities; BoG, *Governor Report for 1979*, pp. 137–43.
106. Kalamotousakis, op. cit., pp. 140–45.
107. BoG, *Governor Report for 1980*, p. 27.
108. Ibid., pp. 80ff.
109. BoG, *Governor Report for 1981*, pp. 24ff.
110. Ibid., p. 27.
111. BoG, *Governor Report for 1982*, pp. 24–6.
112. BoG, *Governor Report for 1983*, pp. 25–6.
113. BoG, *Governor Report for 1981*, pp. 78ff; BoG, *Governor Report for 1982*, pp. 86–7.
114. BoG, *Governor Report for 1983*, pp. 23–5, 81–3.
115. Ibid., pp. 29–30.
116. BoG, *Governor Report for 1984*, pp. 96ff; BoG, *Governor Report for 1985.*
117. BoG, *Governor Report for 1986*, pp. 36–7.
118. BoG, *Governor Report for 1989*, p. 39.
119. *Financial Times*, 27.2.1990.
120. OECD, *Economic Surveys: Greece 1990/91*, Paris: OECD, 1991, pp. 32ff.
121. BoG, *Governor Report for 1990*, pp. 53–4.
122. Article 104A.
123. Cf. K. Grier, 'On the existence of a political monetary cycle', *American Journal of Political Science*, 33 (2), 1989, pp. 376–89.

CHAPTER SEVEN

The History of Nova Ljubljanska Banka (NLB) in the Framework of Slovene Experience with West-European Capital

Franjo Štiblar

Introduction

The geographic position of Slovenia is on the border of Western Europe. The country became fully independent in 1991. For the whole nineteenth century and until 1918 it was a province of the Austro-Hungarian Empire. These geographic and institutional facts make the study of the Slovene national experience with West-European capital somewhat complicated.

At one stage in recent history, during the 1980s, the Ljubljanska banka group included almost the entire banking sector in Slovenia (over 85 per cent of it, to be precise). On these grounds Ljubljanska banka history seems to cover all Slovenia's banking experience.

The subjects of West-European capital and the Slovene banking sector (represented by the Ljubljanska banka) cover in this paper both capital connections (investments) in the country and in affiliates outside the geographic area of Slovenia (in Western Europe), and also business relations (correspondent and other higher levels of cooperation with West-European banks). Non-European banking capital did not enter Slovenia in any form of direct foreign investment. Slovenia established only one bank subsidiary outside Europe (in the USA). Business relations, including Ljubljanska banka representative offices, have been important for the last decade or two. From Eastern Europe only two banks from Belgrade established their branches in Slovenia in the last period of the former Yugoslavia. With Slovene independence they ceased to exist.

The first problem of our study is to identify historical predecessors of the present NLB. In banking circles in Slovenia the Mestna hranilnica ljubljanska (MHL), established as city saving house in 1889, is treated as the first predecessor of the NLB, but it was not an incorporated bank, and was formally integrated into the Ljubljanska banka only in 1976 as one of its branches. The Komunalna banka Ljubljana (KBL), established in 1955, is considered to be a second forerunner of the NLB, although this bank does not have clear traces to the period before the Second World War. To a certain extent, it could be assumed that the first Slovene bank, the Ljubljanska kreditna banka (LKB), incorporated in 1900, represents also one of the roots of the present NLB. This bank existed until the Second World War, but not much specific information on its performance is available at present. And, if it is seriously taken into account that at some stage in history around 1980 the Ljubljanska banka (LB) group included in a special way almost all banks in Slovenia (as 'sisters' to the parent bank Ljubljanska banka), then other Slovene banks, incorporated and established in the early twentieth century, could also be considered as predecessors of the NLB.

Another problem arises from the fact that the Slovene financial system (to which the NLB, MHL and LKB belong) was built in some way parallel to foreign (German) banking systems to become a basis for the economy of Slovenes and to guard against Germans 'occupying' the territory of Slovenia. For that reason there was almost no West-European capital in these Slovene banks and thus also in the NLB and its predecessors. Thus, up until very recent times, discussing simultaneously the history of the NLB and the role of West-European capital represents in a way antagonism by definition. All these are limitations under which this paper was written and which were less well known to the author before the research for this paper started.

The goal of the paper is to describe:

- the history of the Nova Ljubljanska banka (which will include capital connections in Western Europe as only the NLB among all Slovene banks developed a foreign affiliations network from the late 1970s on); and
- the history of the presence of West-European capital in the banking sector of Slovenia both in the form of capital investments and business relations.

The outline of the paper is as follows:

1. The general historical development of the territory of present-day Slovenia is summarized (including institutional arrangements and banking sector arrangements).
2. The history of the NLB is given in detail.
3. The historic development of the role of West-European capital in Slovenia's banking sector is described.

General historical framework

Slovenia was a province in the Austrian part of the Austro-Hungarian Empire during the entire nineteenth century and until 1918, and thus was part of Western Europe. During that period western capital was in fact 'home country' German capital in banking, which dominated Slovenia. It was separated from financial institutions established among Slovenes.

After the First World War Slovenia entered as a constitutive part the newly established Kingdom of Serbs, Croats and Slovenes, which was renamed Yugoslavia at the beginning of the 1930s. During the interwar period German capital in banking became foreign western capital and as such less welcome in the newly formed country. Of all other West-European countries, only Italian capital was present in insignificant size.

During the Second World War Slovenia was occupied by Germans in the north, Italians in the south and in a small north-east region by Hungarians. All foreign forces tried to establish their own banks in Slovenia. Germans (through Austrian banks) were more efficient in that, Italians and Hungarians less so. Germans suspended temporarily all financial institutions and later put them under direct German command. They also opened affiliates of the Vienna banks. Italians prohibited all domestic banks from international business and controlled their other business. Hungarians allowed banks on occupied Slovene territory to continue to operate, but they were required to enter the Hungarian banking association.

On the other hand, the domestic resistance movement started to organize its own simple financial system towards the end of the war. National tax and freedom loans were intended to finance partisans. In 1944 the Slovene monetary institution Denarni zavod Slovenije (a privileged business bank and central monetary authority in the same entity) was established, but it was abolished with the end of the war in 1945 by the central monetary authority of the newly established socialist republic of Yugoslavia, situated in Belgrade.

After the Second World War several types of banks (private, state, local and self-managed) were allowed to operate until 1946, when they were all abolished. A two-tier banking system thus ceased to exist for several years. The National Bank of Yugoslavia (with a large number of offices around the country) became not only the central emission institution, but also the only business bank for the enterprise sector and the population as a whole. After several reform attempts, in 1955 local banks (*komunalne banke*) were established and saving houses were allowed to operate again.

The first economic reform in the former-Yugoslavia in 1961 strengthened the role of banks as independent financial institutions. Besides the central bank there were special federal investment, foreign trade and agriculture banks and several communal banks, which also acquired former saving houses (*hranilnice*). The economic reform of 1965 increased the role of banks further. They acquired former state investment funds. Special federal banks were abolished and business banks were allowed to start up international business on their own, and for five years operated predominantly on a profit motive. But economic reform became dangerous to the monopolistic communist regime. At the beginning of the 1970s market reform was replaced by the special Yugoslav invention of the system of associated labour in economic and social life in general. Banks became officially services of enterprises ('associated labour'). In this way enterprises, the major debtors of banks, became at the same time the banks' owners, leading to incestuous relationships with catastrophic economic results for banks and the economy as a whole.

In June 1991 Slovenia proclaimed independence. For the first time in history the small nation of two million people formed its own nation state. Banking legislation was among the first adopted at the proclamation of independence. It allows entrance of foreign capital although on a somewhat limited basis. As a result, at the beginning of 1997 12 out of 29 banks operating in Slovenia have a foreign ownership stake (four are majority or entirely owned by foreigners) and foreigners have approximately 10 per cent share in total banking sector capital. The owners come mainly from Austria, the rest from Italy, the UK, Switzerland, France, the USA and the European Bank for Reconstruction and Development (EBRD). There are also six representative offices of foreign banks in Slovenia: two Italian, two Austrian, one Hungarian and one EBRD. Banks with at least some foreign ownership control 20 per cent of banking assets and over 10 per cent of capital.

At the same time, the Slovene banking sector has major stakes in five banks in Western Europe and the USA, as well as nine representative offices (at the peak, in 1991, there were 22).

The newly proposed Slovene banking law relaxes further the possibility of entrance of foreign capital into the banking sector, thus indicating Slovenia's adaptation to EU legislation following the country's signing of an Association Agreement with the EU in June 1996.

The history of Slovene banking and Nova Ljubljanska banka (NLB)

Slovenia was controlled by German, Hungarian, Italian and Czech enterprises and financial institutions in the nineteenth century. With the growth of domestic small industry and market-oriented agriculture, internal and external trade became increasingly important, and with it credit.

The strongest among the first financial institutions in Slovenia was the Kranjska Hranilnica (established in 1920 as second to Vienna in Europe), controlled by German wholesalers. Another bank was the German Ljubljanska obrtna banka (1867). Many foreign banks also established affiliates in Slovenia, among them Štajerska eskomptna banka from Graz (1872), Splošna banka za industrijo, trgovino in obrt (1869) from Vienna and Banka Slavija from Prague. Besides banks and their affiliates, German saving houses were established between 1830 and 1880 in Maribor, Radgona, Ptuj, Celje, Slovenska Bistrica, Brežice, Ljutomer, Rogatec, Ormož, and so on.

Alongside the foreign financial institutions, Slovenes wanted to establish their own financial institutions as important economic foundations for national identity and resurrection. From 1870 onwards several attempts to establish a Slovene incorporated bank failed. Finally, in 1900, the first Ljubljanska kreditna banka (LKB) was established under the initiative of city mayor Hribar and with the strong support of the Živnostenska banka Prague (established in 1872). Later, the Jadranska banka was established as the second Slovene bank in Trst in 1905, but it disintegrated during the First World War.

After early attempts to establish Slovene banks failed, regulated saving houses and credit cooperatives started to emerge. The first were established in Slovenj Gradec, Lenart and Kozje between 1869 and 1874. They spread rapidly, thus covering all the territory of Slovenia by the turn of the century. In cities, city saving houses (non-incorporated) were established in Maribor (1862), Celje (1865) and in Ljubljana (1889). Among city saving houses the Mestna hranilnica ljubljanska (MHL) was the largest, forming a counterweight to German financial institutions in Ljubljana.

The legal foundation for saving houses was the Emperor's 'Sparkasseregulativ' of 1844, according to which these institutions should not follow primarily the profit goal favoured by owners (as capitalistic enterprises), but should be used for public benefit. The MHL was state- and city-owned. In 1938 a new state decree regulated these institutions anew.

In the interwar period saving houses were associated in the Yugoslav Saving Houses Association, which had an important role in education and the protection of depositors-savers.

After the First World War the nostrification process affected foreign banking capital, but the domestic banking sector experienced its 'Grün Zeit'. The number of banks in the capital city Ljubljana increased from three to nine with 31 affiliates and, in addition, six other banks had their affiliates in Ljubljana. After the stock exchange was established in 1924 Ljubljana began its development as the financial centre for the economy of Slovenia.

Towards the end of the 1920s, crisis affected the banking sector too. There were three major Slovene banks at the time: Ljubljanska kreditna banka, Zadružna gospodarska banka and Kreditni zavod za trgovino in industrijo. The Slovene banking sector counted for only 9.2 per cent in banking assets and 7 per cent in credits in the total banking sector of the Kingdom at the beginning of 1930. The Slovene share in self-managed saving houses and loan cooperatives was larger. (The Hipotekarna banka was established in 1922 for these purposes.)

The Mestna hranilnica ljubljanska (MHL)

Political foundation for the MHL was given by the 1882 elected Slovene majority in the city council of Ljubljana. But regional government (with German dominance) delayed its establishment for six years. In 1889 it was finally established. In the period 1890–1914 MHL business grew very quickly. During the First World War the MHL more or less vegetated at a low scale of operations. Deposits grew quickly, but mortgage loans were no longer disbursed.

After the First World War the business activity of the MHL started in an unsettled environment. It directed efforts towards population needs related to postwar reconstruction. During the period of worldwide economic crisis at the end of the 1920s the MHL acted with restrictive measures regarding withdrawals of larger amounts of money. Only in 1936 did the situation start to improve again with gradual relaxation of restrictions on withdrawals and increased public deposit activity. The MHL was not much influenced by the approach of the Second World War and was doing business as usual until 1940. During the Second World War the MHL continued to operate as much as circumstances allowed. The volume of savings decreased significantly due to obligatory exchange of former domestic dinars with foreign currency.

After the Second World War the MHL retained its name until 1947, was renamed Komunalna banka Ljubljana in 1948, which lost independent status in 1952 when it became a unit of the National Bank of Yugoslavia. In 1952 the MHL was renewed as an independent financial institution, and expanded banking activities under its name. In 1955 it was again restricted to saving house activities only and as such expanded these activities in the next six years. In 1962 the MHL became a special affiliation (branch) of the Komunalna banka Ljubljana and thus ceased to exist as an independent entity.

The Komunalna banka Ljubljana (KBL)

The KBL was established under the new 1954 legislation at the beginning of 1955. In the period 1955–60 the bank expanded its business quickly (Report: Komunalna banka Ljubljana, 1955–60). It established a number of branch offices around Slovenia, entered into new business (investment banking in relation to housing projects), more than doubled its credit portfolio, increased volume of savings tenfold, introduced modern bank processing machinery and expanded its number of employees from 79 to 715 and improved their qualification skills.

During 1961–65 the KBL acquired several municipal banks, including the above mentioned MHL, secured a licence to operate as a commercial bank and changed its name to Kreditna banka in hranilnica Ljubljana (KBHL).

The first contacts with West-European capital came in 1967, when the KBHL secured authorization to commence international banking operations. Furthermore, in 1968 the KBHL opened its first international representative office in Munich and established correspondent banking relationship with 30 international banks.

In 1970 the KBHL was renamed Ljubljanska banka (LB), the name it carried for the next 24 years. It ranked 181st in the *London Banker* Top 300 commercial banks. In 1978, under new legislation, the LB group was formed consisting of the LB-Associated Bank, and 22 basic banks including former branches and two previously independent banks (Kreditna banka Koper and Kreditna banka Maribor).

In 1986 the LB-Associated Bank established its wholly owned subsidiary LBS-Bank New York, the first bank from Eastern Europe to secure a US licence. Also the LB participated with controlled shares in the Bank Adria, Vienna, the LHB Bank Frankfurt, Proteus Finance Zurich and established a branch in Milan. At the end of the 1980s the LB dealt with 22 representative offices around the world.

In 1990, according to new – and final – legislation of the former Yugoslavia, all banks within the LB group became joint-stock companies. They included the parent bank LBdd, five subsidiaries and 14 member banks. At the beginning of 1991 the largest member bank, the LB-Gospodarska banka, merged with the LBdd thus forming a universal bank which had a significant majority share in the banking sector of Slovenia.

After the proclamation of independence of Slovenia in June 1991 new banking legislation pushed member banks to operate on their own legally, while certain business and ownership relationships were still maintained. In June 1992 the LBdd was put under pre-rehabilitation status (due to losses incurred with the freezing of foreign exchange deposits in the National Bank in Belgrade, losses in other markets of the former Yugoslavia and the weakening position of Slovene enterprises as clients due to transition and economic depression), which was reinforced in full rehabilitation status in January 1993 under new top management and under the auspices of the Central Bank of Slovenia and Agency for Bank Rehabilitation. Larger shares of bad assets were swapped for state bonds and the state replaced the former owners/enterprises as owner of the bank.

The new Constitutional Law adopted in July 1994 established the Nova Ljubljanska banka (New Ljubljanska Bank) (NLB), to which all assets and liabilities were transferred except those related to countries of the former Yugoslavia, which remained in the LB and thus became subject to inheritance negotiations. The NLB established its own subsidiaries in factoring, real-estate business, trading, consulting, and investment funds. The NLB started to widen its domestic network by acquiring smaller banks (E-Banka Maribor in 1995, Banka Krško in 1996) or opening new offices all around Slovenia. At the end of 1996 the rehabilitation process was completed, which is indicated by the positive financial results (cash flow, profit, solvency) and the organizational strengthening of the bank as well as progress with its human resource development. During rehabilitation the NLB decreased its labour force by 30 per cent, much more than its volume of assets was decreased.

Today, the bank fulfils all BIS standards and waits for legal termination of rehabilitation and start of privatization. At the end of 1996 NLB assets were close to US$4 billion, its capital over US$200 million and yearly after tax profits in 1996 were estimated to be in excess of US$50 million. Thus, its CAR is estimated to be around 12 per cent (well above the required minimum 8 per cent), its ROE is above 25 per cent and its ROA around 1.25.

Slovene national experience with West-European capital

History

In the nineteenth century and up to the First World War Slovenia was one of the least developed provinces of the Austrian part of the

Austro-Hungarian Empire. The economy in the region was controlled by German capital and so were financial institutions. The domestic Slovene population was more concentrated in agriculture and craftsmanship. After the 'Spring of Nations' in 1848, national awareness and the quest for larger Slovene autonomy emerged. It was recognized early that economic foundation is necessary for such a quest and that included the establishment of Slovene financial institutions. Thus from the second half of the nineteenth century the Slovene economy (and financial sector) was developed on parallel lines to that on the German territory of present-day Slovenia. It was a kind of dual economy, although regular business relations took place between the two. But during that period West-European capital (Austrian) was controlling the province which, in fact, was part of Western Europe.[1]

In Slovenia, as a backyard province of the Empire, only saving houses represented the financial sector at the beginning. Austrian banks did not bother to establish their independent units or branches in Slovenia until 1900 when the first incorporated Slovene bank, the KBL (followed later by the Jadranska banka in Trst in 1905), forced foreign competitors' capital to enter more seriously.[2] The Austrian Creditanstalt (CA) and the Allgemeine Verkehrsbank (AV) opened their branches in Ljubljana. The First World War caused the collapse of the Jadranska banka and the big problems of the Vienna banks were also felt in Slovenia. However, due to the closeness of the battlefield (the need for transfer of financial resources) and the stronger survival ability of small-size industry with agriculture, Slovene banks were less affected by the war than were Austrian banks.

After the First World War Slovenia became a constitutive part of the Kingdom of Serbs, Croats and Slovenes. Germans and West Europeans became foreigners to Slovenia. The nostrification process immediately after the war aimed to clean the country of foreign (West-European) capital. Thus the branch of the AV bank was taken over by the Prva Hrvaška Štedionica from Zagreb, while the branch of the CA bank was transformed into the Kreditni zavod with domestic majority share. In the mid-1920s, however, Austrian and Italian capital returned and started to control the Slovene economy and especially the banking sector. World economic crisis caused problems for foreign banks, which left Slovene financial institutions on their own. They vegetated for a while.

The Second World War brought occupying forces and with them their capital to Slovenia. Slovene financial institutions were put under direct command of Germans, Italians and Hungarians in the regions of Slovenia they occupied. In addition, they entered with branches of their own banks from Vienna (which represented in fact Berlin), Milan and Trst, at first more and later less successfully.

After the Second World War the enterprise and financial sectors were nationalized under the socialist regime of the Republic of Yugoslavia. The state ownership of means of production was formed first, later transformed into 'social ownership', one of the *sui generis* inventions of the Yugoslav 'communism with a human face'. For more than 20 years the only form of foreign capital to enter the country was some help from the Marshall Plan, after Yugoslavia severed ties with the Soviet bloc (Informbiro).

In 1965 the right to international operations was delegated to commercial banks (among the first to use it was the Ljubljanska banka) and that meant contacts with foreign capital again. During that period of economic reform enterprises obtained the legal possibility of contractual joint ventures with foreign firms. Foreign capital investments in Slovenia were not allowed until the late 1980s. In 1968 the first representative office of the LB was opened abroad and from then on the international network of the LB (as the only Slovene bank with international offices) expanded relatively quickly. Apparently, in Slovenia outward direct investments preceded inward-oriented ones due to legal obstacles at home.

The present situation

Foreign capital was allowed to enter the enterprise and financial sectors only with the last, so called Markovic's, legislation from 1988/89. The latest report of the Bank of Slovenia from 1996 shows that as far as the financial part of direct investments is concerned the value of inward investments to Slovenia up to 1996 was around US$1 259 million, while the value of outward investment from Slovenia is US$250 million. Slovenia remains a significant net importer of foreign capital, an indication of a lower level of development.

Among inward investments in the Slovene banking sector major investors are, again, Austrian banks (Bank Austria, CA, Volksbank), followed by a French bank (Société Générale), and some Italian, Swiss and US capital is also present. They all count for close to 10 per cent of capital of the banking sector in Slovenia. In the last couple of years their share has even decreased. This is partly due to the fact that the present banking law does not allow for foreign affiliates without capital investment and partly to the policy of the Bank of Slovenia which practically has discretionary power regarding issuing licences to foreign banks for operation in Slovenia. The Bank of Slovenia's major criteria for issuing licences to foreign financial institutions are reciprocity and a good domestic record. A newly proposed banking law to be enacted in 1997 will allow establishment of foreign affiliates without capital investment.

Regarding connections with West-European capital through Slovene outward investments in banking, the NLB is the only bank with a developed international network (the only current exception is a representative office of the SKB in London).

The NLB has subsidiaries in New York (100 per cent owned by the NLB), Frankfurt (46.3 per cent share; other owners come from Germany and former Yugoslav states), Vienna (22 per cent share; others come from Austria and former Yugoslav states), Zurich (60 per cent share; others come from Italy, Luxembourg) and France (3.2 per cent share; others come from France and former Yugoslav states). Besides that, the NLB has a branch in Milan, a financial consulting company in Prague and eight representative offices in five superpower countries (the USA, UK, France, Russia, Germany) as well as the world financial centres.

The majority of the 29 operating banks in Slovenia have a licence for international operations. The NLB, as by far the largest bank in Slovenia (with 30 per cent share in the market), has thus correspondent relations with 221 banks from 133 countries, that is 443 opened accounts (127 nostro and 316 loro accounts), and its payment transactions counted in 1995 for one-third of Slovene GDP (Strategija poslovanja NLB v tujini, 1996).

Regarding the size of credit (non-capital) relations of Slovenia with Western Europe one indicator could be the size of foreign debt. The country started independence in 1991 with US$1.7 billion external debt plus unallocated share of the debt of the former Yugoslavia. Today its external debt is around US$4 billion, while reserves are US$4.3 billion. It is still only a slightly indebted country as this debt means 20 per cent of GDP or 35 per cent of receipts from export of goods and services; its debt service coefficient is around 6 per cent. Almost half of the US$2.3 billion debt increase during the first five years of Slovene independence was caused by adding a share of former Yugoslav debt. The remaining share means new foreign credits, predominantly to private sector and from private sources – an indication of the relatively high credit rating of Slovenia (low A by major credit agencies, which is the best among countries in transition).

Concluding remarks

West-European capital was important to the development of the economy and the banking sector of Slovenia during the nineteenth and the beginning of the twentieth century until the First World War, but it was not foreign capital as Slovenia was a province of the Austro-Hungarian Empire. After that, West-European capital was less important in the period until the end of the Second World War and almost non-present during the first 20 years after the war. After 1965 banking ties with Western Europe (and its capital) started to reappear, but very slowly.

Only in the late 1970s were affiliates of Slovene financial institutions allowed abroad and the former Yugoslavia became a highly indebted country (meaning that predominantly West-European loans were extended to the former Yugoslavia). At its peak, foreign debt was US$22 billion for the former Yugoslavia with 23 million inhabitants and GDP around US$50–60 billion. Slovenia had an under-proportional share in the external debt of the former Yugoslavia. Only in the late 1980s, were foreign capital investments allowed to the former Yugoslavia and to independent Slovenia (from June 1991). But the inflow of foreign capital was not so dramatic as in some other countries in transition. Among reasons for that, at the beginning, was the lack of credibility of the newly established state and there is still the somewhat reserved approach of Slovenes towards foreign investment and capital.

For the future, despite the fact that the newly proposed laws liberalize further possibility for foreign capital to enter (related to Slovenia's adaptation to the EU legislation), significant changes in dynamics can not be expected. Slovenia will not follow the experience of Hungary in that sense, where the majority of the banking sector is already in foreign hands and where with the better enterprises the story is the same. The predominant approach of Slovenes is to control their economy (and the banking sector for that matter) by themselves in the foreseeable future, until decisions can be made regarding potential institutional integration into the EU.

Regarding the future development of the Nova Ljubljanska banka (NLB), West-European capital could enter once the privatization of the bank starts after its rehabilitation is formally terminated. For now, the potential share of foreigners could probably not exceed 20–30 per cent. At the same time, regarding business relations, the NLB has a strong ambition to remain an international bank covering predominantly the area of Central Europe. It will further expand its external network and business ties with foreign partners, including those from Western Europe, which are already today the most important to the bank.

Notes

1. F. Štiblar, 'The rise and fall of Yugoslavia', paper for the *Annual Conference of British History Unit*, Leicester, April 1992, pp. 1–26.
2. A. Tosti, 'Denami zavodi v Sloveniji po prvi svetovni vojni', *Banchi Vestnik*, Ljubljana, 1989.

PART II
The Formation of an Economic Area

CHAPTER EIGHT

The Changing Nature of Internationalization of the Greek Financial Sector

Tassos Giannitsis

Introduction

The process of internationalization is dependent on the financial, technological, organizational and knowledge capabilities of firms to expand and to penetrate foreign markets via exports, direct investment and technology transfer. Equally, internationalization is closely associated with the free movement of capital across countries. In this paper the focus will be on the internationalization of the financial sector of the Greek economy in the postwar period, and the particular features it demonstrated during different phases of this longer period.

In particular, our examination will concentrate on the internationalization of the Greek financial system as a process, during which different domestic and foreign actors struggled for market shares, formed alliances, influenced each other's strategy, exerted competitive pressures and modernization effects on the national economy and changed the market structure of this particular sector.

Financial activities represent a field which *par excellence* experienced the widest and most expanded internationalization during the postwar period, and in particular after the first oil crisis and the spread of international financial centres, throughout the world economic system.

This movement swept along the financial systems of a larger number of countries, including Greece.

The evolution of the Greek financial system has been widely affected by this process, especially after 1986, when a profound process of deregulation and liberalization occurred, particularly in terms of adjusting domestic policies to the common regime of the European Community.

During the last four decades the significant changes which can be observed as regards the internationalization of the Greek financial system reflect at least four distinct factors:

1. The internationalization of the Greek financial sector followed

world-wide trends, and reflects largely the characteristics of this process at the world scale.
2. Over the examined period this internationalization process reflects the changing capabilities of the Greek economy with regard to competitiveness, business opportunities, knowledge, differentiation of productive structures and innovative potential. Equally, it reflects the changing power relations of the main actors in the financial market.
3. It reflects the influences exerted from a fundamental change of the broader institutional environment. The change of the basic rules of the game resulting from the liberalization of the financial markets at the international as well as at national level were of critical importance in this respect.
4. It reflects the changing conditions and opportunities that resulted from the transition of neighbouring Balkan countries into market economies, since this process favoured the expansion strategies of the most important domestic banks to this area.

Based on these changes, two major periods in the internationalization process of the Greek financial sector can be distinguished:

1. The period between the early 1960s and the mid-1980s, which can be characterized as a 'period of high protection coupled with administrative regulation'.
2. The period from 1986 up to the present, which is a period of deregulation, increasing internationalization and growing integration of the financial sector into the world market.

Ten key features of the early phase of internationalization

The first period of internationalization was associated with a range of characteristics, the most important of which are presented below.

A gradual penetration of foreign banks into a highly protective domestic financial market

After the Second World War the development of the Greek financial sector took place under heavy protectionist barriers, a factor that characterized almost every other sector of the economy. The market was dominated by publicly controlled banks while government interventions not only set the general rules of the game, but also determined in a very detailed way the functioning of the banking sector.[1]

During this phase internationalization had a passive nature, in the sense that Greece was a host country for direct investments of foreign banks, while at the same time domestic banks were not in a position to expand abroad with similar activities.

Foreign banks were considered as a vehicle, through which the following changes could be introduced into the system.[2]

- Increased competition between financial institutions with positive consequences on cost structures, and on competitiveness of the non-banking productive sectors.
- Provision of new types of services needed for the enhancement of economic development.
- Diffusion of positive externalities throughout the financial system.

The association of Greece to the Common Market as well as the efforts to strengthen the role of the financial system for the acceleration of the development process led in the early 1960s to the creation of two industrial development banks: ETEVA and Bank of Investment.

The participation of foreign banks as minority shareholders in these new institutions was at that time the first step of the internationalization of the Greek financial sector.

The low productivity and the poor quality of existing banking services, the ineffective response of the banking system to the challenges of rapid development, as well as the need for differentiated and innovative investment banking services made the recourse to foreign partners inevitable.

The dominant position of US banks

Since the mid-1960s an increasing number of foreign banks have established branches in Greece, mainly in the area of commercial banking. The firstcomers were of US origin, reflecting the broader trends of internationalization in banking and in other sectors during the 1960s.

Up to the early 1970s, banks of US origin were the main actors in this process. Even after the entrance of banks of a different origin, the dominant position of US banks has remained largely unchanged during this period.[3]

The inward-orientation of domestic financial institutions

The internationalization of the Greek financial sector during that period had an unbalanced nature, since it was not accompanied by a similar expansion of Greek banks abroad. To be more precise, a very limited number of banks started to expand abroad, through branches, offices or subsidiaries, aiming mainly to attract savings from Greek emigrants in these countries. The provision of important incentives from the Greek government to foreign exchange remittances of Greek emigrants created favourable conditions for domestic banks to expand into countries like Germany and the USA with the aim of acting as intermediaries in this type of financial transaction.

An additional factor that favoured the international expansion of Greek financial institutions concerns the opportunity to participate in the financing of Greek shipping activities and/or activities of the Greek emigrants in the USA. Consequently, a range of branches or subsidiaries have been established in some international financial centres such as London and major US cities.

Moderate effects of internationalizaton on oligopolistic market structures ...

A major question with regard to internationalization concerns the implications of this process on the development and performance of the domestic financial system itself. Moreover, due to the central role of the financial sector for a national economy, the same question can be posed with regard to the implications of this process for other productive sectors.

With regard to market structures in the banking sector, the first phase of internationalization led to very moderate changes. Foreign banks as a whole, despite their increasing number, did not contest for significant market shares. Although from 1964 to 1980 18 foreign banks were established in the country leading to an increase of foreign branches from four to 42, it has been estimated that overall they did not account for more than 10 per cent of total deposits or total credits of the banking sector.[4] The market share of each foreign bank was obviously much smaller, and only two of them had comparatively high shares.

In general, the internationalization of the financial sector did not result in a significant change of the prevailing oligopolistic market structures, in which three state-owned banks controlled more than two-thirds of total banking transactions.

... but more differentiated implications for specific financial activities

Despite the fact that internationalization did not contest the broader features of the basic market structure, it did cause more significant changes on particular submarket systems.

Foreign banks developed strategies of targeting either specific groups of clients or particular forms of services.[5] Multinational firms established in Greece, large firms, major exporters and importers, shipping companies, major capital holders and various expanding groups of firms or of personal clients were some of the areas where these banks concentrated their efforts. However, due to their limited network throughout the country, foreign banks were not particularly interested in developing retail banking activities, which are associated with a larger number of branches in the biggest cities and increased costs. Instead, they preferred to concentrate on services like guarantees, trade-related financial transactions, and so on.

Their strategy consisted of the provision of financial services with greater efficiency, better quality, lower cost, and/or more simple procedures. This strategy was very much characterized by a customer-oriented approach for targeted groups of clients' activities. In these particular areas foreign banks achieved much higher market shares than the average figures indicate.

Equally, some of these banks specialized solely in the financing of shipping activities and did not develop any types of relation with other sectors of the economy. In this case, foreign banks played a complementary role to the shipping activities that were established in Greece as a result of the important incentives given to shipping firms to use the country as a location for the management of their international activities.

Positive efficiency gains

An additional area of importance is related to the modernization effects that were exerted on the domestic financial system and which led to efficiency gains for the financial system as a whole.

Since the entrance of new players into the market took place only gradually, competitive pressures were also exerted gradually and affected only parts of the banking system, in particular the commercial banks.

The presence of new actors with more efficient methods in the production of financial services exerted a pressure on domestic banks to introduce more efficient methods of organization, accelerate technical modernization, implement new services, and in general improve productivity. Hence, the transfer of technology that occurred through internationalization led to externalities with a broader positive impact on the banking system.

Cooperative pricing strategies in an oligopolistic market structure

With regard to the structural effects that were expected to arise as a consequence of the attraction of new players into the financial sector, it can be observed that they remained at very moderate levels. Foreign banks did not follow strategies of confrontation with domestic banks. They exploited the possibilities that existed in the host economy within the framework of the current practices of the dominant players and the formal or informal rules of the game. Their refusal to develop retail services and their limited market shares meant that the intensity of competition remained virtually unchanged for very broad parts of the financial market and for the largest part of this period.

In particular, from the point of view of pricing strategies, foreign banks followed strategies of adaptation to price structures and patterns of behaviour of the domestic leaders. The high cost levels and the related high prices of their domestic competitors led foreign banks to adopt the prices set by the domestic leaders and hence to profit from their lower cost level. As a result, foreign banks could achieve much higher profit margins, by concentrating more on the quality and efficiency of their services instead of entering into price competition strategies.

However, the presence of foreign banks was a positive factor for the reinforcement of the competitive position of non-banking firms. The provision of new services, of more efficient banking products, their intermediation for technological agreements, for mergers and acquisitions, their knowledge of foreign markets and of financial assets management, and their role in the provision of useful information were factors that contributed positively to the host economy.

High profitability of foreign banks ...

The main result of the strategies and the stronger competitive basis of foreign banks concerned the profitability levels that could be achieved. Their freedom to expand into selected activities, services and customers led to substantial inequalities with regard to the profits of foreign and domestic banks in the country.[6]

This effect was characterized not only during the first phase of their activity in the country. It was even more pronounced during the most recent period because the liberalization of the financial market provided different opportunities to the major players of the banking system, domestic or foreign ones.[7]

... and weakening dynamism of domestic banks

An adverse implication of this effect was that domestic banks were pushed gradually to less profitable types of financial service and to less dynamic groups of customers. Obviously, this result was due to the interplay of more complex factors and relations and cannot be attributed simply to the internationalization of the financial sector and the strategies of foreign banks. Government policies, trade union pressures and internal capabilities of banks were some among many factors that have triggered this outcome of a more complex process, linked with internationalization.

The more recent period of globalization of financial activities

Following 1986 a second major phase of internationalization of the Greek financial sector can be distinguished. During this phase the internationalization of the financial system expanded significantly and exerted much more profound effects on market structures, sectors and firm strategies in comparison with the previous phase. These effects were not limited to the financial sector itself. They have affected almost all sectors of the economy, from agriculture to manufacturing, trade, services and the public sector as well as the general functioning of the economy.

During this period the financial system of the country took on features that were determined by wider developments concerning the globalization of financial markets. Four main significant differences with the previous phase can be distinguished.

First, this is a period during which the financial sector of the country has been increasingly exposed to deregulation and liberalization procedures. Capital movements, conditions of establishment, abolition of government intervention in the operation of the markets and liberalization of financial services are all elements that led to a substantial transformation of the overall financial scene in Greece.[8]

Second, as a result of this process, competition among financial institutions increased substantially. In a very short period the number of players as well as the nature of the financial services experienced significant changes.[9] In particular, a rapid development of the financial sector took place through the creation of new actors, new services and the advancement of new strategies. The financial sector increased its share of GDP from 2.5 per cent in 1980 to 4.1 per cent in 1995, which, in relative terms, represents one of the highest growth rates among the service or other sectors of the economy. The wave of mergers and acquisitions in industry and services during the second half of the 1980s up to today and the liberalization of capital movements, as well as the privatization policy opened new expansion opportunities to foreign as well as to domestic banks, and enhanced the rapid expansion and the increasing weight of the financial sector in the overall structure of GDP.

The increasing supply of new services was facilitated by the creation of new financial institutions, either of national ownership or of collaboration between Greek and foreign banks. Joint ventures in specialized financial activities such as leasing, factoring, mutual funds, venture capital, financial consulting and investment banking have broadened the range of actors as well as the services offered to users.[10]

As a result, after the deregulation of this sector following 1986 the stable or even declining position of foreign banks in domestic banking activities experienced a reverse trend. The important new element besides the legal form of establishment of foreign banks concerned cooperation with local enterpreneurs. Very often, the initiative came from the local investors themselves, who were interested in such cooperation in order to compensate other weaknesses for their entry into a highly oligopolistic market. Under such conditions, cooperation with a foreign financial institution provided the capabilities and the specialized knowledge needed to cope with the high competition in banking and to offer differentiated and/or innovative services to the market.

A second new feature was the strategy of a range of foreign banks to create a more extensive network in major economic centres around the country, to reinforce their position in retail banking and to expand their spectrum of services.

Third, in contrast to the previous period, the liberalization of the financial market was associated with fundamental changes in interest rates and the cost of financial transactions. The abolition of protection in combination with the deregulation led to interest rates that became positive for the first time in the postwar period. The level of real interest rates was determined by a range of factors, especially by the fiscal deficits. As a consequence, a broader number of firms preferred to cover their needs through foreign loans and other foreign credit facilities, and hence to benefit from the respective low interest rates.

Innovative capabilities, flexibility and knowledge of new activities, especially those linked to foreign exchange markets, increased in importance as factors of competitive advantage.

Hence, during this period competition among domestic and foreign financial institutions increased significantly, as the internationalization of the market played an increasing role for the competitive position of each particular actor.

As a whole, during this phase state-owned banks experienced a gradual but systematic erosion of their competitive position, which was expressed in their weakening market shares. Even more pronounced were the implications in terms of profits and profitability.

A fourth feature of this period concerns the international expansion of Greek financial institutions. Again in contrast to the previous period, the passive form of internationalization of the 1960s was gradually complemented by more active forms of external expansion. To be more precise, during this period a number of domestic banks created branches or subsidiaries in most of the neighbouring Balkan countries. Concurrently, domestic and foreign banks in Greece upgraded their presence in the northern part of Greece aiming to provide better support to their domestic clients, for their expanding activities in Balkan markets. The transition of these latter countries to market economies opened new trade, investment and collaboration opportunities for Greek firms, including financial institutions. The geographical proximity, the income levels, the consumption patterns of their population as well as the small scale of activity gave Greek firms a competitive advantage, and opened significant opportunities for direct investments in these countries.

In total, ten Greek banks opened 14 subsidiaries or branches in Bulgaria, Albania, Romania and the former Yugoslav Republic of Macedonia (FYROM) in order to capture a share of the emerging financial opportunities, to support the expansion of Greek non-banking firms into the Balkan area and to build a potential competitive position for the future, when these economies are expected to achieve more stable and significant levels of economic activity.

Conclusions

Over the last decades the financial system of Greece has played a significant role in the development of the country. Its increasing integration into the world market was associated with effects that influenced its internal structure, the scope and the nature of financial services, the market position of each major actor, the international expansion of the most competitive actors and, in particular, the profitability of the major players.

The different forms under which internationalization gained in importance during the last decade led to significant changes, which exceed the narrow scope of the relations between foreign and domestic banks as in the earlier phases of this process.

The growing importance of the financial sector and of financial capital transactions created conditions of a non-zero-sum game. Despite the increasing presence and the strengthened position of foreign actors in the market, the supply of new financial services and the appearence of new financial needs on the part of firms and the public sector resulted in high growth rates of the financial system and hence created expansion opportunities for all actors, both domestic and foreign.

The combined effect of internationalization and deregulation in the recent period caused a significant change in the attitude and strategies of all large or small actors in the banking sector. A significant restructuring process was initiated in both public and private banks, although of a different intensity. Much tougher competitive relations followed the previous long period of protectionist rigidity and inflexibility of market structures and relations.

The increasing role of foreign exchange transactions and of new financial instruments weakened the relative importance of more traditional financial services for achieving dominant market positions.

In this process domestic banks had to adapt rapidly and to abandon previous patterns of behaviour. This structural transformation is apparent in all financial firms, and especially in the case of private banks, which demonstrated much more flexible and adaptive strategies. Publicly owned banks developed similar efforts, although with much less satisfying results.

However, even in the case of public banks it becomes also more and more obvious that any delay in the implementation of restructuring and adjustment strategies leads to a serious weakening of market positions. Recently, significant efforts can be seen, concerning restructuring and the merging of subsidiaries to give a more active role to specific financial institutions. Concurrently, the efforts undertaken by the government to promote the privatization of a range of smaller banks are also an expression of a policy that aims to increase the efficiency of the public sector of the financial system. The considerable expansion of many domestic banks into neighbouring countries could be an important factor for the strengthening of their overall capabilities and market position.

What becomes crucial during the present situation is the capability of the publicly owned as well as that of the private banks to face the rapidly changing pressures of globalization of markets and competition. A failure or a delay to restructure and to build up more competitive structures will imply higher cost of capital and money for domestic non-banking firms and will further result in increasing gaps in market shares and profitability between the more and the less efficient actors. The experience of the last years shows that a further result is the orientation of domestic firms to foreign loans, with adverse implications for monetary and fiscal policy.

In particular, the participation of Greece in the European Economic and Monetary Union will lead to even more extensive competition in the area of financial services.

Consequently, during the present phase internationalization calls urgently for strategies with two goals:

1. To increase the capabilities of the domestic banks to gain from the broader dynamism that characterizes the financial sector at a world-wide as well as at a national level.
2. To build up a basis of competitive financial services, which will support the competitiveness of the Greek economy as a whole.

Notes

1. For a general description of the evolution of the banking system up to the mid-1970s see the study of D. Chalikias, *Possibilities and Problems of the Credit Policy. The Greek Experience*, Athens: Bank of Greece, 1976 (in Greek).
2. T. Giannitsis, *Foreign Banks in Greece. The Postwar Experience*, Athens, 1982, pp. 75ff. (in Greek).
3. Ibid., pp. 59ff.
4. Ibid., pp. 123ff. and similar estimations in the *Karatzas Report on the Change and Modernization of the Banking system*, Hellenic Bank Association, Athens, 1987, p. 40 (in Greek).
5. Giannitsis, op. cit., pp. 135ff and 143ff, and P. Alexakis, 'Basic developments in the structure, operation and institutional framework of the Greek banking system', in T. Giannitsis (ed.), *Market Liberalization and Transformations in the Greek Banking System*, Athens, 1993, pp. 77–8 (in Greek).
6. Giannitsis, (ed.), op. cit., pp. 156ff.
7. Alexakis, op. cit., pp. 30ff.
8. Ibid., pp. 49ff. and 62ff.
9. T. Giannitsis, 'Conclusions on the shaping of financial policy under conditions of changing competitive structures', in Giannitsis (ed.) op. cit., pp. 250ff. and D. Moschos and D. Fraggetis, *The Present and Future of Greek Banks*, Athens, 1997, pp.30ff. (in Greek).
10. T. Giannitsis, 'The integration of the financial markets and implications for the Greek banking system', in Giannitsis (ed.) op. cit., pp. 237–43.

CHAPTER NINE

Issues of Management Control and Sovereignty in Transnational Banking in the Eastern Mediterranean before the First World War[1]

Christos Hadziiossif

Undoubtedly, the emergence of modern banking as a specialized activity, distinct from commerce and usury, is intimately linked to the rise of capitalism. It is obvious that the saving, borrowing, lending and exchanging of value symbols on a large scale is both a prerequisite for and a consequence of the increase in the social division of labour and the growth of production, the essential features of capitalism. However, histories of banking pay very little attention to the social implications of the linkage between banking and capitalism. The argument of this paper is that we cannot explain the development of the banking sector in a region without referring to the development of the local bourgeoisie, the propertied classes whose economic activity produces capitalist growth and whose demands determine the institutional framework of society. The inviolability of the property rights and the access of the propertied classes to political power are the basic demands of the bourgeoisie. The degree to which they are satisfied reveals the relative strength of the propertied classes in a region and determines further economic growth. At the same time, security of property and political power are essential for the development of modern banking. Without security the accumulation of value symbols is hazardous if not impossible, while political control is needed to avert infringements on the rights of bankers by the government, the single biggest borrower in modern times. The incorporation of the Bank of England in 1694, after the Glorious Revolution, to guarantee the rights of the principal creditors of the English state constitutes the classical, but not the only, example of the relationship between banking and bourgeois institutions.

As a rule the banks played a leading role in the formation of the contemporary nation states. By financing central governments the banks enhanced their autonomy *vis-à-vis* conflicting local and class interests and bolstered their unifying action on the administrative and cultural level. The banks helped also to integrate local economies into wider national markets. Banking acquires an additional political dimension when it crosses the state's borders. Coins, besides representing value, have ever been symbols of sovereignty and means of political propaganda both at home and abroad. In modern times the economic leverage of the stronger states is in great part exercised through the action of their banks that extend loans to foreign rulers and invest in important sectors of alien economies.

Being reminded of these basic relationships is necessary to elucidate the complex history of transnational banking in the Eastern Mediterranean during the nineteenth century and the first decades of the twentieth century. No other part of the world was, at that time, crowded with so many branches and agencies of transnational banking as the Balkans and the Near East. A map drawn by Jacques Thobie shows 14 banks, each of them operating numerous branches and agencies in the principal cities of the area. The note that accompanies the chart is also telling about the density of the web of transnational banks: 'The number of banks in Egypt that were supported by foreign capital is too large to illustrate here.' 'The diversity of forms and structures adopted by European banks' as well as ' the complexity and the flexibility of [their] activities and strategies'[2] renders the analysis of the phenomenon rather difficult. Generally, the existing historical approaches consider banking in the region under the prism of imperialism assuming that the policy of the banks automatically follows capital ownership.[3] Moreover, existing histories assume a linear development of transnational banking from a few French and English banks to a dozen credit establishments operating under various national flags. The picture of transnational banking in current surveys becomes really blurred for the period after 1905, when the number of banks rose exponentially. The difficulties for a global comprehension of the phenomenon are due less to gaps in existing information, as it has been argued, than to the absence of an appropriate analytical framework to deal with the already available data.

The conceptual flaws of the traditional analysis of transnational banking in the Eastern Mediterranean can be summed up in one major point: they do not take local factors adequately into account. Certainly, the political and social conditions in the Eastern Mediterranean were rather complex, as the usual class-determined social cleavages were compounded by national antagonisms. Until the eve of the First World War the greatest part of that area was formed by the territories of the Ottoman Empire, while the other sovereign states or autonomous territorial entities of the region had seceded from it during the previous hundred years. However, the Empire still remained a multinational state and its unity and territorial integrity was threatened by the competing political ambitions of its various nationalities and the conflicting territorial claims of the new nation states of the Balkans. The internal oppositions in the area were exploited by the great European powers which wanted to expand their zones of influence. The nation states of the Balkans as well as the ethnic groups within the Ottoman Empire presented different levels of economic and social development and as a consequence they were not all involved in the same manner in banking activities.

The influence of local societies on transnational banking can be perceived through the analysis of three sets of problems. The first is related to the managerial problems arising from the building up in a short period of time of a network consisting of several branches in many foreign countries and in different cultural environments. The second set of problems is related to the conflicting political pressures put upon transnational banks by the governments of their country of origin as well as by their host countries. The last set of questions concerns the contribution of transnational banking to the development of the host countries and its relative importance for the local economy. I will illustrate these problems with examples taken mainly, but not exclusively, from the activity of two Greek and one Ottoman bank. This perspective will help to break the monolithic view of transnational banking in the Eastern Mediterranean which reduces the whole matter to an exclusive relationship between West-European bankers and oriental pashas.

Greece was the first East-Mediterranean state to create an issue bank in 1841, the National Bank of Greece, which as a universal bank remains the main financial services enterprise of the country today. The reasons for the NBG ushering in the era of modern banking in the region have nothing to do with a supposed superior level of economic development in Greece than in the neighbouring countries. The NBG was the first successful banking corporation in the Balkans and in the Near East because Greece was the first sovereign nation state in that area. Already, the plans for the revolution against the Ottoman Turks provided for the creation of a banking institution. A short-lived National Financial Corporation was founded in 1828, while in the 1830s the demands for a joint-stock bank paralleled the claims for a liberal constitution. Eventually the bank was created three years before the introduction of the constitution of 1844, but subsequently it has become a pivotal element of the economic and political system of Greece.

The importance of the institutional setting for the development of banking is illustrated by the failure of two contemporary banks founded about the same time as the NBG in Alexandria and in Constantinople. The main objective of the first Banque d'Egypte and the first Banque de Constantinople was to regulate the rate of exchange and to stop the depreciation of the local currencies. Both assumed also some financial services to the local governments, while the Banque de Constantinople obtained the right to issue the *kaime*, a kind of banknote. The Banque d'Egypte was a joint venture by the Greek merchant Michail Tossizza and his French colleagues Pastre frères, whereas the Banque de Constantinople was the result of an association of Armenian, Greek and Jewish bankers of the Ottoman capital.[4] The ultimate failure of the two banks was not the result of insufficient funds or wrong entrepreneurial decisions, but was caused by intervention in the bank's affairs by the autocratic rulers. The Ottoman Imperial Bank founded after the Crimean War fared better because the owners were covered by the guarantees accorded to property by the French and the English legal systems, under which was placed the new credit institution.

The development of the NBG has benefited from the bourgeois institutional environment in Greece. Thirty years after its foundation the NBG had already established a network of branches in the main cities of the country and its prestige had outshone the Ionian Bank, an English colonial bank founded in London in 1839. After the cession of the Ionian islands by Great Britain to Greece in 1864 the Ionian bank maintained for a long while its British legal status as well as the right of issue in the islands, but otherwise it has integrated itself into Greek banking. The NBG was also able to overcome the competition of the first investment banks created in Greece by Greek merchants and bankers of the diaspora in 1873.

By means of these new financial institutions, the Bank of General Credit and the Bank for Industrial Credit of Greece, banking in Greece was formally linked to Greek transnational banking operations. These activities passed through three phases. In the first phase from the 1850s to the early 1870s Greek entrepreneurs acted as simple initiators of banking corporations controlled by English and French capital. In the second phase Greeks created their own transnational banks with *siège* (headquarters) in London, Alexandria or Constantinople.[5] During the third phase from 1894 to 1922 the direction of capital flows in Greek transnational banking was reversed. Whereas in the earlier phases the flow of the investments ran from abroad towards Greece, since 1894 the funds invested by Greek transnational banks across the Balkans and the Near East had mainly originated in Greece. Greece was not only the first country of the region to create a bourgeois institutional framework, but also the first to develop an even social distribution of income and wealth, a large middle class capable of saving significant amounts.

The combination of the institutional system with the social equilibrium led in Greece to the emergence of stronger locally controlled banks than in other countries of the region with a higher GDP and more wealthy individuals, as, for example, Romania or Egypt.

In 1914 two transnational banks were based in Greece, the Banque d'Athènes and the Banque d'Orient. The BdA was founded in 1894 and its declared aim was to become the bank of the petite bourgeoisie of which the ranks had swollen during the previous decades of economic expansion and urbanization. However, right from the start it lent principally to some prominent Athens businessmen, several of whom were also its shareholders. The low number of credits accorded to small business notwithstanding, the bank managed through its savings accounts policy to attract the deposits of the petite bourgeoisie, becoming the first Greek deposit bank. The funds collected in this way could not always be profitably invested in Greece, the domestic economy lacking dynamism. The pressure of the idle funds became greater when the remittances of the Greek emigrants to the USA started accruing to the Greek banks after 1900. The possible uses of the surplus funds were shipping and the expansion of banking business abroad. For this purpose the BdA established branches in the main cities of the Ottoman Empire and in Egypt. The artisan of this drive was John Pesmatsoglou, a private banker from Alexandria who merged his bank with the BdA in 1896 to become its chairman. In July 1904 he concluded an alliance with the Banque de l'Union Parisienne (BUP), the youngest of the French bank d'affaires. Under this scheme the French bank patronized the introduction of the shares of the BdA in the Paris stock exchange and extended an important acceptances credit to be used in the Ottoman Empire and in Egypt. With this agreement, the French acknowledged the economic weight of the ethnic Greeks in the region and, indirectly, their political aspirations. They counted on the presumed knowledge of the local conditions by their Greek associates in order to enter a difficult market, where their main competitors in France, like the Crédit Lyonnais and the Comptoir National d'Escompte, were already established.

In the first year of the agreement, in 1905, the BdA owned 11 branches, six of them lying outside Greece (Alexandria, London, Constantinople, Smyrna, Chania, Herakleion). The report for the year 1910 listed 29 branches, 22 of them lying outside Greece. In 1912 the respective numbers were 40 and 31 branches. The rapid expansion of the network required great amounts of capital and significant human resources, as a branch could employ several dozen people. The extra capital needed was secured through successive share issues that raised the equity from initially 2.5 million drachmas in 1894 to 60 million in

1911. The new issues were easily subscribed in Greece and abroad, the group of the BUP controlling more than 35 per cent of the share capital. Recruiting the right people to staff the new branches proved to be more difficult. Exact figures for the staff employed by the bank are not available. However, in 1911 the branch of Salonica employed 32 people, that of Cavala 11, while the amount of business in Serres required the presence of only three people.[6] If we assume an average of ten employees per branch, then the BDA needed about 300 people to staff its services abroad. The expansion of the Banque d'Orient was less spectacular. However, in 1911 the bank possessed an equity of 25 million francs and a network of 11 branches abroad (Salonica, Smyrna, Alexandria, Cairo, Zagazig, Monastirio, Mytilini, Serres, Pergamos, Magnisia, Soma). At that time about a quarter of the total investments by Greek banks were made abroad.[7]

The home labour market was unable to provide so many qualified bank clerks in a short space of a time. It was not only a question of absolute numbers but also of expertise as there were important differences between banking abroad and banking in Greece. On the home market the main business of banks consisted in discounting commercial bills, in change operations, in mortgage loans and in open account credits. In the Ottoman Empire and in Egypt the main business of banks dealing with the private sector of the economy turned around the export of the main commercial crops, credits to the exporters with merchandises as collateral, change operations, etc.[8] Loans guaranteed by government stocks and securities were also a frequent operation. This kind of business was very speculative and required experience in commodity trade and in stock exchange operations as well as a good knowledge of the local commercial and financial conditions. Transnational banks solved this problem by winning over employees from established banks. The Deutsche Orientbank, for example, entrusted a former clerk of the Banque de Salonique in Smyrna with the direction of its branch in Alexandria. A former clerk of the National Bank of Egypt was engaged as deputy director of the Cairo branch.[9] J.Constantinidis, deputy director of the Ottoman Bank in Bassorah, offered his services to the Greek Banque d'Orient to serve it as a director in a great centre of the Ottoman Empire.[10] Hardly a year after his appointment, Roussos, the chief accountant in the Smyrna branch of the same financial institution, a former clerk of the Ottoman Bank, was already being courted by the Deutsche Orientbank which wanted to engage him, probably with a higher salary.[11]

The BdA followed a different tactic for the appointment of the directors of its branches, choosing them among the local merchants and private bankers. These businessmen exchanged their independent status for a good salary and a percentage of the profits of the branch. The Deutsche Orientbank used also local advisory committees as a means to associate prominent local businessmen of German origins with its activities.[12]

If former businessmen and bank clerks could pretend to master the necessary expertise to run a branch, recruiting them raised, however, delicate problems of loyalty. On the one hand, some clerks were accused of keeping too close ties with their previous employers and of passing them confidential information.[13] On the other hand, many of the former merchants placed at the head of BdA branches, both in Greece and abroad, served primarily their personal interests as they borrowed from the bank to speculate on their own account. Thence, they were simultaneously directors and customers of the branches under their care. In 1914 the report of the experts appointed by the Greek government to audit the accounts of the BdA accused eight directors of various branches of mismanagement and embezzlement of funds.[14] Local managers were also solicited by competing banks to accept their credits for the operations of their branch, when the central management, frightened by the rate of expansion, tried to limit the exposure of the bank by curtailing the capital allowances to its branches.[15] The heads of the branches were the more eager to accept those offers as an important part of their emoluments came from the percentage, usually 3 per cent, of the profits of the branch.

In order to keep a firmer grip on their overseas operations transnational banks used inspectors or they dispatched periodically to the branches some senior member of central management. The BUP appointed a permanent representative in Egypt to supervise the progress of its various investments in that country and especially the activities of the Alexandria branch of the BdA. Under the cooperation agreement of 4 July 1904 the BUP had extended to this particular branch credits exceeding 8 million francs.[16] The first to occupy the post of permanent representative was a Frenchman, Maurice Millet, dispatched from France. As were many other bank managers throughout the Near East, Millet was fired after the Egyptian crisis of 1907. He was held responsible for the losses suffered by the BdA in its loans on merchandise and securities and his handling of the affairs were found by his superiors to be a 'mess'.[17] The Cairo director of the Deutsche Orientbank, Said Ruete, had been fired for the same reasons one year earlier than Millet. The French manager was replaced by Rene Ismalun, an Egyptian Jew, Austrian subject, related to the prominent banking family of Cattaui of Cairo.[18] In 1909 Ismalun was made comptroller and another Frenchman from Paris, A. Thierry-Mieg, was named permanent representative in Egypt.[19] Thierry-Mieg was receiving 25 000 francs a year plus a local indemnity of 3 000 francs to keep an eye on the branch of the BdA in Alexandria, the Sucreries et Raffineries d'Egypte, the Egyptian Bonded Warehouse and some other minor investments of the BUP. Thierry-Mieg was replaced, probably in January 1910, by G. Yver de la Bruchellerie who was still acting as special representative of the BUP in Egypt in the year 1913.[20]

The musical chairs of the special representatives prove that the problem in Alexandria was a structural one and did not consist of the occasional mismanagement of the companies' funds by senior clerks. The system pushed the local managers to prefer higher yields to the security of placements. Their essential task was to provide outlets for the idle funds of the head offices. In order to achieve this aim the latecomers among the transnational banks were forced to extend credits to borrowers whose demands were turned down by the older banks as not presenting all the guarantees required. As a result, the recurrent crises in Egypt and in other markets of the Near East between 1907 and 1914 hit the newcomers more than the established banking houses. Another aspect of the problem lay with the tactic of the banks not to make sufficient provisions for bad debts, fearing the adverse effects of such a measure on the value of their shares in the stock exchange. Under the pressure of the markets, the boards opted for 'a gradual amortization'[21] of the bad debts and presented to the shareholders balance sheets with overvalued assets. They hoped that an upsurge of the market would restore the value of their securities portfolios. Sometimes the manipulations of the accounts were so blatant that they could be observed even in the lapidary balance sheets presented to the shareholders, as is the case with the balance sheet of the Banque de Salonique for the year 1909.[22] Eventually, in 1913 the French and the Greek associates of the BdA were forced to recognize the real size of the losses which had not only absorbed the reserves, but also a quarter of the equity of 60 million drachmas. Despite this misfortune of the bank, investors still credited it with a bright future and the new issue of shares, decided to restore share capital to its previous amount, was easily covered.

Whereas bankers were concerned with the expertise and the probity of their clerks, diplomats were principally preoccupied with the political loyalty of the staff. The banks used also to emphasize the national character of their establishments for marketing purposes. The French and the Germans believed that putting their nationals in the management of the branches abroad increased the prestige of their establishments among the potential local customers. The Greek transnational banks appealed systematically to the national feelings of the Greek businessmen in order to win customers from their competitors. However, the

Table 9.1 Nationalities of the employees staffing branches of the major banks in Ottoman Macedonia in 1911

Bank/branch	No. of employees	Nationality of employees	
Banque Impériale Ottomane			
Salonica	42	Ottoman	26
		Austrian	2
		French	4
		German	1
		Greek	3
		Italian	6
Serres	6	Ottoman	4
		Greek	2
Drama	4	Ottoman	3
		French	1
Cavala	10	Ottoman	15
		Austrian	1
		Greek	1
		Italian	3
Uskub	13	Ottoman	9
		French	2
		Italian	1
		Russian	1
Banque d'Orient			
Salonica	41	Ottoman	29
		Greek	10
		Russian	1
		Serb	1
Serres	4	Ottoman	4
Banque de Salonique			
Salonica	122	Ottoman	94
		Austrian	4
		British	3
		Greek	3
		Italian	15
		Spanish	3
Cavala	7	Ottoman	4
		Greek	1
		Italian	2

Table 9.1 concluded

Bank/branch	No. of employees	Nationality of employees	
Uskub	11	Ottoman	6
		Austrian	1
		French	1
		Greek	3
Banque d'Athènes			
Salonica	32	Ottoman	20
		British	2
		French	1
		Greek	8
		Spanish	1
Serres	3	Ottoman	2
		Austrian	1
Cavala	11	Ottoman	7
		Greek	3
		Italian	1

Notes: According to French diplomats the nationality of the bank's clerks was a matter of passport only. This criterion was unreliable in the multi-ethnic and shifting realities of the Near East. For example, according to French data only eight out of 32 employees of the Salonica branch of the BdA were Greek nationals. The respective numbers for the Banque d'Orient are ten out of a total of 41. However, a list of the names of the clerks for the year 1913 shows that almost all the employees of the two branches were ethnic Greeks, see V. Dimitriadis, 'The population of Thessaloniki and the local Greek community in 1913', *Studies on Macedonia*, Thessaloniki: Society for Macedonian Studies, 1996, pp. 68–9.

Source: *AEF* B31284, file Banque de Salonique, Salonica, 28.2.1911.

lack of experienced personnel forced the banks to engage clerks irrespective of their nationality (see Table 9.1). As a result some branches in the great cities of the Ottoman Empire looked like ethnic mosaics. This mix created important communication problems even within the same branch. Some branches of the Banque d'Orient tried to solve the communication problems by keeping the books and the correspondence in French, the lingua franca of the Balkans and the Near East before the First World War.[23] The available information does not allow us to conclude whether Director Herbert Gutman of Dresdner Bank, the promoter of the Deutsche Orientbank, was successful in his endeavour to staff the new establishment with German nationals and to impose the use of German in the communications of the bank with its customers. However, the staff of the Cairo branch was of very mixed origins. Said Ruete, the director, was the son of a Hamburg merchant and of the sister of sultan Said Burgash of Zanzibar. He had German nationality and had served as an officer in the Prussian army. Acting as co-director in the same branch was Albert Erfield, a former accountant at the Ottoman Bank in Port Said, of Jewish-Polish stock and a Persian subject. Salomon Meyer responsible for the securities department, also a Jew, came from England. As for the directors of the Deutsche Orientbank in Alexandria, Ritscher and Zamorani, they were respectively Austrian and Italian subjects.[24]

The diplomats were very suspicious of the international alliances contracted by the bankers and they disapproved of the employment of nationally mixed staffs. They saw the banks as mere instruments of the economic and political interests of their countries and they thought that possessing the majority of the equity allowed the majority shareholders to imprint their national character on the bank and to guide its policies irrespective of the situation in the host countries. According to a French official political influence was the ultimate goal, financial investment being merely the means to achieve that goal. The French minister of foreign affairs judged it to be ' inconvenient to entrust foreigners with the direction of French banks in Turkey'.[25] He referred to cases such as the nomination of Pangiris bey, an Ottoman Greek very well received at the sultan's palace, as director in the central offices of the Ottoman Bank in Constantinople.[26] Correspondingly, his envoy in Turkey had been shocked when another Ottoman Greek took over the branch of the Crédit Lyonnais in the Ottoman capital in 1908.[27] The reactions of the diplomats reflected the imperialist mood in their countries, where some newspapers and colonial lobbies were reclaiming national managers for the transnational enterprises.[28]

Personnel policy was not the only field in which the diplomats encountered difficulties in imposing their views on banks. In their investments strategy too, the banks were not willing executioners of the foreign policy of their home country. Moreover, they often formed alliances with enterprises from countries that their government considered as not friendly. Such politically incorrect cooperation in the Balkan markets was institutionalized by the creation of 'sues' holding societies. The first holding, the Union Ottomane, was created in 1909 in Zürich. It possessed a share capital of 12 million francs and its object was the undertaking of investments in the Ottoman Empire in the sectors of electricity and public transport. It was headed by the Deutsche Bank, but among its shareholders were also the Société Générale and the

Banque de Paris et des Pays-Bas from France (Paribas).[29] The holding was liquidated in 1911 to be replaced by a new one with the participation of the Banque de Bruxelles, Deutsche Bank, Dresdner Bank and 'undoubtedly with the participation of French financiers' too.[30] The more nationalistic aggressive banks were the latecomers like the Deutsche Orientbank, which were forced to win a place on a crowded market. The Greek banks were also among the latecomers, but they had the enormous advantage of finding in place affluent Greek communities.

However, even the Greek transnational banks, some minor services to the national cause notwithstanding, essentially profited from the Greek irredentism and they refused to align their policy with the imperatives of the foreign policy of Greece. Moreover, the alliances with French and German banks served principally as a political caution against a possible backlash in Greek–Turkish relations.[31] On many occasions Greek communities throughout the Balkans and the Near East pressed the BdA and the Banque d'Orient to open a branch in their town in order to bolster the Greek population element there. In other instances, Greek consuls in Ottoman Macedonia and Thrace urged the banks to facilitate, by extending credits, the purchase of Turkish domains by their ethnic Greek cultivators.[32] Generally the banks turned down these proposals. On the one hand, they systematically abstained from mortgage loans to peasants and they were not willing to depart from that line. On the other hand, Greek transnational banks were counting on the Greek ethnic element in choosing the location of their future branches in the Balkans and the Near East. However, their aim was not merely to further 'the economic and industrial development ... of the unredeemed Greeks',[33] as some Greek consuls put it, but to maximize their profits. They could achieve it only by establishing their branches in towns with a flourishing export trade. Contrary to the banks, some Greek insurance companies operating in the same region were more eager to place their business activities under the imperatives of Greek irredentism.[34] Perhaps this policy played a great role in the failure of the biggest of those insurance companies, the Amoibaia (the Mutual) in 1909.

Nevertheless Greek bankers took care not to hurt the feelings of the Greek communities by favouring businessmen belonging to other national communities or ethnic minorities of the region. Their customers were predominantly, if not exclusively, Greeks. For instance the Smyrna branch of the Banque d'Orient accorded credits on current accounts to 172 businessmen of that city. The majority of them, 111, were ethnic Greeks. The rest of the accounts belonged to Armenian, Jewish, Turkish and to some western merchants.[35] In 1908, in two cities more cosmopolitan than Smyrna, in Alexandria and Cairo, out of a list of 79 loans on securities extended by the BdA, 32 belonged to Greek customers.[36]

The distribution of credits among merchants from different communities was one of the main reasons for the divorce between the National Bank of Greece and the Nationalbank für Deutschland. The Greek bank sought the German alliance in order to counter overseas the French connections of its main rival on the home market, the BdA. The German and the Greek group participated equally in a new venture, the Banque d'Orient, which started its operations in February 1905 with a capital of 10 million francs. From the beginning, the German diplomats considered this joint venture with distrust: 'The German shareholders of the bank should always be on guard not to be outmanoeuvred by the experienced, tricky Greeks,' warned the German General Consul in Athens.[37] According to his opinion 'the Greeks hailed the Bank counting on the profit from it, otherwise they have no sympathies whatsoever for the Germans and their endeavours'. Indeed, the association ended within one year. The Greek partners kept the brand name, the headquarters in Athens and all the branches except Constantinople and Hamburg. The German share in the capital was taken over by a Greek–French group headed by the Comptoir National d'Escompte de Paris. The Germans joined forces with the Dresdner Bank and A. Schaffhausenschen Bankverein to launch the Deutsche Orientbank. Officially, the partners parted ways because they disagreed over how to exercise their joint control over the Banque d'Orient. The diplomatic gossip of that time insisted on the animosity between Greeks and German Jews. There were always latent anti-Jewish prejudices among Greek orthodox populations. From the end of the seventeenth century onwards they had been nourished by economic and political antagonism in the framework of the multi-ethnic Ottoman Empire. Economic antagonism between Greeks and Jews had been exacerbated since the middle of the nineteenth century.[38] In the Banque d'Orient the points of conflict between Greeks and German Jews were two. The first was related to the management of the Hamburg branch, which according to the Greeks favoured Jewish merchants and shipping at the expense of the bank's interests. The second had to do with the control and distribution of credits in the Constantinople branch. Favouring too openly Jewish business would alienate their rival Greek shipowners and merchants and throw then into the arms of the BdA, the main rival of the National Bank of Greece, which thence would have failed in its effort to re-equilibrate the balance of forces through the creation of the Banque d'Orient.

Thus beneath the conflict between Greeks and Germans, between Greeks and Jews lay a deeper antagonism for the control of the Balkan and Near-East markets and ultimately for the partition of the anachronistic Ottoman Empire. This antagonism opposed foreign interests and local bourgeoisie, which had been strengthened in the previous decades. There was also antagonism between the local bourgeoisie of different nationalities. Greeks and Jews were both domestic and outside forces in this competition. As domestic bourgeoisie the Greeks benefited from a wider spatial basis and a greater demographic potential than the Jews, who were therefore forced to bet on the preservation of the Ottoman Empire and its integrated market against the partitioning views of the Balkan bourgeoisie. As outsiders the Jews could mobilize wider alliances than the Greeks.

The relationship between national cleavages and financial ties is very well illustrated in the case of the Banque de Salonique. The bank was founded in Salonica in 1888 by Fratelli Allatini, a Jewish businessman of Salonica, with the backing of the group of the Österreichische Länderbank and the Comptoir d'Escompte de Paris. In the 1890s N.Th. Dumba a prominent Viennese Greek banker was sitting on the board of directors, representing the Österreichische Länderbank. In the twentieth century we find another Greek member of the board, John Eliasco, private banker in Constantinople.[39] Progressively the equity was raised to 10 million francs and the bank opened branches in Constantinople, Smyrna, Monastir, Cavala, Uskub and finally in Alexandria and Cairo in 1905. The Egyptian crisis of 1907 caused great losses to the bank, which turned to French capital, the Société Générale and Paribas to consolidate its position.[40] The Jewish directors of the bank supported the coup of the Young Turks and counted on an accelerated economic development of the reformed Ottoman Empire. The outcome of the Balkan Wars 1912–1913, which almost expelled Turkey from the European continent, caused havoc to the plans of the Banque de Salonique. Formally the bank was controlled by the French who possessed the major part of the equity. The French were on good terms with all the Balkan states in whose extended territory lay the branches of the bank. In reality, the rule dear to the diplomats 'who owns the capital fixes the policy' did not hold.[41] The policy of the bank was determined by the minority shareholders, the Jewish businessmen who controlled the local connections. They opted to cede the Balkan branches and to continue as a Turkish bank.[42] However, the disposal of the branches proved to be a thorny affair, because of the political complications. The Quai d'Orsay accepted the redeployement of the bank, but it vetoed the sale of the branches to Austrian-controlled Serbian and Bulgarian banks. When eventually the Banque de Salonique presented as a suitable buyer the Banque Russo-Asiatique of St Petersbourg, because 90 per cent of its equity belonged to French capitalists the French ministry suddenly discovered that, once again, the majority rule did not work. In order to avoid placing French capital under a foreign flag, the Ministry of

Finance suggested the compromise solution of selling the branches to the Russo-Asiatique, but to entrust with their management the Paris committee of the Saint Petersbourg bank.[43] However, this proposal raised many objections in the Quai d'Orsay and the negotiations between bankers and diplomats dragged on until the outbreak of the Great War.

Among the scenarios considered to solve the sovereignty problems linked with the fate of the Banque de Salonique was that of a merger with the National Bank of Turkey. This financial institution was founded by Sir Ernest Cassel after the Young Turks revolution of 1908. Cassel was already involved in the National Bank of Egypt and he became very active in business as well as in politics.[44] The choice of the denomination 'National Bank' for both his financial creations shows that his intentions were not only to please the nationalist feelings of the Young Turks. Inherent in the choice was a vehement criticism of the existing banks in the Balkans and the Near East and especially of the Imperial Ottoman Bank. Cassel argued that the Ottoman Bank had not done enough for the development of the Empire. Cassel innovated in his bank by forming a board of directors with a majority of Ottoman subjects.[45] Cassel's analysis of the economic situation in Turkey coincided with the views of Turkish personalities involved in the new regime or sympathetic to its aims. Besides Cassel's National Bank some other financial institutions expressed similar developmental ambitions. Some had rather a folkloric character, like the Crédit National Ottoman founded by a professor at the Ecole National des Langues Orientales in Paris in 1910. However, if Professor Durand was able to persuade Egyptian and Syrian businessmen of the seriousness of his projects, it was because they felt the need for a different kind of financial institution. Typical of the mood prevailing at that time in Turkey was also the denomination of another bank, the Banque de Turquie pour favoriser le commerce et l'industrie.[46]

These developments revealed that a new Turkish middle class was emerging, with similar but conflicting aspirations to the bourgeoisie of the nation states of the Balkans and the ethnic minorities of the Ottoman Empire. The future of the transnational banks in the region depended on their willingness and ability to respond to the aspirations of the new classes. Eventually, most of the transnational banks perished after the First World War. The main victim of the changing environment was the Ottoman Bank which had tied its fate with the Sultan's regime and was unable to adapt itself to the demands of the new Turkish rulers. The last balance sheets of the bank before the war revealed its inability to follow the growth of the economy. About 20 per cent of its assets were tied to government business, whereas a great part of the rest consisted of credits to official monopolies like the Régie des Tabacs. Credits extended to private business were of the same magnitude as the credits of the BdA.[47] The enormous percentage of gold reserves to banknotes, 318 per cent in 1907 reveals equally the 'Malthusian'[48] policy of the Ottoman Bank. We lack today trustworthy figures that would allow us to relate the activity of the transnational banks to the GDP of the East-Mediterranean region and make a realistic assessment of their economic importance. However, the balance sheets of the state-owned Agricultural Bank give us an idea of the size of the invisible side of the economy. In 1910 the Agricultural Bank extended credits to peasants totalling 5.5 million Turkish pounds, or about a quarter of the assets of the Ottoman Bank. However, it maintained 480 agencies throughout the Balkans and the Near East and it financed more than 1.2 million peasants.[49]

Summing up we can say that during the 50 years before the First World War the East-Mediterranean area formed a rather unified economic space under a remarkably liberal economic regime. Movement of capital and persons was entirely free and the customs duties were much lower than in the following period. In this context, many transnational banks from various origins developed considerable activity. Their operations encountered, however, great difficulties in the field of communications, management control and personnel policy. Most of the banks did not realize that these problems were generally interrelated with wider sovereignty and domestic political issues. Their activity did not take sufficiently into account the needs of local society and as a result the majority of the transnational banks disappeared when the political environment changed, without having contributed sufficiently to the economic development of the region.

Notes

1. Abbreviations: *AA*: Auswärtiges Amt, Bonn, Germany; *AEF*: Archives Economiques et Financières, Paris, France; BdA: Banques d'Athènes, 1893–1953; BUP: Banque de l'Union Parisienne, 1904–1974; *IAETE*: Historical Archives, National Bank of Greece, Athens; *IAYPEX*: Historical Archives of the Greek Ministry of Foreign Affairs, Athens; *NBG*: National Bank of Greece.
2. Jacques Thobie, 'European banks in the Middle East', in R. Cameron and V.I. Bovykin (eds), *International Banking 1870–1914*, New York and Oxford, 1991, p. 440.
3. Ibid.; J. Thobie, *Intérêts et impérialisme français dans l'Empire Ottoman (1895–1914)*, Paris, 1977; P.W. Reuter, *Die Balkanpolitik des französischen imperialismus 1911–1914*, Frankfurt/Main, 1979; K. Loulos, *German Policy towards Greece, 1896–1914*, Athens, 1990 (in Greek).
4. M.D. Sturdja, 'Haute banque et Sublime porte. Préliminaires financiers de

la guerre de Crimée', in Jean Louis Bacqué-Grammond and Paul Dumont, *Contributions à l'histoire économique et sociale de l'Empire Ottoman*, Leuven, 1983, pp. 451–80.

5. Chr. Hadziiossif, 'Banques grecques et banques européennes au XIXe siècle: le point de vue d'Alexandrie', in G.B. Dertilis (ed.), *Banquiers, usuriers et paysans*, Paris, 1988, pp. 157–98; St. Chapman, *The Rise of Merchant Banking*, London, 1984, pp. 127–9, 134–5, 165–6.
6. *AEF*, B31284, File Banque de Salonique, Salonica 28.2.1911.
7. Our own estimates based on the balance sheets for the year 1912.
8. *AA* R14586, Report of Director Kothe of the Deutsche Levant Linie, Hamburg, s.d.s.I (end 1904?).
9. *AA* 14586, Cairo 1.1.1906.
10. *IAETE*, series XXII, file 9, Bassorah 27.1.1905.
11. *IAETE*, series XXII, file 11, Athens 3/16.12.1906.
12. *AA* R14586, Cairo 1.1.1906; R14587, Cairo 10.4.1907.
13. *AA* R14587, Berlin 26.11.1907.
14. *BUP* 580/153 brochure 'Quels sont les faits qui ont motivé les pertes de la B.d.A.'
15. *BUP* 558/16 Wehrung to Barbe, Athens 5.12.1906.
16. *BUP* 558/23, Paris 8.2.1908.
17. *BUP* 558/23 Barbe to Courcelle, Paris 18.12.1908.
18. *BUP* 558/23 Note sur R. Ismalun s.d.s.l. and BUP 577/ 139 BUP to Sergent, Paris 23.9.1910.
19. *BUP* 121, BUP to A. Thierry-Mieg, Paris 18.1.1909.
20. *BUP* 579/152 file Lettres de M. Yver de la Bruchollerie.
21. BdA, *Report to the General Meeting of the shareholders for the year 1912*.
22. *AEF*, B31284 file Banque de Salonique.
23. *IAETE*, series XXII, file 11 Athens 3/16.12.1906.
24. *AA* R14587, Berlin 26.11.1907.
25. *AEF* B31284 file 'Banques', Paris 26.9.1911.
26. *AEF* B31284 file Banque Ottomane, Paris 13.2.1904.
27. *AEF* B31284, file 'Banques', Pera 24.1.1908.
28. *Chemnitzer Tageblatt*, 24.10.1906.
29. *AEF* B31284, file 'Banques', Therapia 9.7.1909.
30. *AEF* B31284, file 'Banques', Paris 28.8.1911.
31. Chr. Hadziiossif, 'Eastern in Alexandria: popular prejudices and intercommunal strife in late nineteenth century Egypt', *Historica*, no. 12–13, 1990, p. 159 (in Greek).
32. Ibid.
33. *IAYPEX*, file B43 (1910–1911), Athens 23.6.1910.
34. Hadziiossif, 'Eastern in Alexandria', op. cit., p. 157.
35. *IAETE* series XXII, file 11, Athens 3/16.12.1906.
36. *BUP*, 121, file Notes, pieces et documents divers.
37. *AA* R14586, Athens 27.1.1905.
38. Hadziiossif, 'Banques grecques', op. cit. and Hadziiossif, 'Eastern in Alexandria', op. cit.
39. See reports of the board to the general meetings of the shareholders in *AEF* B31284, file Banque de Salonique.
40. *AEF* B31384, file Banque de Salonique, Pera 16.6.1909.
41. *AEF* B31284, file 'Banques', London 16.12.1908.

42. *AEF* B31284, file Banque de Salonique, Pera 2.5.1913.
43. *AEF* B31284, file Banque de Salonique, Paris 25.5.1913.
44. Chapman, op. cit., p. 54.
45. *AEF* B31284, file Projets de fondation d'une banque nationale en Turquie, London 16.12.1908.
46. *AEF* B31284, file Banques, Pera 14.1.1910, Paris 23.12.1909, Paris 29.11.1910, Beyrouth 18.4.1910.
47. *AEF* B31284, file Banque Impériale Ottomane, Note s.l. 9.10.1908.
48. Thobie, 'European banks', op. cit., pp. 410–11.
49. *AEF* B31284, file Banque Agricole, *Statistiques graphiques de la Banque Agricole de puis sa fondation* (printed).

CHAPTER TEN

Banking and Politics in Austria-Hungary

Günther Kronenbitter

A couple of years ago, the Fukuyama slogan of the 'end of history' after the collapse of the communist system exposed the utopian aspect of capitalist liberalism. Since then, history has been going on and the interrelationship between political will and market forces is an issue that is still with us. The newspaper-reading or TV-watching European citizen can hardly evade the exhausting and exhaustive discussions on the European Monetary Union or on 'globalization', for example. As a general historian especially interested in the problems of security policy and international relations on the eve of the First World War, I want to focus on some aspects of the often ambivalent role of banks in Austria-Hungary as instruments of political stabilization at the beginning of the twentieth century.

The Dual Monarchy as established by the Compromise with Hungary in 1867 in the wake of the war against Prussia and Italy was a constitutional and political system *sui generis*, highly complex and out of tune with the *Zeitgeist* of the late nineteenth century. At a time when the nation state had become the prevailing model of political integration, the Habsburg Monarchy with its multinational character and the constitutional oddities and paradoxes of dualism looked like an 'anomaly', as the ageing Emperor Franz Joseph I had it.[1] To a certain degree, the project of transforming the more than 500-year-old dynastic Habsburg Empire into a modern state – *one* modern state – was definitely abandoned in 1867. To be sure, at least the Hungarian part of the Dual Monarchy seemed to copy the pattern of western parliamentarism – in its peculiar Hungarian way – and of forming a nation state, but the whole system was based on the suppression of nationalities other than the dominating Magyars and an extreme restriction of voting rights. In Austria, in terms of ethnic composition and regional political subentities even more incoherent, the bureaucracy formed the political backbone of what might well be considered as just the non-Hungarian rest of the Empire. The fragile form of cooperation of Austria and Hungary, both of them sovereign states since 1867, was based on the monarch, the emperor and king, as in early modern times.

The monarch, the common army together with the tiny navy and the foreign policy bureaucracy played the role of institutional bonding agents, the core of what Oscar Jaszi has called the centripetal forces, trying to balance the increasing power of the various centrifugal forces, ranging from dedicated Hungarian separatists to ardently pan-German nationalists. Dynasty, army and diplomacy had been the makers of the Habsburg Empire by cleverly arranged marriages, martial virtues and finesse – now they tried to defend the Dual Monarchy's great power status in order to preserve their own position in society and politics. The methods available to the members of this supranational élite in pursuit of their mission were those of traditional great power politics.[2]

The day-to-day business of domestic and economic policy was run by the Austrian and the Hungarian governments, and it was mainly up to *them* periodically to negotiate the conditions for the terms of tax payments for common purposes and for the prolongation of the customs union and other economic questions, for example concerning the Austro-Hungarian National Bank.[3,4] Quite often the negotiations for the renewal of the economic Compromise, connected with package deals touching on such diverse questions as armaments or constitutional guarantees, caused severe political trouble and made the future of the Monarchy look bleak. Recent studies – I would like to mention those by John Komlos[5] and David F. Good[6] – have suggested that the customs union between Hungary and Austria did *not* reduce Hungary's rate of economic growth and that the remarkably dynamic economic development of the Dual Monarchy was *not* restricted to the highly industrialized areas in Bohemia and Lower Austria. To be sure, the backwardness of the Austro-Hungarian economy compared with Germany, for example, cannot be denied but there is no evidence that it was for *economic* reasons that the Habsburg Monarchy had to be dismembered.[7]

The banking system affected economic development in Austria-Hungary in several ways. Modifying Alexander Gerschenkron's interpretation, Richard L. Rudolph has pointed out that the Austrian banks were reluctant to invest in new industries or other than well-established firms.[8] With hindsight their cautious investment policy, which created a lack of venture capital, can be criticized. But the general lack of available capital in Austria-Hungary aside, the lessons of the disastrous Vienna stock exchange crash of 1873 can explain this conservative mood. As the public had lost its confidence in the stock market, so had the experts. Thanks to the detailed studies of Eduard März on the Creditanstalt, the history of the first and most important *mobilier* bank of the Monarchy can be traced from its founding by the Rothschilds in 1855 up to the early 1920s.[9] Cautiousness and conservative business culture prevailed in the Creditanstalt's board of directors. The traditional *haute finance* of

Vienna, for the most part Jewish private bankers, joined by wealthy aristocrats, and French and British capital initiated the foundation of the major banks in Vienna. With the share of foreign capital in the major banks significantly reduced by the turn of the century, the Bodencreditanstalt and the Anglo-Austrian Bank became Austrian institutions, that is to a great extent controlled by the small banking élite of Vienna.

In the last couple of years before the war, Bohemian banks led by the Zivnostenska banka were very active in industrial investment at home and abroad. They extended their share of the Austrian financial market considerably, not only in Bohemia and Moravia. But all in all, the dominance of the Viennese banks, not only in Austria but in Hungary as well, could not be challenged, and strengthened the economic bonds between both parts of the Dual Monarchy. The consortium formed by the Vienna Rothschilds and the Creditanstalt was able to keep a tight rein on the Hungarian and Austrian state loan business over a long period of time. Bernard Michel has depicted the changes that took place in the Austrian banking system at the beginning of the twentieth century when the Rothschild group lost its hegemony in this field of activities, partly because the Austrian Ministry of Finance favoured the public Postsparkasse. The pre-war regrouping of Austria's most important banks culminated in the joint founding of the Österreichische Kontrollbank für Industrie und Handel.[10] Those changes notwithstanding, stability was the hallmark of the banking system as soon as it had recuperated from the catastrophe of 1873.

The institutes' industrial activities led to the creation of clusters of companies closely connected with one or several of the major Austrian or Hungarian banks and to the cartelization of a number of branches, for example in the sugar industry.[11] This process seems to indicate that an ever-increasing penetration of key industries and the trend towards further concentration might have had important repercussions on political life in the Dual Monarchy. But it would be totally misleading to think of Austria-Hungary as a political system run by a couple of omnipotent bankers. By the very nature of their trade and by the structure of the Austro-Hungarian economy, bankers were interested in stability and a high degree of predictability. Apart from the social climbers in the Bohemian banks, the social composition of the boards of directors of the leading Austro-Hungarian banks was, as mentioned above, remarkably homogenous. With a few exceptions, the high aristocracy had left the business in the wake of 1873 and the majority of the banking élite was formed of Jews or Catholics of Jewish descent from the German-speaking upper bourgeoisie.[12]

At the beginning of the twentieth century, two of the most important banks, the Creditanstalt and the Bodencreditanstalt, decided to hire high-ranking members of the bureaucracy as their managing directors. Both Spitzmüller and Sieghart were experts in financial matters, and they were expected to improve their respective institutes' connections with the administration. In the case of the Creditanstalt this expectation did not indicate an attempt to expand the bank's business aggressively – quite the opposite: Spitzmüller had to *restore* the institute's former ties with the government and he acted as cautiously as his predecessors.[13] On the other hand, the ambitious and less scrupulous Sieghart did not receive a warm reception in the Viennese *haute finance*. Trying to make the most of the skills he had acquired in Austrian politics, Sieghart tried to take a grip on some newspapers by utilizing the Bodencreditanstalt's financial potential and connections. This highly unusual semi-political activity was not only a rare exception but met with the fierce resistance of the heir-apparent Franz Ferdinand.[14] Absolutely loyal to the monarch and brought up in a conservative business culture, the *haute finance* generally accepted the leading social and political position of Austria-Hungary's traditional élites.

This self-restraint did not prevent a close cooperation with political or military authorities whenever the banks were asked to help. As far as patriotism and the opportunity to make a profit went hand in hand, this cooperation does not have to be mentioned here. In some cases, financing railway lines or arms deals at home was the result of government initiatives – an example is the Länderbank's role in financing the construction of battleships by Skoda in 1910 according to an agreement with the navy department.[15] More important were the authorities' attempts to use Austro-Hungarian banks as foreign policy instruments. As I have mentioned above, in the eyes of the decision-making military and diplomatic élite the great power status was of overwhelming importance to their own position. Cut off from domestic policy by the constitutional structure of the Monarchy and alien to economic activities by tradition and training, they lamented the lack of resources without developing realistic concepts to improve the situation and to stop the relative decline of the Dual Monarchy in terms of economic and military power.

The Austro-Hungarian banks could not provide much consolation because most of their business was domestic – not very surprising, given the low profile of the Dual Monarchy's capital export.[16] György Kövér's brief account[17] and Maria Rosa Atzenhofer-Baumgartner's Ph.D. thesis[18] have described the limited volume and the range of Austro-Hungarian capital exports and their place within international financial relations. It was only in the Balkans that the banks of the Dual Monarchy were able to make a difference.[19] With the sole exception of Romania's petrol business, they usually did not invest in industry. Because of political and economic reasons, railways were more attractive fields of activity but in the case of the Novibazar Railway the *haute finance* refused to support a politically motivated project of the foreign minister Aehrenthal that promised to be a loss-maker even in the long run.[20] Sometimes the banks were able to rebut the Austro-Hungarian government's insinuations and proposals but quite often they took economic risks they normally tried to evade. Sometimes, they were pushed by their clients and partners in the armaments industry, for example Skoda.[21] All in all, the political impact of these transactions was very limited in most cases. The exception was the Bulgarian loan on the eve of the First World War that has to be considered a major contribution to the Dual Monarchy's diplomatic strategy of fostering ties between Bulgaria and the Triple Alliance – or to be more exact: the Dual Alliance.[22] In a way, the Bulgarian loan was an important part of a more active Austro-Hungarian Balkan policy – a policy that led to the July crisis.

And yet Austria-Hungary's international financial relations cannot be blamed for the decisions made in 1914. To be sure, the French policy of depriving Germany's ally of the financial resources available at Paris helped to intensify the tensions between the Entente and the Triple/Dual Alliance. The problems with the markets in Paris were partly due to the political confrontation but they were also the result of purely financial quarrels, for example in the context of the crisis of the Südbahn. The deal struck by the French ambassador and Aehrenthal in 1911 was a sign of a *rapprochement* concerning the placing of an Austro-Hungarian loan. Dorizon's Société Générale strengthened its relations with Hungarian banks and with the Länderbank, Paribas cooperated with the Wiener Bankverein and, all in all, there were signs of a cosier financial climate in Austro-Hungarian–French relations in 1914. On the other hand, German and Austro-Hungarian banks – in some cases just rivals – worked hand in hand in a number of financial operations in the Balkans, but there was no implementation of a grand strategy of imperialist penetration by 'teutonic' capital.[23] The competion between German and French institutes saw Austria-Hungary's banks often in the role of spectator, unwilling and unable to play a major role in the drama.

At the very end, the political decision-making was the prerogative of the old élites and both the diplomats and the military based their calculations on their respective 'realms of knowledge'. There was sort of a hunch that in both domains of the traditional élite economic questions had become very important but they proved to be unable to translate this vague idea into action. I think it is quite significant that it was the representative of the Lower Austrian and Viennese business community who initiated intra-governmental talks on the issue of economic preparations for a major war in the last few months before

Sarajevo and *not* the military or the civilian authorities.[24] Any diplomat or high-ranking general officer with a clear picture of Austria-Hungary's economic situation would have come to the conclusion that a protracted great power war in Europe had to be avoided at all costs – little wonder that none of them was willing to realize that the Dual Monarchy was no longer a great power.[25] In accordance with the traditional self-restraint – a few exceptions like Felix Somary[26] notwithstanding – the Austro-Hungarian *haute finance* did not even try to stop the old élites from plunging Europe into war.

The banking system was a stabilizing factor in the crisis-ridden Habsburg Empire at the beginning of the twentieth century, integrating the Dual Monarchy as a financial entity and conservative in its business culture and in its political outlook. Probably too conservative, because a more dynamic economic development spearheaded by daring Schumpeterian entrepreneurs might have strengthened the centripetal forces in the multinational Monarchy; too conservative, because the *haute finance* in Austria-Hungary – as everywhere else in Europe – considered politics to be none of its business.[27] Not these deferential capitalists[28] but the old élites anxious to defend their position considered traditional aggressive great power politics as the best way to stabilize the Dual Monarchy. Political visions of integration and stability by grandeur paved the way to a disastrously risky form of militant diplomacy.[29] In the end this policy resulted in turning a dismembered Austria-Hungary into the north-western appendix of the Balkans which for two decades seemed to be just the European backyard of the Ottoman Empire or a geographical entity.

Notes

1. Carl J. Burckhardt, *Begegnungen*, Zürich, 1958, p. 57.
2. Samuel R. Williamson, Jr, *Austria-Hungary and the Origins of the First World War*, Basingstoke, 1991, pp. 34–57; Lothar Höbelt, 'Das Problem der konservativen Eliten in Österreich-Ungarn', in Jürgen Nautz and Richard Vahrenkamp (eds) *Die Wiener Jahrhundertwende. Einflüsse–Umwelt–Wirkungen*, 2nd edn, Vienna, 1996, pp. 777–87.
3. K. Zuckerkandl, 'The Austro-Hungarian Bank', in National Monetary Commission (ed.) *Banking in Russia, Austro-Hungary, The Netherlands and Japan*, Washington DC, 1911, pp. 35–118.
4. József Galántai, *Der österreichisch-ungarische Dualismus 1867–1918*, Budapest, 1990.
5. John Komlos, *Die Habsburgermonarchie als Zollunion. Die Wirtschaftsentwicklung Österreich-Ungarns im 19. Jahrhundert*, Vienna, 1986.
6. David F. Good, *Der wirtschaftliche Aufstieg des Habsburgerreiches 1750–1914*, Vienna, 1986.

7. Scott Eddie, 'Economic policy and economic development in Austria-Hungary, 1867–1913', in Peter Mathias and Sidney Pollard (eds) *The Cambridge Economic History of Europe. Volume VIII. The Industrial Economies: The Development of Economic and Social Policies*, Cambridge, 1989, pp. 814–85; Roman Sandgruber, *Ökonomie und Politik. Österreichische Wirtschaftsgeschichte vom Mittelalter bis zur Gegenwart*, Vienna, 1995, pp. 292–313.
8. Richard L. Rudolph, *Banking and Industrialization in Austria-Hungary: The Role of Banks in the Industrialization of the Czech Crownlands, 1873–1914*, Cambridge, 1976.
9. Eduard März, *Österreichische Industrie- und Bankpolitik in der Zeit Franz Josephs I. Am Beispiel der k. k. priv. Österreichischen Credit-Anstalt für Handel und Gewerbe*, Vienna, 1968 and *Österreichische Bankpolitik in der Zeit der großen Wende 1913–1923. Am Beispiel der Creditanstalt für Handel und Gewerbe*, Vienna, 1981; Creditanstalt-Bankverein, *Ein Jahrhundert Creditanstalt-Bankverein*, Vienna, 1957.
10. Bernard Michel, *Banques et banquiers en Autriche au début du 20e siècle*, Paris, 1976.
11. Walter Reik, *Die Beziehungen der österreichischen Großbanken zur Industrie*, Vienna, 1932, pp. 13–51.
12. Michel, op. cit., pp. 309–42.
13. Alexander Spitzmüller, *und hat auch Ursach, es zu lieben*, Vienna, 1955, pp. 27–112.
14. Rudolf Sieghart, *Die letzten Jahrzehnte einer Großmacht. Menschen, Völker, Probleme des Habsburger-Reichs*, Berlin, 1932, pp. 16–167.
15. Christoph Ramoser, '*Österreich-Ungarns Weg zur Tegetthoff-Klasse*', Ph.D. thesis, Vienna, 1992, pp. 134–8; Lawrence Sondhaus, *The Naval Policy of Austria-Hungary, 1867–1918. Navalism, Industrial Development, and the Politics of Dualism*, West Lafayette, 1994, pp. 218–20.
16. Franz Bartsch, 'Statistische Daten über die Zahlungsbilanz Österreich-Ungarns vor Ausbruch des Krieges', *Mitteilungen des k.k. Finanzministeriums*, XXII, Vienna, 1917, pp. 1–159.
17. György Kövér, 'The Austro-Hungarian Banking system', in Rondo Cameron and V.I. Bovykin (eds) *International Banking, 1870–1914*, New York, 1991, pp. 319–44.
18. Maria Rosa Atzenhofer-Baumgartner, 'Kapitalexport aus Österreich-Ungarn vor dem Ersten Weltkrieg. Die Stellung der österreichisch-ungarischen Monarchie im System der internationalen Kapitalbeziehungen', Ph.D. thesis, Vienna, 1980.
19. For example, Roland von Hegedüs, *Geschichte der Entstehung und des Bestandes der Pester Ungarischen Commercial Bank. II. Band. 1892–1917*, Budapest, 1917, pp. 263–77.
20. Michel, op. cit., pp. 274–9.
21. Martin Gutsjahr, 'Rüstungsunternehmen Österreich-Ungarns vor und im Ersten Weltkrieg. Die Entwicklung dargestellt an den Firmen Skoda, Steyr, Austro-Daimler und Lohner', Ph.D. thesis, Vienna, 1995, pp. 4–12.
22. Dörte Löding, 'Deutschlands und Österreich-Ungarns Balkanpolitik von 1912–1914 unter besonderer Berücksichtigung ihrer Wirtschaftsinteressen', Ph.D. thesis, Hamburg, 1969, pp. 109–31; Wolfgang-Uwe Friedrich, *Bulgarien und die Mächte 1913–1915. Ein Beitrag zur Weltkriegs- und Imperialismusgeschichte*, Wiesbaden, 1985.

23. Boris Barth, 'Deutsche Banken und Österreich-Ungarn: Eine wirtschaftliche und politische Partnerschaft?', in Helmut Rumpler and Jan Paul Niederkorn (eds), *Der 'Zweibund' 1879. Das deutsch-österreichisch-ungarische Bündnis und die europäische Diplomatie*, Vienna, 1996, pp. 279–97.
24. K. K. Ministerrats-Präsidium (Press-Departement) 1914, Prot. Zahl 518, 519, 526, Österreichisches Staatsarchiv-Allgemeines Verwaltungsarchiv, Ministerrats-Präsidium Presseleitung 1914, Kart. 99.
25. Günther Kronenbitter, '"Nur los lassen". Österreich-Ungarn und der Wille zum Krieg', in Johannes Burkhardt *et al.*, *Lange und kurze Wege in den Ersten Weltkrieg. Vier Augsburger Beiträge zur Kriegsursachenforschung*, Munich, 1997, pp. 159–87.
26. Felix Somary, *Erinnerungen eines politischen Meterologen*, Munich 1994, pp. 70–93, 98–121.
27. Michel, op. cit., pp. 343–69.
28. For a totally different view of the financial élite and the causes of the First World War: Jurij Krizek, 'Beitrag zur Geschichte der Entstehung und des Einflusses des Finanzkapitals in der Habsburger Monarchie in den Jahren 1900–1914', *Die Frage des Finanzkapitals in der Österreichisch-Ungarischen Monarchie 1900–1918*, Bucharest, 1965, pp. 5–51.
29. Williamson, op. cit., pp. 164–216; Günther Kronenbitter, 'Austria-Hungary and the First World War', *Contemporary Austrian Studies*, V, New Brunswick, 1997, pp. 342–56; Helmut Rumpler, *Eine Chance für Mitteleuropa. Bürgerliche Emanzipation und Staatsverfall in der Habsburgermonarchie*, Vienna, 1997, pp. 549–73; Ernst Hanisch, *Der lange Schatten des Staates. Österreichische Gesellschaftsgeschichte im 20. Jahrhundert*, Vienna, 1994, pp. 209–41.

CHAPTER ELEVEN

Capital Markets and Economic Integration in South-east Europe, 1919–89: Lessons from Western Banking in the Two Yugoslavias

John R. Lampe

In the first flush of optimism that followed the collapse of communist regimes across Eastern Europe, our Wilson Center programme convened a conference in Sofia in 1991 to consider the prospects for reconstructing capital markets for private investment. They would be needed to mobilize the resources, domestic and foreign, of competing private companies, replacing subsidies from state budgets to politically managed, monopolistic enterprises. How obvious it had become after 1989, Marvin Jackson noted, that no critic could now challenge the early contention of Ludwig von Mises that 'the Achilles' heel of socialism' was its inability to allocate capital rationally.

Jackson went on to question the prevailing American enthusiasm for replicating the stock markets and investment funds that had dominated US financial history in favour of what he called 'the German model'. The centrepiece of this model would be the universal bank that by definition combines investment with commercial functions. By lending on current account and by underwriting stock issues whose shares may still be voted as proxies for bank customers, such banks exercise a powerful, presumably positive influence over the management of industrial or other enterprises.[1] In late-nineteenth-century Germany that influence often placed bank directors directly on enterprise boards. It also had the negative effect, let us remind ourselves, of favouring the cartel arrangements that kept the least efficient enterprises in business rather than promoting competition between the most efficient.[2] At the same time, the German Great Banks concentrated on the most modern branches of domestic industry, regardless of region, and their integration into a single, modern economy, investing less outside the country and then less for political reasons than either England or France.

Neither of two Yugoslavias formed during the twentieth century was able to integrate its previously disparate regions into a single modern economy. The second state had twice as long a period of time and came closer, but still failed. The six republics' communist leaderships managed to create six complete sets of industrial enterprises in the 1950s and then their own set of financial institutions, to which we shall return, by the 1970s.[3]

This paper will focus on the failure of western banks during both the interwar and postwar periods to promote the integration of Yugoslavia's own economy or its connection to the economic space of South-east Europe as a whole. German participation, for good or ill, will be conspicuous by its absence; an often neglected American role deserves attention, particularly for the recent decades. The western failure should be seen only in lesser measure as evidence of bankers' preference for the guaranteed profits that come from regionally restricted arrangements such as monopolies for mineral extraction or cartels for timber cutting. More important than this echo of the Marxist critique from Rudolf Hilferding's *Finanz Kapitalismus* forward are two distinctly un-Marxist features of Yugoslavia's experience, and indeed that of all South-east Europe. First is the *absence* of either the political will from western governments or the economic interest from western capital markets to coordinate any strong, coherent effort to 'penetrate', that is establish controlling interests in, the Balkan economies. The coincidence of French will and interest in Czechoslovakia was real but simply cannot be read into South-east Europe. Second is the western banks' preference instead for short-term credits granted at high rates of interest largely to finance Yugoslavia's imports. Only the foreign-backed Zagreb banks of the 1920s set this preference aside in favour of industrial investment, and then as we shall see, only for a few years and for short-term advantage in an inflationary period.

None of this is to say that in the world economy of the 1990s both European and American banks would not now respond and support national and South-east initiatives for overdue integration within the area and reconnection with West-European economies, a connection badly reduced by the wars of Yugoslav succession. But, as I argued at a conference staged by the Ost- und Sudosteuropa Institut in Vienna in March 1996, that western support will only come if initiative for the development of South-east Europe emerges from within and also across the economically artificial fault line dividing it from Central Europe. More specifically, I suggested a partnership between Greek and Austrian financial institutions.

Let me turn from the present to the two periods when a single state offered at least the possibility of an integrated modernizing economy within the sizeable space that was Yugoslavia. Obviously central to the Yugoslav state's capacity to survive and succeed was a constructive connection between Serbia and Croatia as well as between Serbs and Croats. For financial institutions that meant a constructive connection between Belgrade and Zagreb. Here western banking tended to reinforce their separate paths. For the interwar period, those paths were set by the state's central bank in Belgrade and by the concentration of the largest private banks in Zagreb. The former became the principal source of rediscounted commercial credit in Serbia while the latter largely ignored those facilities and even avoided the chance to hold significant stock in the central bank.[4]

Like other Balkan central banks of the 1920s, the Yugoslav National Bank joined with its finance ministry to restrict currency emissions at the cost of higher interest rates in order to re-establish the flow of state loans that had constituted the principal presence of western banks before the First World War. For reasons that are well known, the leading European capital markets were neither disposed nor able to resume such loans. One American loan, negotiated through the finance ministry and the Serb-dominated government in Belgrade but targeted for railway construction in Croatia, did hold great promise. The loan through the New York banking house of Blair and Company was originally projected to provide US$100 million, with US$70 million to be spent on constructing the badly needed rail line to connect Zagreb with Split on the Adriatic coast. Linda Killen tells the sad story of how the initial US$100 million was scaled back to US$30 million in 1923, with only US$15 million subscribed and then at a discount that brought the final yield down to US$12 million. Delayed *Skupstina* approval for terms that included a stiff interest rate of 8 per cent bears some of the responsibility for the low yield. Yet Killen places the great share on the lack of enthusiasm among American investors and pressure from the US Departments of State and Commerce to withhold any such lending until Serbia's war debts had been settled.[5] That subsequent settlement smoothed the way for the US$30 million yield that was collected in 1927, with one half devoted to the Zagreb–Split line. Yet after a US$12 million loan through Seligman's, another New York investment firm, to the state's Hipotekarna banka the same year, no more American loans materialized, nor did the US$20 million loan proposed on the London capital market in 1928.

The actual presence of western banks in Belgrade remained minimal throughout the interwar period. The pre-war Banque Franco-Serbe re-emerged but never regained its previous prominence despite backing by the powerful Paribas house. Its industrial interests were confined to a single cement plant. It was at least strong enough to oppose the opening of an American bank in 1920 and to refuse credits for trade with the USA for the rest of the decade. The small Serbo-American bank did open in 1921 with emigrants to the USA subscribing a majority of its capital, but neither it nor the branch of the struggling Wiener Bankverein launched the same year had access to sizeable foreign credits.

Sizeable foreign credit flowed instead through Zagreb, which joined Prague in becoming a main collecting point for Austro-Hungarian capital looking for a safe place to land in the immediate aftermath of the Dual Monarchy's demise. Five large banks led the the way in Zagreb's accounting for fully one half of all Yugoslav bank assets during the early 1920s and still comprising, as may be seen from Table 11.1[6] about 40 per cent in a fourfold larger total in 1927. Rozenberg's authoritative Yugoslav banking survey puts the Austrian share of Croatian bank capital at 30 per cent and the Hungarian share, some of it channelled through the French Banque de l'Union Parisienne, at 10 per cent.[7] Another 10 per cent should be added for a Czech share, primarily through the controlling interest of the Zivnostenska banka in the large Jugoslovenska banka u Zagrebu. For the brief period 1923–25, these banks played the useful domestic role of the German Great Banks in the late nineteenth century by providing some 30 per cent of Croatia's industrial capital. Timber-processing was particularly favoured, but as with other long-term credits or stock purchases, strictly within Croatian plus adjoining Bosnian territory. Bank motivation was in any case less to promote long-term development than to use short-term purchases of stock shares with high dividends to stay ahead of the rate of inflation. Even before the Depression descended, reduced inflation and a more stable financial structure in Yugoslavia prompted the foreign-backed Zagreb banks to shift away from long-term assets and savings deposits into short-term credits and sight deposits.[8]

The Austro-Hungarian presence in the Zagreb banks declined with the Depression, most sharply after the failure of Vienna's Creditanstalt in 1931. Stepping into the breach were French and Czech banks rather than German, much less English houses. Rozenberg's data for 1937 find foreign capital making up 60 per cent of the assets in Yugoslav commercial banks, with 21 per cent from Paris and 19 per cent from Prague. The German share was 15.5 per cent and the English only 4.4 per cent. The five large Zagreb banks still dominated a now shrunken private sector, its assets reduced by one-third from 1929 to 1937 and its share in the Yugoslav total cut from 57 to 41 per cent. Still, these five banks accounted for two-thirds of the total capital in the 12 largest private commercial banks. All of those banks had left long-term investment far behind. Nearly 80 per cent of their liabilities were in three month or sight deposits. The foreign-backed banks did provide 35 per cent of the credit available in a commercial banking system badly strapped for loanable funds; the largely short-term advances available went to cover imports or past debts.[9]

What they did not provide was any significant share of the considerable European and American capital invested primarily in mining and metallurgy during the 1930s. That influx brought the foreign share of joint stock in Yugoslavia's mining and manufacturing up to 51 per cent by 1937. French and English interests took half of that share, with 15.5 and 10.1 per cent respectively. The US share of 6.5 per cent exceeded the German and Czech fractions of 2.5 and 2.4 per cent even when combined as from 1939.[10] The small bank holdings of joint stock were in the now neglected areas of milling, timber and transport.

State support for industry, especially if related to rearmament, and direct French or English investment in mining increasingly predominated in Yugoslavia's access to financial resources as the 1930s wore on. Stojadinovic's 'gamble on the German market', as I have called it, and the decade-long German trade offensive should not obscure this predominance.[11] State enterprises accounted for 15 per cent of Yugoslavia's industrial capital by 1938, adding the one large German investment in the country that year – the rolling mill and other facilities to turn the Zenica iron works into a modern steel mill. Otherwise, state investment for rearmament was concentrated in Serbia, a decision duly noted among the leadership of Zagreb banks and Croatian enterprises. They had just paid a considerable price in lost timber and cement sales to Italy when the same Stojadinovic government in Belgrade decided to honour the League of Nation's sanctions against Italy for the 1935 conquest of Ethiopia.

The Soviet-style economy that Tito's communist regime was initially determined to construct had no place for an independent banking sector, let alone any prospect for western participation. The desire to depart from the Soviet pattern after the break with Stalin in 1948 and an unhappy experience with central planning combined to decentralize the economy's direction. But the republic as well as central party leadership was still determined to industrialize as rapidly as possible. Manufacturing and mining had after all, despite the new investments noted above, comprised just 6 per cent of Yugoslavia's fixed assets in 1929 and 8 per cent in 1939, according to Ivo Vinski's calculations, despite the new investment noted above.[12] By 1960 Yugoslavia's manufacturing sector had caught up with agricultural production and doubled it by 1970 to account for one-third of social product. From 1955 onwards, an initially still centralized set of banks played what Ljubisa Adamovic has called an ambiguous role in that growth.[13]

By the 1970s a decentralized set of large commercial banks, still 'socially owned', was supporting industrial enterprises largely in their own republic with long-term as well as short-term credits. Bank credits had jumped from one per cent to 43 per cent of investment in the entire social sector between 1960 and 1970.[14] As Yugoslav inflation accelerated with budget and trade deficits, West-European and especially American banks became a necessary partner in keeping the supply of new credit coming. Their hard currency was needed first to pay for industrial imports, including suddenly high-priced oil, and then to service repayment of earlier credits. The unhappy end to this connection during the 1980s is well known, but it needs recalling here to understand how the entire process drove a further wedge between Belgrade and Zagreb, and hence the Serbs and Croats whose constructive engagement in the development of the whole country's economy was needed if Yugoslavia was to survive.

We may speak of a separate banking sector in Yugoslavia from 1955, when Tito's regime created three specialized banks in Belgrade outside the central bank to provide credit for foreign trade, investment and agriculture. By the next year, the foreign trade bank, Jugobanka, had already established a commercial relationship for American transactions with the renowned Chase Manhattan Bank of New York. It took until 1967 for the Jugobanka to free itself from the need of a supporting guarantee from the central bank, the Narodna banka Jugoslavije, in order to qualify for import loans from the official US Export–Import Bank in Washington.

The Eximbank's underwriting of some US$3.2 billion in Yugoslav purchases of American goods from 1967 to 1989 would nearly match the total amount of direct US aid over the previous period 1947–66. A further impressive sum for this later period, if backdated to start in 1960, is the US$4 billion in World Bank loans extended to the Yugoslav federal government, primarily to build up infrastructure and agriculture. Here were two sources of official support unavailable to interwar Yugoslavia, set in a framework of falling trade barriers and an unprecedented increase in trade volume across the entire continent of Europe. To what extent either institutions' loans continued to favour the country's economic integration, after a promising start, calls for further study.

Despite a limited amount of short-term trade credit through the Jugobanka, the involvement of western banks with the Yugoslav financial system remained insignificant until the mid-1970s, the start of a less easy period. Western bank readiness to lend rapidly accumulating petrodollars at longer terms and in large amounts brought them to the attention of a new set of Yugoslav banks. These were the republic successors to the single investment bank in Belgrade that was subdivided along with the agricultural bank in 1974 as part of the confederal bargain over a new constitution. They joined some 160 'basic' or commercial banks that also did business largely within republic borders, despite the intention of the 1965 economic reform that created them that they should extend credit countrywide. By 1975 the new republic investment banks were allowed to act for themselves and for associations of republic banks in borrowing directly from the waiting western capital market.[15]

The largest and for our purposes most important successors to the Investbanka were the Beobanka in the Belgrade and the Privredna banka Zagreba (PBZ). By going their separate ways, they weakened the integration of the Yugoslav economy and also stored up debt problems that would accelerate inflation by the 1980s. The PBZ led the turn to medium- and long-term loans from American banks, and the others followed. It secured US$17 million from the Manufacturers Hannover Trust of New York in 1977 and another US$70 million from other American and also West-European banks. The great majority of the PBZ borrowing went directly to Croatia's INA petroleum and Elektroprivreda energy enterprises whose large deposits gave them a decisive influence in bank policy, again under the terms of the 1965 economic reform. From 1977 the PZB and the other republic investment banks could secure their western loans by issuing bonds, instruments somewhat comparable to the stock issues in enterprises themselves that the Zagreb banks had offered in the mid-1920s.

The sum of this activity during the period 1970–79 greatly increased the share of total Yugoslav foreign debt that was private, from 44 to 71 per cent, and unguaranteed, from 26 to 68 per cent. The debt share of financial credits, now increasingly from private western banks, jumped from 28 to 42 per cent, while the proportion owed to the World Bank and other international agencies fell from 19 to 13 per cent. The bulk of the decade's borrowing, some 60 per cent, was none the less used to import industrial equipment, with 35 per cent for repayment of past loans and 5 per cent for import of raw materials.[16]

With the second oil shock of 1979, however, American and West-European banks offered new and longer term loans, now to cover a rising trade deficit as much as more expensive imports. By 1983 the share of these credits largely from western banks had risen again to 52 per cent of Yugoslavia's foreign debt. Those banks had provided US$1.5 billion of new loans in 1979 alone, and Yugoslavia's total foreign debt touched US$20 billion. Individual American banks now banded together with several European partners to consider only syndicated or joint loans to spread perception of growing risk. The PZB was particularly hard pressed because of the INA's need to pay for more expensive oil imports. Its involvement in a once promising petro-chemical project with Dow Chemical on the Adriatic coast was producing no profits. The problems of the Zagreb bank had come to a head in 1982 when it failed to make payments on an oil loan from New York's Citibank. The failure might have been taken less seriously had the Manufacturers Hannover Trust and several partners not failed to raise half a billion dollars for a new syndicated loan to the PZB and other Yugoslav banks just months before. Now Citibank and its partners could not secure even US$200 million from western capital markets for an emergency Yugoslav loan.

The subsequent western effort to reschedule Yugoslavia's foreign debt so as to avoid the renunciation that damaged the Bulgarian economy so badly in 1990 need not be recalled in detail. The official American lead in organizing the Friends of Yugoslavia and the consortium's provision of US$600 million in new credit and rescheduling of US$1.4 billion in existing debt for 1983 and more of both for 1984 is described elsewhere.[17]

More significant for our purposes is the predominance of private American banks and the International Monetary Fund (IMF) in the consortium of creditors and the response of the Yugoslav republic banks most heavily indebted. Six American banks had sufficient commitments in unpaid loans to win places on the consortium; one bank only represented Western Europe and one Japan. Nor could the consortium have been assembled without the financial contribution and direct participation in the negotiations of the IMF, another of the post-1945 international institutions that did not exist in the interwar period. Its terms for subsequent standby credits to complete the Yugoslav recovery in 1985–86 were criticized by the country's communist leadership and the credits abandoned by 1987. In the meantime, however, the PZB and the other republic investment banks had prudently allocated the credits received for reprogramming their outstanding debts.[18]

What did not happen, until it was too late in 1990, was the political decision by that communist leadership to follow the IMF's principal if belated recommendation to face up to the same task that has confronted literally every European government in the 1990s. That is to reduce its own budgetary deficits to a manageable level and to allow its central bank independent of political control to use its powers to restrain currency emissions regardless of regional demands. Within such a framework western banks cautious after their losses from reckless lending of petro-dollars in the 1970s can still provide essential credit to the South-east European economies starved of capital by the wars of Yugoslav succession. But the initiative, as I have argued earlier in this paper, will have to come from the commercial banks of South-east Europe, hopefully free from the bonds to politically managed enterprises from which the investment banks of the former Yugoslavia could not free themselves until, like much else of promise in that lost land, it was too late. Western banks will at the same time have to reward such austerity more significantly than they did during the 1920s.

Notes

1. Marvin R. Jackson, 'Company management and capital market development in transition', in J.R. Lampe (ed.) *Creating Capital Markets in Eastern Europe*, Washington DC: Woodrow Wilson Center Press, 1992, pp. 57–74.
2. Jurgen Kocka, 'Entrepreneurs and managers in German Industrialization', in P. Mathias and M.M. Postan (eds) *Cambridge Economic History of Europe*, vol. VII, pt 1, Cambridge: Cambridge University Press, 1978, pp. 555–70.
3. For details see John R. Lampe, *Yugoslavia as History. Twice there was a Country*, Cambridge: Cambridge University Press, 1996, pp. 271–92 and 308–15.
4. John R. Lampe, 'Unifying the Yugoslav economy: misery and early misunderstanding, 1918–1921', in D. Djordjevic, *The Creation of Yugoslavia, 1914–1918*, Santa Barbara, Calif.: ABC Clio Press, 1980, pp. 139–56.
5. Linda Killen, *Testing the Peripheries: US–Yugoslav Economic Relations in the Interwar Years*, East European Monographs, New York: Columbia University Press, 1994, pp. 55–6 and 100–101.
6. J.R. Lampe and M.R. Jackson, *Balkan Economic History, 1550–1950. From Imperial Borderlands to Developing Nations*, Bloomington, Ind.: Indiana University Press, 1982, p. 396.
7. V. Rozenberg and J. Kostic, *Ko financira jugoslovensku privredu* (Who finances the Yugoslav economy), Belgrade: Balkanska stampa, 1940, pp. 66–72.
8. Lampe and Jackson, op. cit., p. 425.
9. Rosenberg and Kostic, op. cit., pp. 25–68.
10. R. Notel, 'International finance and monetary reforms', in M.C. Kaser and E.A. Radice, *The Economic History of Eastern Europe, 1919–1975*, vol. II, Oxford: Clarendon Press, 1986, pp. 277–83.
11. Lampe, *Yugoslavia as History*, op. cit., pp. 177–80.
12. Alice Teichova, 'Industry', in M.C. Kaser and E.A. Radice, *The Economic History of Eastern Europe, 1919–1975*, vol. I., Oxford: Clarendon Press, 1986, p. 290.
13. J.R. Lampe, R.O. Prickett and L. Adamovic, *Yugoslav–American Economic Relations since the Second World War*, Durham, NC: Duke University Press, 1990, pp. 89–92.
14. Table 10.1 in Lampe, *Yugoslavia as History*, op. cit., p. 311.
15. Lampe, Prickett and Adamovic, op. cit., pp. 89–91 and S.L. Woodward, *Socialist Unemployment. The Political Economy of Yugoslavia, 1945–1990*, Princeton, NJ: Princeton University Press, 1995, pp. 230, 253.
16. Lampe, Prickett and Adamovic, op. cit., pp. 154–8.
17. Ibid., pp. 159–80.
18. Momcilo Cemovic, *Zasto, kako I koliko smo se duzili* (Why, how and how much we became indebted), Belgrade: Institut za unapredjenje robnog prometa, 1985, pp. 235–41.

CHAPTER TWELVE

The Role of Jews in Serbian Banking until the First World War

Danica Milić

Since the establishment of the Prva srpska banka (First Serbian Bank) in 1869 and its collapse two years later, followed by the establishment of the Prva kreditna banka (First Credit Bank) in 1882 and the Narodna banka (National Bank) in 1884, the number of financial institutions in Serbia grew year after year. They may be classified into three groups – savings banks, banks and cooperatives – and their functions as savings and credit institutions were limited to minor interventions in monetary and credit relations. The volume of available capital in banks was rather modest, particularly compared with the banks in other, economically developed communities. All major projects for the needs of domestic entrepreneurs, merchants and others required the use of capital provided through loans from foreign banks, while local credits were used if the amounts were not too high. On the eve of the Balkan Wars the sum of available capital in banks in Serbia reached 51 million current dinars of paid equity. By the end of the nineteenth century 72 banks of various types had been founded in Serbia, and by the beginning of the First World War another 115. This numerous and dispersed network of financial institutions spread throughout the country, although fragmentation and lack of concentration were its weak points. This was the main reason for immobility of available capital, hampering its faster action in efficient engagement for the country's economic development. Banks were frequently used as instruments in party confrontations. In smaller towns there were as many banks as there were political parties and instead of acting as creditors for the economy they acted as creditors of voters. Money circulation was limited and all proceeds from export trade in one year had to be paid next spring for interest on loans.[1]

Besides local banks, some foreign banks also engaged in the establishment and operation of the first domestic banks. They concluded that it was safer and more efficient to operate through direct contact and by having better insight into the method and aims of operation, as well as achieved results. Brother Andrejević's banking house was founded towards the end of the nineteenth century with the assistance of an

Austro-Hungarian banking loan, originating from the Budapest Hungarian Commercial Bank, which was affiliated with international Jewish capital. At the end of the first decade of the twentieth century the French-Serbian Bank was founded in a similar way, owing to capital originating from similar sources and acquired from French banks. Approximately at the same time the Bank of Prague also opened in Belgrade. The main tasks assumed by these banks were taking and investing foreign loans, financing industrial companies, crediting the construction of public utilities in Belgrade, and so on. Although domestic capital was insufficient to meet the credit requirement of businesses, supply of foreign capital in this way was nevertheless regarded with considerable reserve. This was exacerbated by negative experiences from the time of political crises, when banks suddenly used to raise interest rates, tighten credit terms, request repayment of debt and threaten to withdraw capital.

As far as foreign banking capital is concerned, which came through special banks organized for these purposes, there was an obvious discrepancy between a large number of attempts and very modest success. Bankers from richer countries, with well-established banking traditions and operations that yielded good results participated in these attempts. In other Balkan countries – Romania, Turkey, Greece and Bulgaria – foreign banks were founded in different ways and compared with these countries, the smallest number of foreign banks was founded in Serbia. There were some attempts to set up foreign banks with headquarters outside Serbia, with the aim of financing loans necessary to Serbia, primarily for capital construction, public utilities, construction and development of industry and some larger commercial deals. There is no doubt that favourable conditions in Serbia attracted foreign banking capital, which ultimately benefited the Serbian economy because it increased the supply of credit on the local financial market and pushed interest rates down. Local banks were reluctant to take this move because their available credit capital was limited and they believed that only higher interest rates might help them survive.

Owing to better living and working conditions the number of Jewish participants in the country's economic life was steadily increasing as the nineteenth century approached its end. Jews mainly engaged in some branches of the urban economy, crafts and trade and hardly anywhere else. Even in the urban economy they were not present in all activities. This was the consequence of their particular habits, inclination or stands regarding certain businesses. There is no doubt that wholesale and retail trade in some products, above all manufactured and industrial such as clothing and footwear, were most attractive to Jewish businessmen. They gave preference to imported products, while on the export side they preferred to deal in grain. Jewish businessmen were also middlemen, agents and freight forwarders, while their number was negligible in foodstuffs and grocery staples trade. They were not particularly involved in crafts, with the exception of tinsmiths, where Jewish contractors and craftsmen were very active in Belgrade and other cities. They also earned their living as watchmakers, opticians, making women's hats, cords, braids and decorations, etc. Moneychangers appeared in these circles, downtown and everywhere where trading took place, as early as the first decades of the nineteenth century and some of them performed larger financial transactions on behalf of rich merchants, even the Prince himself, as happened to be the case during the reign of Miloš Obrenović.

Their relative involvement in different activities changed over the years and, as we will see from the data presented here for the end of the nineteenth century and the years before the First World War, these differences are sometimes quite conspicuous. In later years, with the new development, the number of Jewish craftsmen and merchants in larger cities outside Belgrade grew. The following data about the occupation of the Jewish population in Belgrade are available for 1896–97:[2]

Agents and commissioners	15
Technical agents	3
Lawyers	3
Umbrella makers	3
Bazaar trade	2
Grocers	6
Lumber trader	1
Tobacconists	4
Grain traders	2
Dressmakers	5
PTT installers	4
Coffee shop owners	2
Cord and braid makers	3
Hat makers	1
Raw hide exporters	5
Importers of American hides	2
Tailors	11
Military uniform tailors	2
Lamps – sale, warehouse	2
Physicians	4
Tinsmiths	10
Wholesalers of manufactured goods	7
Retailers of manufactured goods	25
Furniture forwarding	1

Moneychangers	17
Milliner	1
Musical instruments, trade	3
Nuremberg goods	2
Footwear – trade	2
Footwear – making	10
Clothing trade	11
Opticians	2
Linen traders	5
Tin kitchenware, trade	3
Miscellaneous goods	8
Glass – porcelain	4
Glass cutters	2
Junk dealers	12
Upholsterers	7
Funeral company	1
Watchmaker	6
Sewing machines, sale	1
Freight forwarders	6
Dealers in agricultural products	7

Additional data about each of listed craftsmen and members of other professions reveal that some of them had been living in Belgrade for a longer time, while some were even born there. This was not the case at the end of the nineteenth century with other cities with Jewish populations which actively participated in economic and public life:[3]

Niš	
Agents and commissioners	3
Grain traders	9
Leather traders	2
Dressmaker	1
Traders in manufactured goods	11
Moneychangers	9
Mixed stores	1
Milliner	1
Clothes makers	3
Shoemaker	1
Junk dealers	2
Speculators	6
Šabac	
Grain trader	1

Tailors	2
Tinsmiths	4
Traders in manufactured goods	7
Pirot	
Trader in manufactured goods	1
Livestock trader	1
Moneychangers	2
Smederevo	
Agents/commissioners	2
Grain traders	5
Freight forwarder	1
Broker	1
Watchmakers	2
Kragujevac	
Trade in mixed goods	1
Coffee shop owner	1
Watchmaker	1
Broker	1

Data about businessmen of Jewish descent in Serbian cities have been elaborated for subsequent years, such as, for example, 1911, considered as the best in terms of economic development in Serbia in the years preceding the Balkan Wars and the First World War. Compared with previous periods, data for this year point to a higher diversity of economic occupations and more people who engaged in them. Shifts are noticeable toward occupations which render possible greater volume of operations and higher profit, which may be attributed to the progress, modernization and Europeanization of the Serbian economy at that time. There was an increasing number of businessmen who were able to contribute as shareholders to the establishment and operation of financial institutions, investing part of their accumulated profits in facilities of permanent value, either in public services or production, as well as to improve personal and family standards of living. There was an obvious differentiation among the population in the country, as well as among its segments, such as the Jewish community, as our subject of interest. Here are the relevant data:[4]

Belgrade	
Agents of foreign companies	22
Umbrella makers	2

Bazaars	3
Midwife	1
Grocers	9
Bankers	3
Embroiderers	5
Cord and braid makers	4
Hardware stores	1
Scrap metal	1
Engravers	3
Tobacconists	8
Electrical technicians	2
Class lottery	3
Bookstore	1
Leatherwear stores	2
Raw hide export	4
Export commissioners and agents	3
Suitcase making	2
Tailors	6
Dressmakers	5
Military uniform tailor	1
Upholsterer	4
Iron smelting	1
Tinsmiths	12
Pottery	1
Wholesale in manufactured products	4
Retailers in manufactured products	31
Tie makers	2
Moneychangers	10
Miscellaneous goods	19
Mill	1
Fashion accessories	1
Milliners	3
Nuremberg goods	12
Men's clothing trade	9
Women's clothing trade	3
Chemical cleaning	1
Scrap export	1
Optician	1
Sharpeners	2
Prune exporters	4
Grain exporters	5
Agricultural produce exporters	17
Trade in linen and manufactured goods	15

Pleating	4
Middleman-trade shop	1
Clothing accessories	1
Mirrors	3
Glove maker	1
Harnessing equipment	1
Glass cutters	7
Glassware – porcelain	8
Junk dealers	3
Wicker chairs	3
Carpenter's glue fabrication	1
Coal warehouse	1
Photographers	1
Customs agents – forwarders	9
Constantinople goods	1
Stockings, knitwear	2
Watchmakers	2
Chocolate production	1
Production of heavy fabrics	2
Underwear seamstresses	4
Felt hat fabrication	1
Fur hat and cap fabrication	1
Furrier	1
Bone and animal offal processing	1
Printing shop	1

The following data are available for other larger cities in the country:[5]

Kragujevac	
Export trade and warehousing	3
Traders in manufactured goods	1
Mixed goods	1
Clothing trade	3
Forwarder	1
Speculators	3
Leskovac	
Grain traders	3
Speculators	3
Niš	
Agent and commissioner	1
Grain and hide export	8

Class lottery	1
Tailors	3
Traders in manufactured goods	2
Moneychangers	3
Mechanic	1
Milliners	4
Clothing warehouse	3
Printing shop	1
Požarevac	
Trader in manufactured goods	1
Livestock traders	6
Mixed goods	2
Clothing trade	2
Soap maker	1
Freight forwarder	1
Smederevo	
Agents-commissioners	2
Vine growers	3
Grain export	3
Quilt maker	1
Traders in manufactured goods	2
Trade relations	1
Freight forwarder	1
Pirot	
Egg export	2
Tinsmith	1
Moneychangers	3
Blacksmith	1
Photographer	1
Šabac	
Cord and braid maker	1
Electrical technician	1
Grain and prune exporters	3
Tailor	3
Tinsmiths	5
Traders in manufactured goods	5
Mixed goods	3
Clothing warehouse	2

As these data show, an increase in the number of economically active members of the Jewish community by 25 per cent (from 315 to 413) within the span of some 15 years is noticeable not only in Belgrade, but in other major cities and towns in the provinces. The number of occupations also increased from 44 to 70, primarily in some lucrative businesses with considerable impact on savings, monetary and credit arrangements. The need for development of credit relations appeared quite naturally because business expansion without credit would hardly be possible. The Jewish population, which was accustomed to reliance on mutual cooperation and assistance in life and work, in most cases had the same stand when credit relations were concerned. Therefore, the emergence of the first financial institutions founded by the deposits of the Jewish population was no surprise. Among the banks established and run by Jewish capital, many were characterized by having solely Jews as founders, officers and clients. In some major Serbian banks with high capital at their disposal, some members of the board of directors were Jews, often from the most reputable and affluent families.

The following banks, in order of their emergence, belong to the first group of banks founded and operated with Jewish capital:[6]

Beogradska trgovačka štedionica, Belgrade, 1893–94
Srpsko-jevrejska trgovačka zadruga, Niš, 1893
Industrijska banka, Belgrade, 1900
Srpska banka, Belgrade, 1906
Banka Merkur, Belgrade, 1906
Saobraćajna banka, Belgrade, 1912
Kolonijalna banka, Belgrade, 1912
Jadranska banka, Belgrade, 1914

The common feature of all these banks is that they were managed and founded by Jewish businessmen with an intention to cooperate with and assist their founders and shareholders. In most cases they were not particularly rich financial organizations; by the amount of equity capital and volume of operations they were classified in the 3rd or 4th group. The first group encompassed banks with authorized capital of over 1 million dinars, enjoying the reputation of big banks; the second group with capital between 500 000 and 1 million dinars; the third group with 250 000–500 000 dinars capital; the fourth group with under 250 000 dinars. Of all the banks in Belgrade that operated before the Balkan Wars, according to this criterion ten banks would be classified in the first group, seven in the second, 13 in the third and another 13 in the fourth group.[7]

The Beogradska trgovačka štedionica (Belgrade Commercial Savings Bank) started its operation with the pooled capital of Jewish businessmen from Belgrade amounting to 320 000 dinars in silver, divided into 1 122 shares, whose 53 owners carried out this venture by themselves. The bank received deposits in silver and gold and gave loans on the basis of domestic drafts in silver and gold. According to the report for 1904, the number of drafts for loans in silver was 171, and in gold 1 251. The number of depositors in silver was 156, and in gold 48. The bank also discounted drafts. It invested its reserve fund, amounting to over 40 per cent of the paid capital, in securities issued by the Narodna banka, the Izvozna banka and the Srpsko brodarsko društvo, in lottery loans, and so on. Although this was a relatively small bank, or even a family bank given the family relations between its shareholders, the annual capital turnover could be considered satisfactory. The annual value of all transactions in 1904 exceeded 25 million dinars, and distributed dividends were 9 dinars per share, that is 9 per cent. The Beogradska trgovačka štedionica distributed 9 per cent dividends the next year too and by this indicator was the second best bank, after the Prometna banka. This was unquestionably one of the indicators of successful performance.[8] The bank was under the management of prominent businessmen: president Dr David Alkalai, lawyer and member of the management; Benzion Buli, banker and MP; Abraham Mošić, industrialist; Isaac Azriel, merchant; Isaac Tajtacaković, also merchant; Solomon Nisim, exporter; David Cohen, merchant; and Nachman Amar, trade agent. Adolf Reshovsky, merchant, was the president of the supervisory committee and members included A.M. Mevorah, trade agent; A.S. Lević, bookkeeper; Isaac M. Farki, merchant; and Reuben Farki, commissioner and freight forwarder.[9] Among the shareholders, the following families were represented: Michael, Armand, Mida, Alfred and Rika M. Levi with 55 shares; David J. Cohen and children Pepi, Leon, Burlući, Sultana with 105 shares; Nachman S. Amar and children Sali, Solomon, Meti and N. Amar with 39 shares; Chaim D. Azriel and children Victor, Rachel and Leon with 84 shares; Max and Sabina Alkalai with 35 shares; Abraham Mošić and children Buhas, Nathalie, Leon and David with 95 shares; Benzion Buli with 42 shares, Dr David Alkalai with 125 shares, and so on. Among the shareholders there was a negligible number of Serbs, including Josif Manojlović with ten shares, Kosta Marković with 22 shares and Milan Stojilović with six shares.[10]

One of the early financial institutions was the Srpsko-jevrejska trgovačka zadruga u Nišu (Serbian-Jewish Commercial Cooperative in Niš), founded in 1883, with Solomon Ruso as president.[11] This bank had 1 884 paid shares, and in 1904, according to the annual financial statement, it operated with positive result, while dividend per share was 4.5 per cent.

Both economic and political circumstances at the time of the establishment of the Srpska banka (Serbian Bank) in 1906 differed considerably from those when the first Jewish banks began operations. These differences were rather favourable taking into consideration the accelerated development pace of the Serbian economy, credit and financial market, better organization of the government and legislation, and increased interest of the European market for Serbian goods and vice-versa. However, at that time a crisis was caused by the Austro-Hungarian–Serbian Customs War (1906–1911), which considerably deteriorated some of the conditions. All former contractual relations with Austria-Hungary, under which business had been going on, became questioned, particularly those governing foreign trade. The Serbian export trade, which used to export mainly raw materials and intermediaries, faced the problem of finding new ways and opportunities to penetrate new markets to maintain its uninterrupted continuity. Modification of the structure of Serbian exports was also contemplated, partially through the establishment of the country's own consumer products industry, particularly canning. This allowed access to farther markets.

The newly founded Srpska banka, with authorized capital of 300 000, ranked in the fourth group by size, and among 54 shareholders 19 were from the Jewish community. As in other cases, they represented several families: Robert, Ilona, Charlotte, Marianne and Rene Azriel, a merchant family possessing 160 shares; Nachman Abraham, merchant, with 30 shares; Jacob M. Azriel, employee of this bank, with his family Victor, Rudi, Solomon and Leon, also merchants, owned 150 shares; Bertold Goldstein, merchant, had 30 shares; Nandor Gutman, bank employee, 15 shares; Mita Azriel, merchant, 30 shares; Jacob Alfandari, merchant, 15 shares; Elias Levi, merchant, 16 shares; Josif Levi, freight-forwarder, six shares; Abraham S. Barukić had three shares, as much as Moshe Amar, employee. This bank was considered Jewish, although only some shareholders came from that community. However, the way shares were distributed offered the opportunity to this section of shareholders, who shared not only business interests but family ties, to agree upon and vote for what they found favourable disregarding the intentions of other shareholders, who came from different sides and did not have much communication with each other. The bank also dealt with credits, loans and other transactions. It was connected to certain economic sectors and this fact is reflected in its organization: the technical department used to solely sell steam threshing machines manufactured by the English firm Marshall, Son and Co., while another department engaged in purchase, storage and sale of high-caloric coal, above all from Silesia and Bosnia.[12]

Another Jewish bank – the Merkur – was also founded in 1906, with equity capital amounting to 250 000 dinars, divided into 2 500 shares. The predecessor of this bank was the Merkur Insurance Company founded in 1896 for operation with lottery. It collected savings from the poorer and middle-class population and bought lottery tickets and later distributed proceeds to depositors for their daughters' dowries or for expansion of business activity. In changing economic and political circumstances at the beginning of the twentieth century, conditions for successful operation of this company deteriorated because the value of government and tobacco lottery tickets and bonds increased considerably above their nominal value and it was no longer profitable to buy them for profit through resale or lottery, which previously yielded good returns as a supplement for profit distribution. This new development motivated the members of the management to ask the authorities for permission to transform the company into 'a modern banking institution to ensure better business operation, deposits and support to the members when needed'. At the end of their application the founders of the new bank added comment on the company's former operation: 'the company gathered a large number of members of average and poorer material-standing and developed companionship'.[13] This move again enabled a larger number of shareholders – including poorer ones – to pool their resources. There was a total of 203 shareholders. In this mass, we encounter some familiar names from business circles: Solomon Azriel with 20 shares; brothers Alien de Mayo 50 shares and Ams de Mayo 30 shares; Adolf Reshovsky 20 shares; Michael Aaron Levi 20 shares; Abraham S. Amar 25 shares; David M. Levi 50 shares; Leventay Joshua 25 shares; David Israel Ruso 50 shares; Israel Josif Ruso 20 shares; Sabina de Majorović 20 shares. Among larger shareholders we notice several Serb names, already familiar from cooperation in mixed banks: Miloš Zdravković with 30 shares; Pera Natošević 50 shares; P.P. Bajić 40 shares; Aleksa Ilić 30 shares; Josif Manojlović 30 shares. The bank's founders, quite predictably, were well-known merchants Abraham H. Geran, Elim Rauman, Michael A. Levi, Sabitaj de Majorović, Solomon M. de Mayo, Jacob Benvenista, David Adanya, Isaac J. Arosti and Nisim Calderon. Then there were moneychangers David M. Levi and Josif Manojlović, as well as trade agents Pera D. Natošević, Josif S. Melanon and, among others, Jacob K. Čelebonović, lawyer.

In the reports for subsequent years, which record the bank's successful performance, a smaller number of shareholders is mentioned, probably as the result of greater mobility in operation.[14]

In 1911 another Jewish bank was founded under the name Kolonijalna banka (Colonial Bank). Its equity capital was 500 000 dinars, ranking it in the third group by amount of capital. According to the balance for

1912 the assets were four times the amount of equity, but the operation did not yield any considerable profit, which is why the bank did not distribute dividend to its shareholders. The bank manager was David M. Levi, president of the board of directors was Adolf Reshovsky and members were Jacob Benvenista, Isaac J. Levi, Josif Alkalai, Jacques Buli, Nachman J. Levi and Samuel A. Amar. Max S. Alkalai and Jacob S. Daviĉo were members of the supervisory committee. As we can see, many names of these prominent businessmen are already familiar as shareholders or officials of other banks.[15]

The Saobraćajna banka (Traffic Bank) was founded in 1912 with Serbian and Jewish capital with the aim of mediating in export trade, engaging in agency deals, discount, loans and other banking transactions. The equity capital of this bank was only 125 000 dinars, but already in the first year of operation the assets reached four times that amount. Other data about the bank are not available.[16]

In some banks with higher capital, which participated in financing and other banking operations, among officials, besides the Serbian businessmen and politicians, appear some wealthier Jews, who were engaged in operation and management of these banks. This was the case with the Eskontna banka (Discount Bank), founded with capital of 500 000 dinars in silver. The first board of directors included Solomon Azriel and Abraham S. Cohen, merchants, who were also involved in other banks, above all Jewish. As a shareholder, S. Azriel owned 20 shares and the right to six votes, and A. Cohen ten shares and three votes. Compared to other shareholders, this was obviously insufficient to ensure any considerable influence on the bank's operation. Their presence was certainly aimed at providing links with other banks and similar financial institutions or companies. The biggest shareholder of this bank was Dragomir V. Radulović, banker, who owned 800 shares of the 1 245 issued. The Eskontna banka performed very well within its scope of operation, both as creditor, financier of industrial enterprises, and as a savings bank. More deals were transacted using the gold standard than silver, mostly in savings deposits and taking loans against drafts, although at Lombard more depositors (1 446) deposited their money in silver than in gold (only 208). What is interesting is that the total amount of deposits was identical in both cases. However, in giving loans against lien, more transactions were with gold than with silver. Such operations rendered possible the distribution of dividends amounting to 9 per cent, while 5 per cent of the profits were allocated to a reserve fund. Although containing the word 'discount' in its name, this bank was not the leader in this type of transaction because other larger banks with higher capital could discount to a greater extent. The leader in discount deals was certainly the Beogradska zadruga, followed by the Vračarska zadruga i štedionica, and so on.[17]

The Izvozna banka (Export Bank) was undoubtedly above many other banks very significant in the economic life of the country, particularly in foreign trade. At its establishment in 1901 its equity was declared in the amount of 5 million dinars and 50 000 shares. However, annual balance sheets for subsequent years reveal that the amount of paid capital was considerably lower: in 1904 only 2 348 460 dinars were paid, and in 1911 the bank's capital was declared in the amount of 2 500 000 dinars, that is 25 000 shares at 1 000 dinars each. Transactions of the Izvozna banka defined in its statute in 1901 include giving loan against lien for livestock, grain, prunes and construction of storage facilities, purchase of miscellaneous goods and their sale, discount and rediscount of drafts issued by merchants-exporters, issuing of cheques and other financial and banking operations.[18]

The founders and later members of the board of directors and supervisory committee were the most reputable Belgrade merchants-exporters, commissioners, industrialists and rentiers, as well as politicians, such as, for example Milovan Milovanović. In 1904 a member of the bank's supervisory committee was Abraham Cohen, and in 1911 Chaim D. Azriel and Dr David Alkalai were on the bank's board of directors. We do not know whether and how the participation of these businessmen from Jewish circles influenced the operation of the Izvozna banka, and whether it rendered any benefit to themselves and their fellow countrymen. We are also lacking many other data that would enlighten the inside life of that business community, since the archives of the Belgrade banks for the early years of their operation have been destroyed. This fact is very unfortunate because this archive contained data not only on the banking operation but also about the financial power of individuals, about capital formation from accumulated profit generated in foreign trade and about investments, mutual credit relations and so on. As for the Izvozna banka, its performance was rather successful, although its dividends did not exceed 6 per cent. In this bank, 10 per cent of profit was allocated to a reserve fund. The bank was particularly active during the export season, when all resources were employed for credits to finance export, storage space, trips to foreign markets and export control. Then this bank too, lacking sufficient amounts of its own resources, took loans from the National Bank.[19]

Although the Industrijska banka (Industrial Bank), founded in 1890, was not considered purely Jewish, its top officials were all Jewish businessmen, with the exceptions of Vladislav Kostović, director and president of the board of directors and Mihailo Ilić and Joca Marković, members of the management. Benzion Buli and Chaim Melamed were members of the board of directors, while A.S. Lević, Friedrich Pops and Moshe Melamed were members of the supervisory committee.[20]

Among the founders of the Jadranska banka, headed by Dragoljub Milovanović, director of the French company Union, we encounter many familiar names of merchants from Belgrade as well as those from Smederevo, Požarevac, Kragujevac and Negotin. Marko Baruh was the only Jewish businessman. The authorized capital of this bank was stated at 1 million dinars in silver. The main tasks of the bank were to organize domestic and foreign consortia to create cooperative communities and general consumer cooperatives for staple foods, developing the dairy industry, building bakeries in Belgrade and Serbia, four hotels, the construction of shared flats in Belgrade and surroundings and the construction of summer resorts and sanatoriums, public transport facilities and public baths. The bank also performed other banking operations.[21]

A separate group of banks with some Jewish capital were the biggest banks in Serbia, founded by foreign capital, which was partly Jewish. We do not know to what extent this capital was involved because the archives of these banks were not accessible to us. As early as 1882 the Srpska kreditna banka (Serbian Credit Bank) was founded in Belgrade with capital from the Länderbank Wien and French capital, which was reflected in the composition of the board of directors: baron Otton Bourgoin, of French descent, member of the administration of the Länderbank Wien and the Union-bank; Charles Dührenberg, member of the administrative council of the Monopoly Administration in Serbia; Moritz Koritschoner, former director of the Länderbank; Hans Schuschmi, director of the Länderbank; Maximilian Marski, director of the Srpska kreditna banka; and Maurice Dumie, railway director. Oscar Ritter, Markus Robert, Arnold Deitsch, Fleischer and others were influential representatives of Austrian-Jewish capital in the work of the Srpska kreditna banka.[22] From Belgrade business circles came Abraham Ozerović, merchant and member of Parliament, David Simić and another four Serbian merchants. The equity capital, amounting to 1.2 million dinars, was paid in gold, and annual financial statements indicate that 10 per cent of profits were allocated to a reserve fund, while dividends to shareholders were paid at the rate of 5 per cent. It is interesting that as a rule the dividend rate in larger and more successful banks was lower than in some smaller banks, which may be explained by their desire to attract more shareholders by this demagogic gesture.

For nearly three decades the Srpska kreditna banka was the only bank in Serbia founded by foreign capital, used to lend credit to merchants and industrialists. It had branch offices in Obrenovac, Smederevo and Šabac. The director of the Länderbank Wien, Maximilian Kraus, as the vice-president of this bank participated in the expansion of its operation: leather factory Đurić-Barlovac, joint-stock company. Furthermore, during the annexation crisis, contrary to many expectations that a bank with Austrian capital would cease lending to merchants in Serbia, M. Kraus insisted on quite contrary policy. He even demanded that the credits increase, and he pursued the same policy at the time of the Balkan Wars.[23]

The Peštanska mađarska trgovačka banka (Hungarian Commercial Bank of Pest),[24] which was thought to have been founded by Jewish capital, had already in the nineteenth century established business connections with the Belgrade bank of Dimitrije and Lazar Andrejevič, founded in 1882, turning it gradually into its stronghold. The operations of this Budapest bank in Serbia referred to trade in tobacco, government loans and the purchase of Serbian government bonds, minting of Serbian silver coins, etc.[25] In 1910 this Pest bank, together with the Berlin Commercial Company – another bank – turned the banking house Andrejević and Co. into a joint-stock bank with a new branch office in Niš, besides the existing business foothold in Pavle Bojić's bank in Šabac, later renamed the Ńabačka štedionica (Šabac Savings Bank).[26] Paid authorized capital amounting to 1 million dinars ranked this bank among the larger. The bank manager was Maximilian Oppenheimer, while members of the board of directors, besides Vasa Radulović and Milisav Radivojević, and other major businessmen from Belgrade and Pest, included Chaim Israel, Louis Büchler, Charles Dührenberg, Charles Fürstenberg, Edmund Schweiger, Filip Weiss and James Zutrauen. Besides Vasa M. Mijović and Jovan D. Andrejević, members of the supervisory committee were Leon von Bido, Karl Sonnenfeld and Isidor Horowitz. The bank was considered to be very successful and was treated as the dominant in Belgrade, according to French sources. However, unlike other banks, it affected the price of gold by artificially raising agio on gold.[27] It was also involved with large loans which came from France. The bank's task was to receive the loan proceeds, carefully and purposefully administer the loan and make sure that creditors' assets were not wasted.

Besides other indicators of economic stabilization and emancipation in foreign trade through penetration of new markets, trends on the financial market in Serbia are also mentioned among the facts that illustrate ways to overcome the economic crisis caused by the Customs War. The novelty was in the fact that large foreign money suppliers appeared in the form of the Francusko-srpska banka (French-Serbian Bank) and a branch of the Praška banka (Bank of Prague). Our attention here is drawn to a group of French banks which decided to expand into Serbia, primarily offering credit. They had in view some major projects in Belgrade, such as sewerage construction and paving of streets, as well as the construction of four railway lines: Niš–Knjaževac, Belgrade–Mala Krsna, Gornji Milanovac–Čačak and Požarevac–Mala Krsna.[28] At the same time, capital of the existing Belgrade banks also increased. For example, 20 per cent growth was recorded during 1911 alone, taking into consideration cash collections and transactions with drafts and cheques. Already towards the end of the first year in business the Francusko-srpska banka had a higher amount of available resources than other Belgrade banks and in case of greater need for capital to meet its obligations, the bank could always get additional resources and loans from its parent bank in Paris. It could also sell its securities. Towards the end of 1911 it was the second-largest Serbian bank in Belgrade (after the Srpska kreditna banka), and the amount of credit it took from its foreign founders was eight- or nine-fold higher than its equity.[29] From the history of this successful bank we learn that its founders were the following French banks: Banque Impériale Ottoman, Banque de l'Union Parisienne, Banque française pour Commerce et l'Industrie de Paris, Société financière d'Orient, Société Générale pour favoriser le developement de Commerce et de l'Industrie en France, Banque N.J.A. Bardac and Banque Hoskier and S. The authorized capital amounted to 12 million francs, divided into 24 000 shares at 500 francs each. The bank was managed by an eightmember board of directors and the director. From among influential Serbian citizens the board of directors elected the advisory committee for a two-year term. Members of the first advisory committee were L. Paču, representing the board of directors of the Zemaljska banka, a certain Drašković, president of the board of the Izvozna banka, Milovan Milovanović, one of the bank's main shareholders and Minister of Foreign Affairs in the Radical's government and, finally, Voja Veljković, representative of the Vračarska zadruga, considered to be the Liberals' bank.[30]

As the exponent of foreign capital, which used the bank as its mediator in lending capital and in closing major deals with the government, for example military purchases and capital construction, the bank was quite naturally the focus of attention of many observers. Above all, domestic businessmen critically accepted the arrival of foreign capital and then monitored its actions proceeding from both the interests of the country and their own. As with the previously founded bank Andrejević i kompanija (Andréevitch et Cie), this bank was considered to be founded with a special task – to exploit government and private securities and participate in attractive tenders and thus ensure advantage, although its terms were often no better than those offered by other bidders. The bank was even suspected of engaging in some behind-the-scenes activities, above all between members of the board of directors and creditors, and even other persons involved in decision-making about loan and tender.[31]

On the eve of the First World War another Jewish-Serbian bank was founded with capital from the Budapest Hungarian Bank and the Commercial Joint-Stock Company of the same city. The following names are mentioned among the founders of the bank Otadžbina (Fatherland):[32] Franz Szekely, director of the Budapest bank, and besides him Bruno Brun, Bela Selai, Julius Bern, Alkan Gerasi (the latter from Belgrade), as well as Michael Levi and E.M. Raumann, merchants from Belgrade, Jacques Buli, rentier from Belgrade, and Shemaya de Mayo. The other five members-founders were Serbian merchants from Belgrade. Other details about the operation of this bank are not available.

The presented data, which depend on the availability of archive material and the extent of its research, as well as known facts about the development of banking capital in Serbia in general, offer ground for conclusions about the participation of Jewish capital in banking. All available data are certainly insufficient to meet the requirements of a monograph and call for further research, additions and comparative research in other Balkan countries as well as additional study of the development of banking in Serbia. However, what appears clearly according to the available data is one specific feature associated with the development of Jewish banks. According to their function, they focused above all on a kind of mutual assistance to their fellow countrymen, either merchants with higher needs and requirements or craftsmen, whose needs for financing were much more modest, and even to other parts of the population in emergency situations. Quite naturally, in their operation these banks followed the same practices that were customary in other banks, with whom they cooperated in professional matters. Furthermore, Jewish capital was not excluded from the operation of other banks, either domestic, where merchants and wealthier members of the Serbian business community played the main role, or where the banks were founded and supported by foreign capital. Whether the participation of Jewish businessmen was fully identical and equitable to that of the others can hardly be concluded on the basis of available data, particularly since in such cases the Jews were a numerical minority. However, this is subject to some assumptions because affluent businessmen, quite certainly, were much more numerous among the Serbian population than among the minority Jewish population, and this could as well be the criterion to assess the number and influence of participants. Certain confusion is caused by blank statements occasionally encountered in literature about the wealth and power of Jewish banking circles and which cannot be ascertained in the cases discussed here. This more refers to a phenomenon that normally fits into the general development of social and economic relations of the given period, where successful functioning of banks – when Jewish banking capital, either domestic or foreign was concerned – was solely or in most cases the result of good organization, professional attitude and observance of the rules of the game.

Notes

1. V. Balkitch, *Monnaies, banques et bourses en Serbie*, Paris, 1919. S. Kukla, *Razvitak kreditne organizacije u Srbiji* (Development of credit organization in Serbia), Zagreb, 1924; N. Stanarević, *Razvitak kreditne organizacije u Srbiji* (Development of credit organization in Serbia), Zagreb, 1924; D. Milić, 'Pregled delatnosti stranog kapitala u Srbiji do Prvog svetskog rata' (Review of activity of foreign capital in Serbia until the First World War), *Istorijski pregled*, 2, Zagreb, 1964, pp. 94–111.
2. *Trgovinsko-zanatlijsko-industrijski šematizam Srbije za 1986–7* (Professional directory of trade, crafts and industry in Serbia for 1986–7); this directory lists names, often the addresses of members of certain professions, although not data on their national affiliation. In the case of Jewish businessmen, members of this nationality could be identified with fair certainty by name, although in the case of Ashkenazis this was sometimes difficult, since their names were Germanized and therefore very similar to German, so that mistakes are possible. However, we think that these mistakes could be only minor and would not substantially affect the value of the data.
3. Ibid.
4. *Trgovinsko-zanatlijsko-industrijski šematizam Kraljevine Srbije za 1911. godinu* (Professional directory of trade, crafts and industry in the Kingdom of Serbia for 1911).
5. Ibid.
6. *Compas*, 1924/III.
7. Stanarevič, op. cit., *Ekonomist*, No. 2, 1912, p. 22.
8. *Archives of Serbia* (hereinafteer: *AS*), Ministry of National Economy (MNP), T, 1908, section V, gr. 6, 3; MNP, T, 1906, F. II, Rn 66.
9. *AS*, MNP, T, 1905, F. II, Rn 66.
10. *AS*, MNP, T, 1908, section V, gr. 6, 3; *Compas*, 1924/III.
11. *AS*, MNP, T, 1905, F. II, Rn 66; *Compas*, 1924/III; *Sloboda* paper, No. 63, Niš 1893.
12. *AS*, MNP, T, 1912, unfiled, 251–1007; T, 1913, b.b.; T, 1914, No. 634; *Compas*, 1924/III.
13. *AS*, MNP, T, 1906, F. XXV, 3.
14. *AS*, MNP, T, 1912, unfiled 5–231, 1085.
15. *AS*, MNP, T, 1912, unfiled, no number.
16. *AS*, MNP, T, 1914, 2627.
17. Stanarević, op. cit., *Ekonomist*, 1912, No. 3, p. 38.
18. Kukla, op. cit.; *Archives of Yugoslavia*, F. 152; Izvozna banka, Beograd, 1901, 30.
19. Ibid.

20. *AS*, MNP, T, 1914, No. 6014–7498.
21. *AS*, MNP, T, 1914, No. 3108–3998.
22. *AS*, MNP, T, 1905, F. II, Rn 66.
23. *AS*, Military General Government of Serbia, K 20, 0214.
24. *Encyclopedia Judaica*, V, 4, B, p. 176, mentions that the *Pester Ungarische Commerzialbank* was founded in 1841 by Moritz Ullmann.
25. A. Mitrović, 'Pester Ungarische Commerzialbank na Balkanu do 1918. godine' (Pester Ungarische Commerzialbank in the Balkans until 1918), *Zbornik matice srpske za istoriju*, No. 34, 1986, p. 47.
26. Kukla, op. cit., p. 74; Mitrović, op. cit.; *AS*, MNP, T, 1910, unfiled.
27. Mitrović, op. cit.; Kukla, op. cit., p. 74.
28. Stanarević, op. cit., *Ekonomist*, 1912, p. 21.
29. Ibid., p. 54.
30. Lj. Aleksić-Pejković, *Odnosi Srbije sa Francuskom i Engleskom* (Serbia's relations with France and England), Belgrade, 1965, pp. 289–91; *Haus-, Hof- und Staatsarhiv*, Vienna, AR, F 23, Sub 5/50836, 1917.
31. *Trgovinski glasnik*, 1912, No. 12; *Mali žurnal*, 11–18 August 1910; *Štampa*, 10 August 1910, No. 218; *Samouprava*, 17 August 1910.
32. *Otadžbina* bank according to the data in *AS*, MNP, T, 1914, No. 6014–7498.

CHAPTER THIRTEEN

The Position and Role of French Finance in the Balkans from the Late Nineteenth Century until the Second World War

Alain Plessis and Olivier Feiertag

The place and role of French finance in the Balkans at the end of the nineteenth century
(by Alain Plessis)

At the end of the last century, the Balkan states did not present much interest to French finance. French capital registered in the area amounted in 1902 to 970 million French francs, that is one-seventh of the French capital placed in Russia and 3 per cent of all the 'French fortune in foreign countries'.[1] To what degree did this situation change, during the years preceding the Great War, a period of new vigour for capitalism, and during which the Balkan states appeared as the European powder keg?

Just before the First World War, the Balkan states were still a region of secondary interest for French capital. According to some estimates its total amount represented 2.5 to 3 million francs,[2] that is approximately 1 million in Greece, slightly less in Serbia, and half that in Bulgaria and in Romania. By that time capital placed in Russia amounted to 11.3 million francs according to H. Feis. French capital in this area was far inferior to British capital (4.3 million francs) and barely surpassed that from Germany.

However, it is in this area that the flow of French capital increased faster after the end of the nineteenth century. Between 1902 and 1914 its stock doubled or trebled, when it was only progressing by 60 per cent in Russia and in the rest of the world.

This acceleration of French investments in the area took place during the Balkan Wars. These young states had increasing capital needs for arming themselves and modernizing their countries; at the same time other powerful countries, such as Russia, inspired less confidence.

This is why the Balkan securities, with their high interest, concerned people who were looking for a personal income; they were then considered 'additional sources of value', recommended warmly by economists and financial newspapers. The persistent demand for capital from this part of Europe was a powerful motive for French banks to develop their relations with the Balkan countries.

As usual, the export of capital was mostly organized and guided by banks, who set up financial operations and constituted syndicates of loans issue. Here, it was the old families representing the 'Haute Banque' who played the leading role. At first, indirectly, they were involved in many businesses through the Banque Impériale Ottomane and through the Banque de l'Union Parisienne (BUP). Up to 80 per cent of the capital of the Banque Impériale Ottomane, created in 1863, had belonged since 1880 to French capitalists and its board of management consisted of representatives of the 'Haute Banque' such as Mallet, Hottinguer, Mirabaud, etc.[3] While this bank was mostly concerned with the Asiatic part of the Ottoman Empire, the BUP, created in 1904 by the same families, favoured investments in Eastern Europe.

Moreover, as the Rothschild name rarely appears (particularly concerning Romanian petroleum), the above mentioned Protestant Haute Banque companies operated for their proper account in the placing of many Balkan securities in the West-European capital markets. They also preserved significant quantities of them in their portfolios, testifying in this way to the permanent relations thus maintained with this part of Europe. In the Banque Mallet et Cie's balance sheet, a bank which nevertheless is not the most dynamic of the time, one can find in the assets side for 1912 and 1913 credits to the Serbian government, treasury bonds from the kingdom of Bulgaria, various loans from other states of the same area, bonds from Crédit Foncier of Serbia and shares from Astra Romania.[4]

On the Haute Banque side and in collaboration with it, some other Banques d'Affaires intervened in these financial operations: apart from the BUP, the Banque de Paris et des Pays-Bas (Paribas) – which then intensified its intervention in Eastern Europe – was active.[5] Besides, new companies appeared, such as the Banque française pour le Commerce et l'Industrie, created in 1901. Amongst the deposit banks, the financial support of which was essential when loans were to be offered to a large public, the Société Générale and the Comptoir National d'Escompte seem to have been more active than the Crédit Lyonnais: the first French bank intervened only occasionally and in order only to propose alternative sources of income to its clients.

The Haute Banque companies, with the active collaboration of the Banques d'Affaires, were instrumental in the exportation of capital to the Balkan countries. They found businesses that suited their size, when the Russian loans became too important for them, and they profited from the relative disinterest of the important banks; lastly they could depend, in these fragmented countries, upon solid relations networks that had long been in place.

These capital exportations mainly aimed to cover the public expenses of states that suffered from permanent financial distress. Government stocks represented in 1902 more than 77 per cent of the French capital in the area.[6] In 1914 their relative importance increased even more; they represented 90 per cent of French capital in Romania.[7] Even if the largest part of the loans in this country were subscribed in Germany, and even if in 1903 and 1908 the French government had refused in Paris the issue of new Romanian loans, unless their product was to be used to purchase French industrial products, France had absorbed one-third of the Romanian national debt, the rest being covered in Germany. In Bulgaria 80 per cent of French capital was represented by public loans and France then held half of the public debt.[8]

The same is true of Serbia: more than 80 per cent of French capital was represented by bonds held by individuals and two-thirds of the public debt was owned by the French people. Greece had sold most of her 1910 and early 1914 loans (the latter of a nominal value amounting to 500 million francs) on the Paris market, and in 1914 French finance dominated in Athens.[9]

These public loans were not simple assets in the French balance of payments: France attempted very often either to influence their employment, by obtaining industrial orders, particularly arms buying from Schneider, at the expense of Krupp,[10] or to use its 'financial arm' in such a way as to influence the political orientation of these countries. But these operations were mainly conducted according to the decisions of banks acting in their own best interests. As concerns the use of these funds by the beneficiary countries, they served political and closely financial goals (paying off previous loans) or supported military efforts, much more than indirectly financing investments in railways or public works.

French capital also directly financed most traditional public works such as the construction of railway lines, the development of harbours, and so on, works often carried out by French companies. In this sector France had from early on excellent engineers as well as high performances and very efficient companies.[11] Thus, in Romania, French companies built the bridge of Cernavoda on the Danube as well as the harbour of Constanza. In Bulgaria several railway lines were under the control of the Régie Générale des Chemins de Fer et des Travaux Publics owned by the Comte Vitali and by the Maison Guilloux, and the Société des Batignolles was in charge of the building of the Varna and Bourgas harbours. In Greece the construction of the railway network was the result of a series of French initiatives which started with the Athens-Piraeus line in 1857 and continued to the Athens-Larissa and Larissa-Salonika lines. Lastly, in the European part of the Ottoman Empire, the building and the operating of a line joining Salonika to Constantinople required the collaboration of the Banque Impériale Ottomane and the Régie Générale des Chemins de Fer.

But, and this was new, investments in the Balkan economies multiplied during the years immediately preceding the Great War. Some took the form of participation in banks, or of the creation of new banks, so as to meet the credit needs that arose locally because of the economic development of the countries. In Romania, there was little French capital in banking: Paribas only obtained a minor participation in the Bank Marmorosch as did the BUP in the Banca Comerciala Romana. This is one of the causes of the weakness of French influence in this country. In Greece the success of French finance was more evident: in 1904 the BUP obtained two positions on the board of directors of the Bank of Athens; after 1906 the Comptoir National d'Escompte de Paris eliminated Germans from the Banque d'Orient and in 1909 French interests from the Société Générale and Paribas, predominated in the Bank of Salonika. After 1906 France played an essential role in the creation of a credit system in Bulgaria. She owned, via Paribas, the Société Générale and the BUP, one-quarter of the capital of the four main banks in the country (the General Bank of Bulgaria, the Balkan Bank, the Crédit Foncier Franco-Bulgare and the Banque Commerciale et Foncière des Balkans), through which deposits or credit operations quickly increased.[12]

In Serbia French capital, of secondary importance in the first credit companies functioning in this country, predominated in 1910: it ousted the Germans from the Crédit Foncier Serbe and under the leadership of the BUP created the Bank Franco-Serbe, with a capital amounting to 12 million; this latter bank created the firm Franco-Serbe of Industrial and Public Works Companies, with a capital of 4 million, and immediately obtained a railway concession. Thus, under French influence a credit system was born that would attract profitable concessions and then motivate economic development.

Direct investments in industry according to the strictest definition of the term had been limited for a long time. But we should bear in mind that probably some of the enterprises belonging to this category may escape the attention of historical research and statistics because they functioned not as joint-stock companies publishing balance sheets but as family companies (belonging for example to the Haute Banque), avoiding at the same time the issue of loans in the international capital market.

In all these countries French capital was present in financing in part at least some small or medium-sized companies in various sectors:

paper or cardboard or matches manufacturing, wood, salt, tobacco, metallurgy, sugar refinery, distillery, gas and electricity furnishing (for Bucharest). It was French capital that permitted the exploitation of some mine resources, for example the Travna coal basin in Bulgaria and the Selenitza asphalt mines in Albania. The Laurium deposits of silver and lead brought about the constitution of the Compagnie Française des Mines du Laurium in 1875; French engineers equiped with modern machinery who worked for this company were linked to the Comptoir National d'Escompte de Paris as its President Thiebault had also been a member of the 'conseil d'administration' of this bank since 1900.

In Romania various French groups (Rothschild, Desmarais Frères, Paribas) showed interest in petroleum resources, creating some small companies or participating in a minor way in other German-dominated ones. In total these investments represented 37.8 million francs only, that is 8.7 per cent of all invested capital in this area, and even if this figure was to reach 45 million,[13] it was still limited by the importance of German finance in this area.

There is at least one significant example of industrial investment in Serbia, where until this time capital investment in industry was, however, rare: that of the Bor mines.[14] This town, at a distance of 30 kms from the Bulgarian frontier in the Timok subdivision of North-east Serbia, harbours a copper deposit discovered in 1876 by a Serbian engineer. Georges Weifert, the recipient of the concession granted in 1903 by the King of Serbia, appealed to the Mirabaud Bank to finance this operation. Things moved fast: the Mirabaud Bank entrusted an engineer of the Société française d'Etude et d'Entreprises – one of its subsidiaries – to evaluate the importance of this discovery, and as early as 6 June 1904 they created the Compagnie française des Mines de Bor, with a capital of 505 million francs. The amount is not large but it surpassed the bank's resources. The Mirabaud family then called upon their parents and friends, the relatives with whom they worked, the whole 'gens', in the latin sense of the term, to participate in this lucrative project. In a short time they had to invest more capital, subscribe a capital increase and buy the bonds of a loan, but this affair was exceptionally interesting: this copper-rich mine yielded a metal that was in great demand at the time. This business immediately made a big profit for the Mirabaud family as their bank kept control of the company, as well as taking profit of 1 per cent royalty on the gross income realized by the sale of the ore. This is how the first copper-producing company in Europe was created before the Second World War. But as with the Laurium mines, the extracted metal, after its first treatment, was exported and did not give rise to the development of any metallurgical industry in the country.

At the beginning of the twentieth century French finance, mostly represented in the Balkan states by the old banks, was tenacious. This accounts for the accelerated flow of French capital to the area. French influence did not contribute to the industrial delay there; it helped set up a modern transport network. But these capital was still intended, above all, to inflate the public debt of states that never used it for development.

Most certainly, there were new French investments after the creation of modern banks. They aimed at attracting new public works. Direct investments in industry, despite the case of the Bor mines – which can be explained by its high profitability – were too limited in scope and quantity to bring about real development of modern industry. French bankers favoured 'the big deals' of public or railway loans, with high profits, to more risky industrial companies which at the most, could only yield low profits.[15]

French banks, capital strategies and financial diplomacy in the Balkans in the interwar period

(by Olivier Feiertag)

The Balkan Wars and the First World War profoundly changed the political and economic organization of South-east Europe.[16] More generally speaking, the whole of Europe was transformed by the Great War: in 1918 France emerged militarily victorious but financially weakened by a long war won at the cost of suspending the convertibility of its currency, an unprecedented increase in its public debt and the sacrifice of most of its credits abroad. In 1919 its international portfolio, badly hit by the collapse of Czarist Russia and the Ottoman Empire, was reduced by two-thirds of its maximum value in 1913.[17]

We can therefore raise the question of how these many upheavals contributed to changing the conditions of French financial presence in the Balkans which, as we have seen, had reached its apogee at the eve of the war. Much work has covered the penetration of French capital in Eastern Europe in the interwar period. But it tends either to concentrate on one country only – Romania for example which has been studied by many historians – or to cover a much larger geographical area, Central and Eastern Europe. As a result, the existence of specific French financial influence in the Balkans has not really been examined. What indeed could there be in common, during this period, between Czechoslovakia, Austria and Hungary – with their pre-war industrialized economies and considerable national capital – and the situation of the newly created Yugoslavia, Bulgaria and Romania, mainly agricultural countries, where the capital accumulation process had barely started and which were marked by a weak state organization and strong nationalism? Greece, besides a few small differences owing to the specific role of its diaspora, shared these general characteristics but is usually excluded from general studies of the history of South-east Europe. Its role as part of the Balkans has barely been studied, at least by western, Slav and Romanian historians. Finally, Albania, even by default, is practically never taken into account. It is, however, possible to identify the position and role of French banking in the Balkans considered in their entirety on the basis of existing work and research carried out in the archives of the Banque de France which, as we know, was led to intervene outside the purely national context from the end of the war, and is a privileged observatory, at the intersection of the state and the market, of the development of French capital abroad.[18] Three major questions are now raised:

1. Did the growing trend in the increase in French investments in South-east Europe, identifiable before 1912, continue or was it reinforced in the renewed geopolitical Balkan context of the postwar period, considering that the disappearance of Czarist Russia in 1917 had suddenly put an end to the main external outlet for French capital? How did portfolio investment made through the market and direct non-market investments develop in terms of total exported capital, which was known to represent a very small share of the external portfolio of France before 1914? Was not this preference for liquidity heightened by the obvious political instability of the Balkan states during this period? This instability was eloquently reflected by the constantly high price of foreign currency in the Balkans.
2. After 1919 was there a clear consolidation of the links created between French banks and industry ('financial capital'), especially in this part of the world, since the early twentieth century? What were the effects of French capital on the development of the Balkan economies, namely in the industrialization of countries that were still mainly agricultural before the outbreak of the Second World War? This question leads us finally to examine the relationship between capital flows and merchandise flows between France and the Balkan zone during this period: did French capital flows translate attempts to establish a type of international division of labour between peripheral Balkan countries and France? Or, on the contrary, did they lead to the formation of a regional economic unit or did they sanction the balkanization of South-east Europe?
3. Finally, it is necessary to examine whether state involvement in the foreign policy of French banks was reinforced in the area. France,

namely with the constitution of the Petite Entente, including Romania and Yugoslavia, intended to establish a military alliance in the Balkans capable of compensating for the defection of its Russian ally and of countering the rise of totalitarian imperialism, first Italian, then German. Herein lies the delicate problem of the use of the 'financial weapon' and the ambiguous relations between genuine financial interests and the supposedly superior interest of French diplomacy during this period.[19]

Three sub-periods can be quite easily identified, according to the evolution of the monetary and economic situation of the time:

1. From the military victory of 1918 to the monetary stabilization linked to the return to power of Poincare in 1926, French finance in the Balkans was clearly backtracking, despite the imperialist illusion of the postwar period which in fact encountered the weakness of the franc and the undamaged financial strength of Great Britain.
2. Between 1927 and 1934, on the contrary, there is a return to a certain 'golden age' (R. Girault) of French financial presence in the Balkans, founded on the return of the franc gold standard, on the restored financial strength of the Paris stock exchange and on genuine monetary diplomacy conducted closely between the Ministry of Foreign Affairs, the General Fund Movement at the Finance Ministry and the Banque de France.
3. From 1935 until the declaration of war, the backward surge was obvious, in the context of an international depression which reduced exchanges (capital and goods) and led to the partial withdrawal of French capital towards the colonial empire, giving free reign to the Axis powers in their commercial and military expansion in the Balkans.

1919–1926: disillusionment of the postwar period and the financial withdrawal of France

The victory in 1918 mainly appeared as a French victory. Its army was considered at the time as the strongest in the world, its military and industrial potential was considerably reinforced and modernized by the war effort and the military and economic superiority over the Central Powers left it free to extend its influence in Central and Eastern Europe. But these dreams of grandeur soon came crashing down with the reality of the weakening financial power of France in the wake of the First World War.

In the new context of the Gold Exchange Standard, French economic expansion policy in the Balkans was heavily handicapped by the international weakness of the franc, taken off the gold standard in 1914 and undermined by inflation during the war and postwar period. The unprecedented growth of the public debt, mainly in the short term, affected the availability of French savings and the constantly high requirements of the Treasury between 1919 and 1926 prevented the reconstitution of the French international portfolio. The fact that the Act of April 1918 establishing administrative control on all external capital movements was maintained until 1928 effectively illustrates the difficulties explaining the relative withdrawal of French investment in the Balkans in the postwar period. The disengagement of French finance in Greece in the 1920s clearly shows the state of the international financial situation at that time.

The financial restoration of Greece, ruined by the consequences of war and of the loss of territories in Asia Minor in 1922, was established under the aegis of the League of Nations, and its financial committee in particular, dominated by British experts. Significantly, the two international loans of 1924 and 1927, arranged within the framework of the League of Nations, were mainly contracted on the London and New York markets (by Hambros Bank and the National City Bank respectively).[20] The weakness of the Paris stock exchange at this time is indisputable. It can also explain the regression of the influence of French banks in Greece after 1918. As from 1919 the Société Générale tried to withdraw its participation (dating back to 1880) in the capital of the Bank of Salonica, which it eventually transferred to the Crédit Foncier of Algeria and Tunisia which developed a strategy tending to focus on the Levant rather than on the Balkans, although the latter had been the privileged expansion zone of the Bank of Salonica until the war. Similarly, in 1920, the Banque de l'Union Parisienne (BUP), against its will, was once more forced to consolidate stakes in the capital of the Bank of Athens with which it had been linked since 1904 and whose shares it had easily invested at the Paris stock exchange during the capital increase in 1911. Likewise, after the war, the BUP sought to withdraw from the capital of the Banque Franco-Serbe which it had helped set up in partnership with the Imperial Ottoman Bank in 1910 and had directed towards an enthusiastic expansion policy in the Balkans (opening a branch in Zagreb in 1919 and in Salonica in 1920).

This general retreat by French banks, apparently contrary to the grandiose projects nourished by the French governments of the time (Clemenceau), evidently finds immediate justification in the geopolitical upheavals following the collapse of the Ottoman Empire. The fragmentation of the Balkans that occurred in the wake of the Treaty of Sevres in 1922 suddenly put an end to the banking and financial networks that had been woven from Alexandria to Odessa, from Smyrne to Trieste, through the action of Jewish and Greek bankers on the eve of the start of the conflict.[21] The memoirs of a French banker, Jean Morin, who managed the Crédit Lyonnais branch in Smyrne in 1921–22, then the Constantinople branch between 1923 and 1926, clearly reveal the scale of this major breakdown. They show how the expulsion of Greeks from the coast of Asia Minor in 1922 suddenly stopped the funding of tobacco and cotton crops, and the difficulties encountered by the Crédit Lyonnais when it tried to make secret contacts with Greek bankers exiled in Athens. More generally, having arrived in Constantinople in 1923, Morin observed the financial decadence of the Crédit Lyonnais which had nevertheless been established on the Gold Horn since 1875 and whose prosperity had hitherto been closely linked to Ottoman dominance; 'the glorious days', he wrote, 'are drawing to a close. I myself arrived to witness the decline of the Crédit Lyonnais'.[22] Obviously, the First World War and its consequences, the sudden disappearance of the Russian and Ottoman Empires and the Austro-Hungarian Monarchy, interrupted the reinforcement of French banking imperialism in the Balkans in the form it had taken at the beginning of the twentieth century by suddenly smashing the capital networks operating in this region both all over the Eastern Mediterranean and, more generally, within Central and Eastern Europe. The weakness of the links between French banks and national industries, already apparent before 1914, prevented the real development of French imperialism in the Balkans founded on the alliance between diplomacy and major French military and industrial companies. The development of French investment in Romania after the war shows this quite clearly.

Great Romania in 1919 appeared as the darling of French diplomacy immediately after the war. French banking strategy was established on the existence of two local banks controlled by the two most important French merchant banks at the time: the Banque de Paris et des Pays-Bas which set up the Banque de Crédit Roumain, and the Banque de l'Union Parisienne which, since 1906, had had a stake in the Banque Commerciale de Roumanie.[23] After 1919 the BUP aimed to gain full control of the Banque Commerciale de Roumanie. To do so, between 1924 and 1928 it gradually acquired the share of the capital owned by the group of Greek and Romanian bankers, namely Chrissoveloni and Economos, who owned the majority stake before the war, and by supplying the largest share of the capital increase in 1925. This strategy was clearly aimed at opposing competition from its rival, the Banque de Paris et des Pays-Bas, whose vice-president, Jules Cambon, was appointed to the board of Banque de Crédit Roumain at the same time.

Competition between the two merchant banks in Romania in the 1920s should, however, be set in the context of France's attempt from 1918 to develop a strategy of direct industrial investment in Romania, based on the French banking system and on the reinforcement of the military and diplomatic alliance between the two countries. The BUP, from late 1918, was therefore party to the initiatives of Schneider and Batignolles who created the Société Franco-Roumaine d'Etudes et d'Entreprises, specializing in civil engineering and railway construction. In the same way, the Banque Commerciale de Roumanie was involved in the creation of the Industrie Aéronautique de Roumanie in 1925, in partnership with the French aeronautics companies Lorraine-Dietrich and Blériot Aéronautique. It also owned two-thirds of the capital of the chemicals company Maraseti (sulfuric acid and fertilizers) which it helped merge with the French chemicals group Saint-Gobain in 1925. Is it possible to say on the basis of these examples that after the war the merger between French banks and industry, still weak in 1914, was considerably reinforced? In fact this policy resulted in a series of failures which, to the contrary, reveal the persistent weakness of French 'financial capital' after 1919: from 1922 the BUP broke with Schneider and withdrew from projects launched in 1918; its financial support to the Romanian aeronautics industry was always hesitant and the aeronautics company finally filed for bankruptcy in May 1932, having failed to achieve a partnership with Schneider and Skoda who nevertheless offered the possibility of concentrating French influence in the Romanian aeronautics industry. As for its participation in the chemicals sector, the BUP sold its stake at the same time to Solway, the Belgian company. Industrial participation of the BUP in Romania through its subsidiary Banque Commerciale de Roumanie in the 1920s was therefore disastrous. The relative success during the same period in the well-studied sector of the Romanian oil industry by Banque de Paris et des Pays-Bas, in partnership with the local Marmorosch Blank Bank, should not delude us: Paribas mainly owed the good results of the oil company it controlled, Steaua Romana, to its partnership with powerful Anglo-Saxon interests, formed on the initiative of Horace Finaly with Standard Oil from 1920.[24] Isolated, French finance in the wake of the First World War was powerless to impose itself in the new political and economic context of the Balkans. Against the strong pressure of the City and the action of the Bank of England, against the growing influence of the New York stock exchange, France, at least until 1927, was reduced to practising 'poor man's imperialism' in the Balkans[25] which was also the consequence of the international weakness of the franc at the time. Monetary stabilization in 1926–28 was therefore, from this angle, a turning point which opened new prospects for French banks in the Balkans.

1927–33: French banking imperialism and franc diplomacy

The official stabilization of the franc in June 1928, preceded in late 1926 by an actual period of stabilization, undoubtedly opened the door to a new era in the history of French imperialism in the interwar period.[26] It resulted in the French financial market gaining a top-ranking position in Europe, effectively competing with the power of Great Britain. The new factor was the complete involvement of the Banque de France in this international expansion policy, under the new team appointed at its head in June 1926: Governor Emile Moreau, assisted by Charles Rist, the deputy-governor, and Pierre Quesnay, director of studies, both experts in international monetary affairs since their involvement in the work of the Financial Committee of the League of Nations. The often quoted memoirs of Emile Moreau explain the new financial strategy of France in Eastern Europe at the end of the 1920s:

> I had an important conversation with M. Poincaré on the question of the imperialism of the Bank of England. I explained to the president of the council that England, having been the first European country to regain a stable currency after the war, took advantage of this to establish the foundations of real financial domination in Europe ... England is thereby completely or partially established in Austria, Hungary, Belgium, Norway and Italy. It will establish itself in Greece and Portugal. It aims to find a base in Yugoslavia and it is insidiously fighting us in Romania.[27]

This is admirable proof – perhaps too admirable – of the close links that appear to have been established in the late 1920s between the French banks, the bank of issue and the government, with the aim of giving France political and economic influence in Eastern Europe through real franc diplomacy.

The reality of this new situation is perfectly illustrated by the dominant role France played in monetary stabilization operations in Bulgaria in 1928, in Romania in 1929 and in Yugoslavia in 1931. These operations show the personal role of Emile Moreau and his team at the head of the Banque de France until 1930, then as president of the Banque de Paris et des Pays-Bas from 1930. The well-documented example of the stabilization of the Romanian leu in 1929 also illustrates the new forms taken by the influence of French finance in this part of the world during this period.[28] It was expressed first in the launch of an international stabilization loan of a total value equivalent to 100 million dollars, at the high rate of 7 per cent. The stake subscribed by the group of French banks led by Paribas, which was the real force behind the whole operation, represented in fact 22 per cent of the total, that is the highest subscription after the stake taken by the Swedish group Kreuger (30 per cent) but well in front of the British stake (9.8 per cent).[29] In April 1931 a second international loan was granted to Romania, for the sum of 1.35 billion francs, that is 52 million dollars, at the rate of 7.5 per cent. This time it was completely subscribed by the Paris market by a banking syndicate once more led by Paribas equally representing the Crédit Lyonnais, the Société Générale and the Comptoir National d'Escompte. Was this a pure and simple return to financial investment practices characterizing French capital exports during the belle époque?

In reality it is important to note that these loans were part of the General stabilization programme of the Romanian currency defined from autumn 1927 by the deputy governor of the Banque de France, Charles Rist, who was repeatedly sent on missions to Bucharest.[30] The programme adopted by the Romanian government in early 1929, coinciding with the stabilization loan floatation, provided for a 'technical adviser' who would work for three years at the Banque Nationale de Roumanie to supervise the proper execution of the programme. Roger Auboin, who on his return to France was appointed secretary general of the Banque de France, fulfilled this role until 1935, the initial duration of his mandate being extended with the second 'development' loan granted in 1931.[31] A point that has been often neglected is that the application of the 1929 programme led to the real modernization of financial and monetary structures in Romania, reorganizing the statutes of the Romanian bank of issue, codifying its relations with the state and setting the rules of discount aimed at organizing the monetary market and commercial loans. In addition, the Romanian Ministry of Finance was also reformed, namely with the creation of a Treasury department which provided the basis of the revision of the whole tax system.[32] The direct influence of the Banque de France in the attempt to modernize the Romanian financial system between 1929 and 1935 is therefore indisputable. Its role in the stabilization of the Yugoslavian dinar between 1931 and 1934, namely through the successive assignments to Belgrade undertaken by Jean Bolgert, an inspector at the Banque de France who was to become the director of the Foreign Department of the Banque de France after the war, was similar in outline to the Romanian operation.[33]

In both cases, in Romania and in Yugoslavia, increased penetration from 1929 of French capital occurred within the general framework of the monetary stabilization of the two countries and was backed up by the modernization of local financial structures. This effort, to a certain extent, reflected the development of deposit banks induced by the subsidiaries of French banks established in the Balkans. The Banque Commerciale Roumaine, instigated by the BUP, was thereby oriented in the late 1920s towards a strategy to extend its network of branches, namely with the takeover in 1929 of branches owned by the Banque Belge pour l'Etranger, itself a subsidiary of Société Générale de Belgique, in Romania and in Bulgaria. The Banque Commerciale de Roumanie henceforth played a considerable part in animating the Bucharest money market, acting as a clearing house for most banks in the market. This direction effectively translated the overall liquidity strategy adopted by the BUP in the Balkans at a time when its industrial fixed assets, contracted in the first half of the 1920s, were leading to real disappointments, namely with the arrival of the Depression in Eastern Europe in the 1930s.[34] In some ways, the reinforcement of the financial presence of France in certain Balkan countries therefore corresponded to an attempt to modernize the financial structures of these countries. On the other hand, the effects of a possible economic modernization of the Balkan states in question are much harder to grasp.

The apparent determination of French diplomacy to link stabilization loans to industrial, and mainly military, orders came up against both the reticence of French banks, traditionally unconcerned with implementing tied loans, and the opposition of experts at the Banque de France itself who, in the name of monetary orthodoxy, did not encourage the use of funds on military spending instead of on currency reserves to guarantee the legal cover percentage of monetary circulation set by stabilization programmes.[35]

In total, in 1932 20 per cent of loans contracted through the French financial market abroad were concentrated in Petite Entente countries. France at that time was by far the top-ranking creditor of Yugoslavia and Romania where its total commitments respectively reached five and three times the sum of British loans. On the other hand, investment remained low in Bulgaria and in Greece, and non-existent in Albania, which since 1925 had been completely controlled by the Italian orbit of the National Bank of Italy.[36] Total direct investment from France, which is very difficult to assess, shows the relative modesty of this type of investment, which remained generally lower than market investment, and also shows that Romania and Yugoslavia, the military allies of France, were its main beneficiaries. In 1933 investment represented some 2 500 million francs in Romania, which placed France behind Great Britain and just ahead of the USA; in Yugoslavia, industrial investment represented 400 million francs only, mostly represented by the Banque Mirabaud's stake in the Bor copper mines. This shows the extent to which French financial penetration in the Balkans, which grew between 1928 and 1933, was primarily governed by diplomatic and military considerations and was not a factor contributing to the development of trade relations between France and the Balkan states, which, on the contrary, were tending to decline over the period, as is clearly shown by the example of Bulgaria.[37] There were apparently no attempts to organize a form of division of labour, capable of establishing a sort of complementarity between an industrial, technology-exporting centre and a developing Balkan peripheral, with French money. Basically, the economy of the two areas were barely complementary. The importance of the agricultural sector in both economies even established an objective competition, which was also perceived by French farmers at the time. As before 1914, merchandise in the interwar period did not follow capital. This structural situation allows us to understand how, when the Depression hit France, the French financial and economic presence in the Balkans was rapidly withdrawn mostly to the advantage of Nazi Germany, whereas the diplomatic impotence of France contributed to the increased economic fragmentation of the Balkan area.

1934–39: financial withdrawal and the external impotence of France

The arrival of the Great Depression in the Balkans in the 1930s was accelerated by the effects of the monetary torment experienced in Central Europe in the summer of 1931, starting in Vienna with the collapse of the Creditanstalt. At first France, backed up by the Bank International Settlements (BIS), which it controlled, helped attenuate the scale of the monetary crisis in the countries of many of its clients: in this way, for example, the Banque de France agreed in 1931–32 to readjust part of the commercial portfolio of the National Bank of Yugoslavia against the franc.[38] However, the removal of French interests in Bulgaria was felt from 1931. At that time, in response to measures taken by the Bulgarian government to control the movement of foreign capital, the Balkan Bank, the main Bulgarian bank controlled by French capital, closed six out of seven branches in the country and withdrew massively from its industrial subsidiaries (the Fabriques des Tabacs Reunies). The French withdrawal left room for strong German commercial expansion in Bulgaria from 1933, mainly on the basis of clearing agreements perfectly adapted to the dearth in convertible currency in Bulgaria, as in most Balkan states. The financial weapon was thereby tempered ... the German commercial drive, based on the clearing system, was increasingly reinforced throughout South-east Europe until the eve of the Second World War as the weakness of the foreign policy of France became increasingly apparent.[39]

France's diplomatic backtracking in the Balkans is, of course, explained by the pro-Italian errors of its foreign policy in 1935 and its passivity with regard to the remilitarization of the Rhineland in 1936, and even more so by the Munich agreement which, following Great Britain's cue, confirmed the dismantling of Czechoslovakia by Hitler.

But it may also be explained by France's inability to appreciate the scale of the Balkan Entente formed in 1934 and to reply favourably, for example, to applications to join the BIS by the member states of the Balkan Entente between 1934 and 1936.[40] Parallel to the decline in France's political power and the worsening of the world's economic situation, genuine commercial relations between countries in the Petite Entente, after having grown between 1928 and 1930, constantly declined throughout the 1930s, reaching practical insignificance on the eve of the war.[41] The tendency towards economic fragmentation of the Balkan peninsula was therefore apparent at this date. From 1937 King Carol's Romania and Stojadinovic's Yugoslavia therefore resolutely moved towards Germany and Italy, thereby marking the real end to French financial influence in the Balkans which the late efforts of the Daladier government (which sent Herve Alphand to Belgrade and Sofia in November 1938) were unable to prevent. The withdrawal of French financial interests from the Balkans was part of a general French retreat from its empire, to the benefit of the North African colonies.

Therefore, on the eve of the Second World War, the presence of French capital in the South-European states had melted away: very low in Bulgaria and Greece, in Romania it was reduced to the increasingly unprofitable oil industry and the Bor mines in Yugoslavia. There remained many credits in Balkan states but they became worthless with the suspension of the servicing of the debt decided by debtor countries. The Second World War led to the transfer of remaining French industrial interests to Nazi Germany. The integration of most Balkan states in the Soviet bloc after 1945 once more raised the problem of unpaid French credits. French capital strategies in the Balkans were therefore faced with renewed failure in the aftermath of the Second World War.

General conclusions

The position and role of French finance in the Balkans from the late nineteenth century to the Second World War remained relatively modest, even though it experienced a surge in the early twentieth century this was interrupted by the war. The disappearance of the Ottoman Empire, followed by that of the Russian Empire and the dual Austro-Hungarian Monarchy after 1918, led to the dismantling of financial networks that had been gradually set up in the Balkans, mainly thanks to the input of foreign capital. During the interwar period, South-east Europe, however, seemed a privileged market for French capital exports as a consequence of the collapse of the Russian and Ottoman empires which had provided the main outlets for French capital before the war.

But French banking imperialism, with a few brilliant exceptions (Romanian oil industry or the Bor mines), was generally passive and only vaguely tied to French economic penetration in the region, owing to the persistent weakness of French financial capital before and after 1914.

Its impact on the economic development of the Balkan states was therefore small, owing to the absence of true complementarity between the French and Balkan economies and of political stability, a permanent factor in this 'powder keg' of Europe before and after 1914. From this point of view, the role played by French finance, far from unifying the Balkan zone into a more homogeneous market, contributed to seriously aggravating the fragmentation of South-east Europe by closely associating diplomacy and financial penetration.

Nevertheless, industrial and financial alliances formed at the start of the century, for example in Greece or Bulgaria, the technical action of the interventions of the Banque de France in Romania and Yugoslavia between 1929 and 1932 and the development throughout the period of deposit banking in Romania, Yugoslavia and Bulgaria were factors of modernization that were prevented from developing fully by the troubled economic and political situation.

Notes

1. Data established by the French government in 1902 and published in the *Bulletin de Statistique et de Législation comparée*, October 1902. According to Herbert Feis, *Europe. The World's Banker 1870-1914*, New York, 1930, reprint 1964, p. 51, french investments in the Balkans in 1900 reached, however, the amount of 700 million francs.
2. According to Feis, op. cit., p. 51, who gives the global amount of 2 500 million in 1914. See also S. Damianov, 'Aspects économiques de la politique française dans les Balkans au début du XXe siècle', *Etudes balkaniques*, Sofia, 1974, n. 4, who gives 3 032 million at the eve of the war (respectively 980 million in Serbia, 522 million in Romania, 530 million in Bulgaria and 1 000 million in Greece). For his part, R. Girault, 'Les Balkans dans les relations franco-russes en 1912', *Revue historique*, January–March 1975 reached a total of 2 792 million in 1914 (800 million in Serbia, 780 million in Romania, 512 million in Bulgaria and 700 million in Greece).
3. About the activities of the Banque Impériale Ottomane in the east part of the Ottoman Empire, cf. J. Thobie, *Intérêts et impérialisme français dans l'Empire Ottoman (1895–1914)*, Paris, 1977, and A. Autheman, *La Banque Impériale Ottomane*, Paris: Comité pour l'histoire économique et financière de la France, 1996.
4. According to the annual inventories of the Banque Mallet, private archives, Paris.
5. Cf. E. Bussière, *Paribas, 1872–1992, l'Europe et le monde*, Antwerp: Fonds Mercator, 1992.

6. According to the inquiry of 1902 (*Bulletin de Statistique*, op. cit.), the repartition of the use of French capital in the Balkans would be at this date (in millions of francs):

	Business houses	Insurance, banks	Navigation ports	Mining, industry	Public funds	Total
Romania	12	1	—	37	328	378
Bulgaria	1	2	4	4	37	48
Serbia	—	—	—	1	200	201
Greece	4	—	60	34	185	283
Total						910

Surprisingly, no mention is made in this data about French capital in the railway sector.

7. Cf. J. Thobie, *La France impériale, 1880–1914*, Paris: Megrelis, 1982, and C. Durandin, 'La politique française et les Roumains, 1878–1903', unpublished Ph.D. dissertation, Paris III, 1996.
8. Thobie, *La France impérial*, pp. 264 ff.
9. Thobie, ibid. and S. Damianov, 'Les placements français en Bulgarie, 1878–1940', in M. Lévy-Leboyer, *La position internationale de la France. Aspects économiques et financiers, XIXe–XXe siècles*, Paris, 1977.
10. R. Poidevin, *Les relations commerciales et financières entre la France et l'Allemagne de 1898 à 1914*, Paris: Comité pour l'histoire économique et financière de la France, 1969, reprint 1998.
11. Cf. Dominique Barjot, 'La grande entreprise de travaux publics (1883–1974)', unpublished Ph.D. dissertation, Université de Paris IV, 1989.
12. According to Damianov, op. cit., these four banks, controlled by French capital, owned in 1914 55 million francs as capital and 70 million francs as deposits.
13. According to Durandin, op. cit.
14. The Archives of the Mirabaud Bank, which include many important files on the Bor mines, are now deposited at the Archives National, series AQ.
15. The reasons why the foreign capital did not contribute to the industrialization of Greece, according to G.B. Dertilis, *Banquiers, usuriers et paysans. Réseaux de crédits et stratégies du capital en Grèce (1780–1930)*, Paris: Ed. de la Découverte, 1988, pp. 218 ff., could also explain the role of French capital in the Balkans at the beginning of the twentieth century. The great investments in public debt (with a few exceptions like the Bor mines) were more profitable than the industrial investments. Moreover it was easier to sell to private investors public loans than industrial shares.
16. Cf. M.C. Kaser and E.A. Radice, *The Economic History of Eastern Europe, 1919–1975*, vols I and II, Oxford: Clarendon Press, 1986. Concerning Greece, cf. *A. Andréades et al., Les effets économiques et sociaux de la guerre en Grèce*, New Haven, 1929.
17. According to L. Rist and Ph. Swob, *De la France d'avant guerre à la France d'aujourd'hui*, Paris: Librairie du Recueil Sirey, 1939, pp. 532–3.
18. O. Feiertag, 'La Banque de France et les problèmes monétaires européens de la conférence de Gênes (1922) à la création de la BRI (1930)', in

Milieux économiques et intégration européenne en Europe occidentale au XXe siècle, Arras, Presses Université, 1998.
19. Cf. R. Girault, 'Economie et politique internationale: diplomatie et banques pendant l'entre-deux-guerres', *Relations internationales*, no. 21, spring 1980, pp. 7–22.
20. Cf. P. Dertilis, *La reconstruction financière de la Grèce et la Société des Nations*, Paris: Librairie A. Rousseau, 1929, pp. 132–40.
21. Cf. Chr. Hadziiossif, 'Banques grecques et banques européennes au XIXe siècle: le point de vue d'Alexandrie', in G.B. Dertilis, op. cit., pp. 157–98.
22. Jean Morin, *Souvenirs d'un banquier français, 1875–1947*, Paris, 1983, p. 270.
23. Cf. H. Bonin, 'La Banque de l'Union Parisienne en Roumanie (1919–1935). Influence bancaire ou impérialisme du pauvre?', *Revue historique*, no. 2, 1985, pp. 349–81 and E. Bussière, op. cit., Anvers: Fonds Mercator, 1992, pp. 118–20.
24. Cf. E. Bussière, *Horace Finaly, banquier, 1871–1945*, Paris: Fayard, 1996, pp. 181–93.
25. Cf. G. Soutou, 'L'impérialisme du pauvre: la politique économique du gouvernement français en Europe centrale et orientale de 1918 à 1929. Essai d'interprétation', *Relations internationales*, no. 7, 1976, pp. 219–39.
26. Cf. J. Bouvier and R. Girault, *L'impérialisme à la française, 1914–1960*, Paris: Ed. la Découverte, 1986, pp. 199 ff.
27. E. Moreau, *Souvenirs d'un Gouverneur de la Banque de France, Histoire de la stabilisation du Franc (1926–1928)*, Paris: Librairie de Medicis, 1954, p. 488.
28. Cf. R.H. Meyer (R.H.), *Banker's Diplomacy. Monetary Stabilization in the Twenties*, New York and London, 1970; Philippe Marguerat, 'Banque de France et politique de puissance dans l'entre-deux-guerres: le problème des stabilisations monétaires en Europe orientale, 1927–1931', *Relations internationales*, no. 56, winter 1988, pp. 475–85.
29. Cf. R. Notel, in Kaser and Radice, op. cit., vol. II, tables 12–17, p. 208.
30. Archives of the Banque de France (ABF), files about the stabilization in Romania, 4e N 384, 20–25.
31. ABF, Reports of the French technical advisor in Bucharest (1929–1935), 4e N 384, 22.
32. ABF, Ch. Rist and R. Auboin, *Rapport général sur la réforme financière et monétaire en Roumanie*, 1932, Imprimerie R. Dupont, 4e N 384, 23.
33. ABF, *Mission de M. Bolgert en Yougoslavie*, 3 liasses, 17/12/1945.
34. The poor industrial portfolio of the Banque Commerciale again unleashed 55 per cent of its value in 1932, cf. Bonin, op. cit., pp. 360–61.
35. ABF, 7e Q 647, *Crédits ouverts à la Yougoslavie*, 1931–32. Cf. also Ph. Marguerat, op. cit.
36. According to Girault, 'Economie et politique', op. cit. on the basis of a memo of the Mouvement général des Fonds, 30 September 1932, p. 213.
37. Cf. Damianov, 'Les placements', op. cit., pp. 325–30.
38. ABF, 7e Q647, box 36.
39. Cf. J. Thobie, 'La France, la Grèce et les Balkans dans les années Trente', *Balkan Studies*, 29, 1988, pp. 3–28 and D. J. Delivanis, 'La politique économique et financière de la France dans les Balkans pendant les années Trente', *Balkan Studies*, 29, 1988, pp. 39–45.

40. ABF, 7e J 273, box 6.
41. Cf. N. Dascâlu, 'The economic Little Entente. An attempt at setting up a European Economic Community (1922–1938)', *Revue des Etudes Sud-Est Européennes*, t. XIX, 1981, pp. 81–96.

Bibliography

100 let Mestne hranilnice ljubljanske, Ljubljana, 1989
Akyıldız, A. (1996) *Osmanlı Finans Sisteminde Dönüm Noktası. Kâğıt Para ve Sosyo-Ekonomik Etkileri*, Eren: Istanbul
Aleksić-Pejković, L. (1965) *Odnosi Srbije sa Francuskom i Engleskom 1903–1914* (Serbia's relations with France and England 1903–1914), Belgrade
Alexakis, P. (1993) 'Basic developments with regard to the structure, the functioning and the institutional framework of the Greek financial system', in T. Giannitsis (ed.) *Liberalization of Markets and Transformation of the Greek Banking System*, Athens, pp. 77–8. (in Greek)
Alexakis, P. (1995) 'Basic developments in the structure, operation and institutional framework of the Greek banking system', in T. Giannitsis (ed.) *Market Liberalisation and Transformations in the Greek Banking System*, Athens: Papazissis (in Greek)
Alexakis, P. and Petrakis, P. (1988) *Commercial and Development Banks*, Athens: Papazissis (in Greek)
Anderson, R.W. and Kegel Ch.(1998) *Transition Banking. Financial development of Central and Eastern Europe*, Oxford: Clarendon Press
Andréades, A. et al. (1929) *Les effets économiques et sociaux de la guerre en Grèce*, New Haven, Conn.
Arsenis, G. (1987) *Political Statement*, Athens: Odysseas (in Greek)
Atzenhofer-Baumgartner, M.R. (1980) 'Kapitalexport aus Österreich-Ungarns vor dem Ersten Weltkrieg. Die Stellung der österreichisch-ungarischen Monarchie im System der internationalen Kapitalbeziehungen', Ph.D. thesis, Vienna
Autheman, A. (1996) *La Banque Impériale Ottomane*, Paris
Balkitch, V. (1919) *Monnaies, banques et bourses en Serbie*, Paris
Banca Nationale Romaniei (1938) *Contributii la problema reorganizarii creditului in Romania* (Contributions regarding the issue of the reorganization of the credit system in Romania), vol. 1, Bucharest
Bančni Vestnik, Ljubljana, 1989
Bank of Greece (1965) *Investment Banks–Placement Companies: Role and Importance in the Capital Market*, Athens: Bank of Greece (in Greek)
Bankov pregled (Banking review), 1908–1914, Sofia
Barjot, D. (1989) 'La grande entreprise de travaux publics (1883–1974)', unpublished Ph.D. dissertation, Université de Paris IV
Barth, B. (1996) 'Deutsche Banken und Österreich-Ungarn: Eine

wirtschaftliche und politische Partnerschaft?', in Helmut Rumpler and Jan Paul Niederkorn (eds) *Der 'Zweibund' 1879. Das deutsch-österreichisch-ungarische Bündnis und die europäische Diplomatie*, Vienna, pp. 279–97

Bartsch, Fr. (1917) 'Statistische Daten über die Zahlungsbilanz Österreich-Ungarns vor Ausbruch des Krieges', *Mitteilungen des k.k. Finanzministeriums*, XXII Vienna, pp. 1–159

Beaud, C. (1985) 'De l'expansion internationale à la multinationale Schneider en Russie (1896–1914)', *Histoire économique et société*, pp. 562–626

Beaud, C. (1995) 'Les Schneider marchands de canons 1870–1914', *Histoire économique et société*, pp. 107–130

Berendt, I.T. and Ranki, G. (1974) *Economic Development in East-Central Europe in the 19th and 20th Centuries*, New York and London: Columbia University Press

Berendt, I.T. and Ranki, G. (1982) *The European periphery and Industrialization, 1780–1914*, Cambridge: Cambridge University Press

Berov, L. (1965) 'Le capital financier occidental et les pays balkaniques pendant les années vingt', *Etudes balkaniques*, 2–3, pp. 139–69

Berov, L. (1971), 'The withdrawing of western capitals from Bulgaria on the eve of the Second World War', *Studia Balkanica*, 4

Berov, L. (ed.) (1989) *Ikonomikata na Bălgarija do socialističeskata revoljucija* (The Economy of Bulgaria until the Socialist Revolution), Sofia

Biliotti, A.(1909) *La Banque Impériale Ottomane*, Paris: Henri Jouve

Bisignano, J. (1990) 'Banking in the EEC: structure, competition and public policy', in G. Kaufman (ed.) *Bank Structure in Major Countries*, New York: Kluwer

Bočev, St. (1911) *Ipotekarnijat kredit u nas* (Mortgage credit in our country), Sofia

Bonin, H. (1985) 'La Banque de l'Union Parisienne en Roumanie (1919–1935). Influence bancaire ou impérialisme du pauvre?', *Revue historique*, no. 2, pp. 349–81

Bonin, H. (1992) *La Banque et les banquiers en France du Moyen Age à nos jours*, Paris

Born, K.E. (1977) *Geld und Banken in 19. und 20. Jahrhundert*, Stuttgart

Borges, A. (1993) 'Portuguese banking in the Single European Market', in J. Dermine (ed.) *European Banking in the 1990s*, Oxford: Blackwell

Boué, A. (1940) *La Turquie d'Europe*, I–IV, Paris

Bouvier, J. (1973) *Un siècle de banque française*, Paris: Hachette

Bouvier, J. and Girault, R. (1976) *L'impérialisme français d'avant 1914. Recueil de textes*, Paris

Bouvier J. and Girault, R. (1986) *L'impérialisme à la française, 1914–1960*, Paris: Ed. la Découverte

Buchanan, N.S. and Ellis, H.S. (1955) *Approaches to Economic Development*, New York: The Twentieth Century Fund

Burckhardt, C.J. (1958) *Begegnungen*, Zürich

Bussière, E. (1983) 'The interests of the Banque de l'Union Parisienne in Czechoslovakia, Hungary and the Balkans, 1919–30', in P.L. Cottrell and A. Teichova (eds) *International Business and Central Europe, 1918–1939*, Leicester: Leicester University Press

Bussière, E. (1992) *Paribas, l'Europe et le monde, 1872–1992*, Antwerp

Bussière, E. (1996) *Horace Finaly, banquier, 1871–1945*, Paris: Fayard

Čakalov, As. (1962) *Formi, razmer i dejnost na čuzdija kapital v Bălgarija, 1878–1944* (Form, extent and activity of foreign capital, 1878–1944), Sofia

Caloghirou, Y. (1993) 'Problematic structures in Greek industry', in T. Giannitsis (ed.) *Industrial and Technological Policy in Greece*, Athens: Themelio (in Greek)

Cameron, R. (1971) *La France et le développement économique de l'Europe, 1800–1914*, Paris: Seuil

Cemovic, M. (1985) *Zasto, kako I koliko smo se duzili* (Why, how and how much we became indebted), Belgrade: Institut za unapredjenje robnog prometa

Cezar, Y. (1986) *Osmanlı Maliyesinde Bunalım ve Değişim Dönemi*, Istanbul

Chalikias, D. (1976) *Possibilities and Problems of the Credit Policy. The Greek Experience*, Athens: Bank of Greece (in Greek)

Chapman, St. (1984) *The Rise of Merchant Banking*, London

Charissopoulos Study on the Banking System (1981) Athens: Bank of Greece (in Greek)

Clay, C. (1990) 'The Imperial Ottoman Bank in the later nineteenth century: a multinational "national" bank?', in G. Jones (ed.) *Banks as Multinationals*, London and New York: Routledge, pp. 142–59

Clay, C., 'The financial collapse of the Ottoman state, 1863–1875', paper presented at the Sixth International Conference of Economic and Social History of the Ottoman Empire and Turkey (1326–1960), 1–4 July 1992, Aix-en-Provence

Coleman, W.D. (1993) 'Reforming corporatism: the French banking policy community, 1941–90', *West European Politics*, 16 (2)

Courakis, A. (1984) 'On the rationale and implications of constraints on the choices of deposit-taking financial intermediaries (with particular reference to seven European countries)', in D. Fair and L. de Juvigny (eds) *Government Policies and the Workings of Financial Systems in Industrialized Countries*, Dordrecht: Martinus Nijhoff

Creditanstalt-Bankverein (1957) *Ein Jahrhundert Creditanstalt-Bankverein,* Vienna
Damianov, S. (1971) *Frenskoto ikonomičesko pronikvane v Bălgarija, 1878–1914* (French economic penetration in Bulgaria, 1878–1914), Sofia
Damianov, S. (1974) 'Aspects économiques de la politique française dans les Balkans au début du XXe siècle', *Etudes balkaniques*, Sofia
Damianov, S. (1977) 'Les placements français en Bulgarie, 1878–1940', in M. Levy-Leboyer, *La position international de la France. Aspects économiques et financiers, XIXe–XXe siècles*, Paris
Danailov, G.T. (1908) 'Nezavisimostta I čuzdite banki u nas' (Independence and the foreign banks in our country), *Bankov pregled,* 8
Daskaloff, R. (1912) *Das auslaendische Kapital in Bulgarien*, Berlin
Dascâlu, N. (1981) 'The economic Little Entente. An attempt at setting up a European Economic Community (1922–1938)', *Revue des Etudes Sud-Est Européennes*, XIX, pp. 81–96
de Boissieu, C. (1989) 'The "Overdraft Economy", the "Auto-Economy" and the rate of interest', in A. Barrère (ed.) *Money, Credit and Prices in Keynesian Perspective*, London: Macmillan
de Boissieu, C. (1993) 'The French banking sector in the light of European financial integration', in J. Dermine (ed.) *European Banking in the 1990s*, Oxford: Blackwell
de Cecco, M. (1994) 'The Italian banking system at a historic turning-point', *Review of Economic Conditions in Italy*, 1, January–June
Delivanis, D.J. (1988) 'La politique économique et financière de la France dans les Balkans pendant les années Trente', *Balkan Studies*, 29, pp. 39–45
Dermine, J. (ed.) (1993) *European Banking in the 1990s*, Oxford: Blackwell
Dertilis, G.B. (1980) *The Banking Issue, 1871–1873*, Athens: National Bank Educational Foundation (in Greek)
Dertilis, G.B. (1984) *Greek Economy, 1830–1910, and Industrial Revolution*, Athens: Sakkoulas (in Greek)
Dertilis, G.B. (ed.) (1988) *Banquiers, usuriers et paysans. Réseaux de crédits et strategies du capital en Grèce (1780–1930)*, Paris: Ed. de la Découverte
Dertilis, P. (1929) *La reconstruction financière de la Grèce et la Société des Nations*, Paris: Librairie A. Rousseau
Dimitrijević, M. (1913) 'Carsko-otomanska Banka' (Imperial Ottoman Bank), *Ekonomist*, I, pp. 278–80
Djordjević, D. (1962) *Carinski rat Austro-Ugarske i Srbije 1906–1911* (The Customs War between Austria-Hungary and Serbia 1906–1911), Belgrade

Dritsa, M. (1990) *Industry and Banks in Interwar Greece*, Athens: National Bank Educational Foundation (in Greek)

Durandin, C. (1996) 'La politique française et les Roumains, 1878–1903', unpublished Ph.D. dissertation, Université de Paris III

Eddie, S. (1989) 'Economic policy and economic development in Austria-Hungary, 1867–1913', in Peter Mathias and Sidney Pollard (eds) *The Cambridge Economic History of Europe. Volume VIII. The Industrial Economies: The Development of Economic and Social Policies*, Cambridge, pp. 814–85

Eldem, E. (1994) *Banque Impériale Ottomane. Inventaire commenté des archives*, Istanbul: IFEA–Osmanlı Bankası, Collection Varia Turcica, XXV

Eldem, E., 'Osmanlı Bankası Arşivi ve Tasnif Çalışmaları Hakkında Bir Sunuş' (A presentation on the Ottoman Bank archives and their classification), *Toplum ve Ekonomi*, 3, pp. 5–12

Eldem, E. (1992) 'Galata'nın Etnik Yapısı' (The ethnic structure of Galata), *İstanbul*, 1, pp. 58–63

Eldem, E. (1993) 'The ethnic structure of Galata', *Biannual Istanbul*, 1, pp. 28–33

Eldem, E. (1993) 'Culture et signature: quelques remarques sur les signatures de clients de la Banque Impériale Ottomane au début du XXe siècle', *Études turques et ottomanes. Documents de travail n° 2*, June and *L'oral et l'écrit*, June, Paris, pp. 63–74

Eldem, E. (1993) 'Batılılaşma, Modernleşme ve Kozmopolitizm: 19. Yüzyıl Sonu ve 20. Yüzyıl Başında İstanbul' (Westernization, modernization and cosmopolitanism: Istanbul at the end of the nineteenth and beginning of the twentieth centuries), in R. Zeynep (ed.) *Osman Hamdi Bey ve Dönemi*, Istanbul: Tarih Vakfı Yurt Yayınları, pp. 12–26

Eldem, E. (1995) 'Culture et signature: quelques remarques sur les signatures de clients de la Banque Impériale Ottomane au début du XXe siècle', in *Revue du Monde Musulman et de la Méditerranée. Oral et écrit dans le monde turco-ottoman*, 75–6 (1–2), pp. 181–95

Eldem, E. (1997) 'Istanbul 1903–1918: a quantitative analysis of a bourgeoisie', *Boğaziçi Journal. Review of Social, Economic and Administrative Studies*, 11 (1–2), *Istanbul Past and Present*, Special Issue, pp. 53–98

Ellis, H.S. (1965) *Industrial Capital in Greek Development*, Athens: Center of Planning and Economic Research

Erčić M. (1929) 'Naši predratni i ratni dugovi Francuskoj' (Our prewar and war debts to France), *Ekonomist*, January–February, pp. 188–202

Eulambio, M. (1924) *The National Bank of Greece: A History of the Financial and Economic Evolution of Greece*, Athens: Vlastos

Evelpidis, C. (1930) *Les Etats Balkaniques. Etude comparée politique, sociale, économique et financière*, Paris

Exertzoglou, H.A. (1986) 'Greek banking in Constantinople, 1850–1881', Ph.D. thesis submitted to King's College, London University

Feiertag, O. (1998) 'La Banque de France et les problèmes monétaires européens de la conférence de Gênes (1922) à la création de la BRI (1930)', in *Milieux économiques et intégration européenne en Europe occidentale au XXe siècle*, Arras: Presses Université

Feis, H. (1930) *Europe. The World's Banker 1870–1914. An Account of European Foreign Investment and the Connection of World Finance with Diplomacy before the War*, New York and London

Fischer, F. (1969) *Krieg der Illusionen*, Düsseldorf

Friedrich, W.-U. (1985) *Bulgarien und die Mächte 1913–1915. Ein Beitrag zur Weltkriegs- und Imperialismusgeschichte*, Wiesbaden

Fürstenberg, C. (1968) *Die Lebengeschichte eines deutschen Bankiers, niedergeschrieben von Hans Fürstenberg*, Düsseldorf

Galanis, T. (1946) *Banking Studies*, Athens: Papazissis (in Greek)

Galántai, J.(1990) *Der österreichisch-ungarische Dualismus 1867–1918*, Budapest

Gardener, E. (1992) 'Banking strategies and 1992', in A. Mullineux (ed.) *European Banking*, Oxford: Blackwell

Georgiades, D. (1893) *La Grèce économique et financière en 1893*, Paris

Gerschenkron, A. (1966) *Economic Backwardness in Historical Perspective*, Cambridge, Mass.: Harvard University Press

Ghizari, E. (1992) 'Banking Reform in Romania', in D. Kemme and A. Rudka (eds) *Monetary and Banking Reform in Post-communist Economies*, New York: Westview Press, pp. 115–22

Giannitsis, T. (1982) *Foreign Banks in Greece: the Postwar Experience*, Athens: Gutenberg (in Greek)

Giannitsis, T. (ed.) (1993) *Market Liberalisation and Transformations in the Greek Banking System*, Athens: ETVA, Papazissis (in Greek)

Gibson, H. and Tsakalotos, E. (1992) 'Economic theory and the limits to financial liberalization: domestic financial liberalization in Greece, Portugal and Spain', in H. Gibson and E. Tsakalotos (eds) *Economic Integration and Financial Liberalization: Prospects for Southern Europe*, London: St Antony's/ Macmillan

Girault, R. (1975) 'Les Balkans dans les relations franco-russes en 1912', *Revue historique*, January–March

Girault, R. (1980) 'Economie et politique internationale: diplomatie et banques pendant l'entre-deux-guerres', *Relations internationales*, no. 21, spring, pp. 7–22

Gnjatović Dr. (1991) *Stari državni dugovi. Prilog ekonomskoj i političkoj istoriji Srbije i Jugoslavije 1862–1941* (Old government debts. A contribution to the economic and political history of Serbia and Yugoslavia 1862–1941), Belgrade

Good, D.F. (1986) *Der wirtschaftliche Aufstieg des Habsburgerreiches 1750–1914*, Vienna

Gortsos, C. (1992) *The Greek Banking System*, Athens: Hellenic Bank Association

Gounaris, B.C. (1993) *Steam over Macedonia, 1870–1912. Socio-economic Change and the Railway Factor*, East European Monographs, New York: Columbia University Press

Grier, K. (1989) 'On the existence of a political monetary cycle', *American Journal of Political Science*, 33 (2), pp. 376–89

Gusti, P.D. (ed.) (1940) *Enciclopedia Romana*, Bucharest

Gutsjahr, M. (1995) 'Rüstungsunternehmen Österreich-Ungarns vor und im Ersten Weltkrieg. Die Entwicklung dargestellt an den Firmen Skoda, Steyr, Austro-Daimler und Lohner', Ph.D. thesis, Vienna

Hadziiossif, Chr. (1988) 'Banques grecques et banques européennes au XIXe siècle: le point de vue d'Alexandrie', in G.B. Dertilis (ed.) *Banquiers, usuriers et paysans*, Paris, pp. 157–98

Hadziiossif, Chr. (1990) 'Eastern in Alexandria: popular prejudices and intercommunal strife in late 19th century Egypt', *Historica*, no. 12–13 (in Greek)

Hadziiossif, C. (1993) *The Old Moon: Industry in the Greek Economy, 1830–1940*, Athens: Themelio

Halikias, D.J. (1978) *Money and Credit in a Developing Economy: The Greek Case*, New York: New York University Press

Hanisch, E. (1994) *Der lange Schatten des Staates. Österreichische Gesellschaftsgeschichte im 20. Jahrhundert*, Vienna

Herman, K. (1958) 'Novoslovanstvi a česka buržoasie', in *Kapitoly z dejin vzajemnych vztahu narodu ČSR a SSSR*, Prague: sbornik praci, pp. 235–312

Hicks, J. (1974) *The Crisis in Keynesian Economics*, Oxford: Blackwell

Höbelt, L. (1996) 'Das Problem der konservativen Eliten in Österreich-Ungarn', in Jürgen Nautz and Richard Vahrenkamp (eds) *Die Wiener Jahrhundertwende. Einflüsse–Umwelt–Wirkungen*, 2nd edn, Vienna

Hristoforov, A. (1937) 'Akcionernite banki prez perioda na krizata' (The joint-stock banks during the crisis period), *Spisanie na Sajuza na Populjarnite Banki*, 1

İnalcık, H. (1980) 'Military and fiscal transformation in the Ottoman Empire, 1600–1700', *Archivum Ottomanicum*, VI, pp. 283–337

Jackson, Marvin R. (1992) 'Company management and capital market development in transition', in J.R. Lampe (ed.) *Creating Capital Mar-*

kets in Eastern Europe, Washington, DC: Woodrow Wilson Center Press, pp. 57–74

Johri, C.K. (1965) *Monetary Policy in a Developing Economy*, Calcutta: World Press

Jouganatos, G. (1992) *The Development of the Greek Economy, 1950–1991*, Westport Conn.: Greenwood

Kalamotousakis, G. (1981) 'Monetary and special credit restrictions of the Greek banking system. Interest rate and investment policy in Greece and the EEC member states. Currency Committee', in Harissopoulos Committee *Summaries of Papers*, Athens

Karamihailov, M. (1939) *Kreditnoto delo v Balgarija i stopanskata kriza* (The credit system in Bulgaria and the economic crisis), Sofia

Karatzas Report on the Change and Modernization of the Banking System, Athens: Hellenic Bank Association (in Greek), 1987

Kaser, M.C. and Radice, E.A. (1986) *The Economic History of Eastern Europe, 1919–1975*, 2 vols, Oxford: Clarendon Press

Katseli, L. (1990) 'Economic integration in the enlarged European Community: structural adjustment of the Greek economy', in C. Bliss and J. Braga de Macedo (eds) *Unity with Diversity in the European Community: The Community's Southern Frontier*, Cambridge: Cambridge University Press

Kefalas, A. (1995) 'Reforms and state banks', *Economicos Tahydromos*, 22 June

Killen, L. (1994) *Testing the Peripheries: US–Yugoslav Economic Relations in the Interwar Years*. East European Monographs, New York: Columbia University Press

Kiritescu, C. (1971) *Sistemul banesc al leului* (The monetary system of the leu), Bucharest: Ed. Academiei RSR

Kocka, J. (1978) 'Entrepreneurs and managers in German industrialization', in P. Mathias and M.M. Postan (eds) *Cambridge Economic History of Europe*, VII, pt 1, Cambridge: Cambridge University Press, pp. 492–589

Komlos, J. (1986) *Die Habsburgermonarchie als Zollunion. Die Wirtschaftsentwicklung Österreich-Ungarns im 19. Jahrhundert*, Vienna

Komunalna banka Ljubljana, 1955–1960, Ljubljana, 1960

Kostis, K. (1997) *Collaboration and Competition. The 70 Years of the Hellenic Bank Association*, Athens (in Greek)

Kostis, K. and Tsokopoulos, V. (1988) *The Banks in Greece, 1898–1928*, Athens (in Greek)

Kostopoulos, I. (1981) 'Greek banking competitiveness compared to that of banking systems of EC member states', in Harissopoulos Committee *Summaries of Papers*, Athens (in Greek)

Kostopoulos, S. (1953) *The Policy of Bank Merger*, Athens: Alfa (in Greek)

Kostov, A. (1989) 'The Belgian Capital in the Balkans, 1878–1914', unpublished dissertation, Sofia

Kövér, G. (1991) 'The Austro-Hungarian banking system', in Rondo Cameron and V.I. Bovykin (eds) *International Banking, 1870–1914*, New York, pp. 319–44

Krizek, J. (1965) 'Beitrag zur Geschichte der Entstehung und des Einflusses des Finanzkapitals in der Habsburger Monarchie in den Jahren 1900–1914', *Die Frage des Finanzkapitals in der Österreichisch-Ungarischen Monarchie 1900–1918*, Bucharest, pp. 5–51

Kronenbitter, G. (1997) '"Nur los lassen". Österreich-Ungarn und der Wille zum Krieg', in Johannes Burkhardt et al., *Lange und kurze Wege in den Ersten Weltkrieg. Vier Augsburger Beiträge zur Kriegsursachenforschung*, Munich, pp. 159–87

Kronenbitter, G. (1997) 'Austria-Hungary and World War I', *Contemporary Austrian Studies*, V, New Brunswick, NJ, pp. 342–56

Krontiras, D. (1995) 'Conflict of modernization and protection', *Hellenic Bank Association Bulletin*, March (in Greek)

Kukla, St. (1924) *Razvitak kreditne organizacije u Srbiji do svetskog rata. Ekonomsko-istorijska strudija* (Development of the credit organization in Serbia until the First World War. An economic-historic study), Zagreb

Lampe, John R. (1980) 'Unifying the Yugoslav economy: misery and early misunderstanding, 1918–1921', in D. Djordjevic (ed.) *The Creation of Yugoslavia, 1914–1918*, Santa Barbara, Calif.: ABC Clio Press, pp. 139–56

Lampe, J.R. (1986) *The Bulgarian Economy in the 20th Century*, London/Sydney: Croom Helm

Lampe, J.R. (1996) *Yugoslavia as History, Twice there was a Country*, Cambridge: Cambridge University Press

Lampe, J.R. and Jackson, M.R. (1982) *Balkan Economic History, 1550–1950. From Imperial Borderlands to Developing Nations*, Bloomington, Ind.: Indiana University Press

Lampe, J.R., Prickett, R.O. and Adamovic, L. (1990) *Yugoslav–American Economic Relations Since World War II*. Durham, NC: Duke University Press

Landes, D. (1956) 'Vieille banque et banque nouvelle: La Révolution Financière du dix-neuvième siècle', *Revue d'Histoire Moderne et Contemporaine*, 3, pp. 204–22

Lesourd, J.A. and Gérard, Cl. (1976) *Nouvelle histoire économique*, I, Paris

Löding, D. (1969) 'Deutschlands und Österreich-Ungarns Balkanpolitik von 1912–1914 unter besonderer Berücksichtigung ihrer Wirtschaftsinteressen', Ph.D. thesis, Hamburg

Loulos, K. (1990) *German Policy towards Greece, 1896–1914*, Athens (in Greek)

Lukauskas, A. (1994) 'The political economy of financial restriction: the case of Spain', *Comparative Politics*, 27 (4), pp. 53–76

Manesis, A., Manitakis, A. and Papadimitriou, G. (1991) *The 'Andreadis Affair' and the Economic Constitution*, Athens: Sakkoulas (in Greek)

Maravall, J.M. and Santamaria, J. (1986) 'Political change in Spain and the prospects for democracy', in G. O'Donnell, P. Schmitter and L. Whitehead (eds) *Transition from Authoritarian Rule: Southern Europe*, Baltimore, Md.: Johns Hopkins University Press

Marguerat, Ph. (1988) 'Banque de France et politique de puissance dans l'entre-deux-guerres: le problème des stabilisations monétaires en Europe orientale, 1927–1931', *Relations internationales*, no. 56, winter pp. 475–85

März, E. (1968) *Österreichische Industrie- und Bankpolitik in der Zeit Franz Josephs I. Am Beispiel der k. k. priv. Österreichischen Credit-Anstalt für Handel und Gewerbe*, Vienna

März, E. (1981) *Österreichische Bankpolitik in der Zeit der großen Wende 1913–1923. Am Beispiel der Creditanstalt für Handel und Gewerbe*, Vienna

Mazower, M. (1991) *Greece and the Inter-War Economic Crisis*, Oxford: Oxford University Press

Meyer, R.H. (1970) *Banker's Diplomacy. Monetary Stabilization in the Twenties*, New York and London

Michel, B. (1976) *Banques et banquiers en Autriche au début du 20e siècle*, Paris

Milenković, P. (1936) *Istorija gradjenja železnica i železnička politika kod nas 1850–1935* (Railway construction history and our railway policy 1850–1935), Belgrade pp.12–13

Milić, D. (1964) 'Pregled delatnosti stranog kapitala u Srbiji do Prvog svetskog rata' (Review of activity of foreign capital in Serbia until World War I), *Istorijski pregled*, 2, Zagreb pp. 94–111

Milić, D. (1970) *Strani kapital u rudarstvu Srbije do 1918*, (Foreign capital in Serbian Mining until 1918), Belgrade

Milić, D. (1992) 'Učešće Jevreja u bankarstvu Srbije do Prvog svetskog rata' (The role of Jews in Serbian banking until World War I), *Zbornik Jevrejskog istorijskog muzeja u Beogradu*, 6, pp. 168–82

Mitrović, A. (1985) 'Berliner Handelsgesellschaft u Srbiji' (Berliner Handelsgesellschaft in Serbia), *Zbornik Filozofskog fakulteta u Beogradu*, XVI, pp. 167–97

Mitrović, A. (1986) 'Pester Ungarische Commerzialbank na Balkanu do 1918 godine' (Pester Ungarische Commerzialbank in the Balkans until 1918), *Zbornik matice srpske za istoriju*, 34, pp. 43–80

Mitrović, A. (1988) 'Mreža austrougarskih I nemačkih banaka na Balkanu pred prvi svetski rat' (The network of Austro-Hungarian and German banks in the Balkans on the eve of the First World War), *Jugoslvenski istorijski časopis* (Belgrade), 23 (3–4), pp. 51–75

Mitrović, A. (1995) 'Les intérêts français en Serbie à la veille de la première guerre mondiale', *Godišnjak za društvenu istoriju*, II(3), pp. 365–78

Mitsis, V. (1987) *The Issue Privilege of the Ionian Bank, 1839–1920*, Athens: Ionian Bank (in Greek)

Moran, M. (1984) *The Politics of Banking. The Strange Case of Competition and Credit Control*, London: Macmillan

Moreau, E. (1954) *Souvenirs d'un Gouverneur de la Banque de France, Histoire de la stabilisation du Franc (1926–1928)*, Paris: Librairie de Medicis

Morin, J. (1983) *Souvenirs d'un banquier français, 1875–1947*, Paris

Moschos, D. and Fraggetis, D. (1997) *The Present and the Future of Greek Banks*, Athens: IOBE (in Greek)

Mouzelis, N. (1986) *Politics in the Semi-Periphery: Early Parliamentarism and Late Industrialisation in the Balkans and Latin America*, London: Macmillan

Murgescu, C. and Constantinescu, N.N. (eds) (1960) *Contributii la istoria capitalului strain in Romania* (Contributions regarding the history of foreign capital in Romania), Bucharest: Ed. Academiei RPR

Natan, Z. and Berov, L. (1958) *Monopolističeskijat kapitalisam v Bălgarija* (Monopolist capitalism in Bulgaria), Sofia

National Monetary Commission (ed.) (1911) *Banking in Russia, Austro-Hungary, The Netherlands and Japan*, Washington DC

Nedeljković, M. (1909) *Istorija srpskih državnih dugova* (History of Serbian government debts), Belgrade

Neven, D. (1993) 'Structural adjustment in European retail banking: some views from industrial organization', in J. Dermine (ed.) *European Banking in the 1990s*, Oxford: Blackwell

Notel, R. (1986) 'International finance and monetary reforms', in M.C. Kaser and E.A. Radice (eds) *The Economic History of Eastern Europe, 1919–1975*, 2 vols, Oxford: Clarendon Press

Nova Ljubljanska banka, *Annual Report*, Ljubljana, 1989, 1995, 1996

Nova Ljubljanska banka (1996) *Strategija poslovanja NLB v tujini*, Ljubljana, May

Pagoulatos, G. (1996) 'Governing in a constrained environment: policy-making in the Greek banking deregulation and privatisation reform', *West European Politics*, 19 (4), pp. 744–69

Pagoulatos, G. (1997) *Institutions and public policy making: the politics of Greek banking deregulation and privatisation*, D.Phil. thesis, University of Oxford

Pagoulatos, G. (forthcoming) 'Liberalizing Southern Europe: financial systems and their Europeanization', in K. Lavdas (ed.) *Junctures of Stateness: Politics and Policy Change in Southern Europe*, Aldershot: Ashgate

Pagoulatos, G. and Wright, V. (forthcoming) 'The politics of industrial privatization: Spain, Portugal and Greece in a European perspective', in H. Gibson (ed.) *Economic Change in Southern Europe*, Baltimore, Md.: Johns Hopkins University Press

Palairet, M. (1997) *The Balkan Economies c.1800–1914. Evolution without Development*, Cambridge: Cambridge University Press

Pamuk, S. (1987) *The Ottoman Empire and European Capitalism, 1820–1913. Trade, Investment and Production*, Cambridge: Cambridge University Press

Papagiannakis, E. (1982) *The Greek railways (1882–1910). Geopolitical, Economic and Social Dimensions*, Athens (in Greek)

Peltzman, S. (1976) 'Toward a more general theory of regulation', *Journal of Law and Economics*, 19(2), pp. 211–40

Pesmazoglu, J. (1965) *The Relation Between Monetary and Fiscal Policy*, Athens: Bank of Greece

Pirerger, A. (1980) *100 Jahre der Österreichischen Länderbank 1880–1980*, Vienna

Poidevin, R. (1964) 'Les intérêts financiers français et allemands en Serbie de 1895 à 1914', *Revue historique*, 232, July–September, pp. 49–66

Poidevin, R. (1969) *Les relations commerciales et financières entre la France et l'Allemagne de 1898 à 1914*, Paris: Comité pour l'histoire économique et financière de la France, reprint 1998

Poulis, P. (1994) 'Banking system modernization and modern management information systems', *Hellenic Bank Association Bulletin*, November (in Greek)

Pougli-Bey, D. (1910) 'La Banque Impériale Ottomane', *Annales des sciences politiques*, 24, pp. 346–89

Provopoulos, G. (1985) *Public Sector in the Greek Economy: Recent Trends and Financial Effects*, Athens (in Greek)

Provopoulos, G. (ed.) (1995) *The Greek Financial System*, Athens: IOBE (in Greek)

Psilos, D. (1964) *Capital Market in Greece*, Athens: Center of Economic Research

Quataert D. (1994) 'The age of reforms, 1812–1914' in H. İnalcık and D. Quataert *An Economic and Social History of the Ottoman Empire, 1300–1914*, Cambridge: Cambridge University Press

Ramoser, Chr. (1992) 'Österreich-Ungarns Weg zur Tegetthoff-Klasse', Ph.D. thesis, Vienna

Reik, W. (1932) *Die Beziehungen der österreichischen Großbanken zur Industrie*, Vienna

Reuter, P.W. (1979) *Die Balkanpolitik des französischen imperialismus 1911–1914*, Frankfurt/Main

Riesser, J. (1911) *The German Great Banks and their Concentration with Connection of the Economic Development of Germany*, Washington DC: Government Printing House, reprint 1977 by Arno Press Inc.

Rist, L. and Ph. Swob (1939) *De la France d'avant guerre à la France d'aujourd'hui*, Paris: Librairie du Recueil Sirey

Rozenberg, V. and Kostic, J. (1940) *Ko financira jugoslovensku privredu* (Who finances the Yugoslav economy), Belgrade: Balkanska stampa

Rudolph, R.L. (1976) *Banking and Industrialization in Austria-Hungary: The Role of Banks in the Industrialization of the Czech Crownlands, 1873–1914*, Cambridge: Cambridge University Press

Rumpler, H. (1997) *Eine Chance für Mitteleuropa. Bürgerliche Emanzipation und Staatsverfall in der Habsburgermonarchie*, Vienna

Rusenov, M. (ed.) (1983) *Istorija na finansovata i kreditnata sistema v Bălgarija* (History of Bulgaria's financial and credit system), vol. 2, Varna

Sandgruber, R. (1995) *Ökonomie und Politik. Österreichische Wirtschaftsgeschichte vom Mittelalter bis zur Gegenwart*, Vienna

Sieghart, R. (1932) *Die letzten Jahrzehnte einer Großmacht. Menschen, Völker, Probleme des Habsburger-Reichs*, Berlin

Simidčiev, D.I. (1930) *Cuzdite kapitali v naseto narodno stopanstvo* (Foreign capital in our economy), Sofia

Simitch, M. (1925) *La dette publique de la Serbie de l'origine à la guerre de 1914*, Paris

Slavescu, V. (1915) *Marile banci comerciale din Romania* (The big commercial banks in Romania), Bucharest: Institutul de Arte Grafice 'Universala'

Soldatos, G. (1991) 'The post-war Greek economy: politics and economics', *Suedosteuropa*, 40 (5), pp. 226–39

Somary, F. (1994) *Erinnerungen eines politischen Meterologen*, Munich

Sondhaus, L. (1994) *The Naval Policy of Austria-Hungary, 1867–1918. Navalism, Industrial Development, and the Politics of Dualism*, West Lafayette

Soutou, G. (1976) 'L'impérialisme du pauvre: la politique économique du gouvernement français en Europe centrale et orientale de 1918 à 1929. Essai d'interprétation', *Relations internationales*, no. 7, pp. 219–39

Spitzmüller, A. (1955) ... *und hat auch Ursach, es zu lieben*, Vienna

Stanarević, N. (1912) 'Beogradske banke u 1911' (Belgrade Banks in 1911), *Ekonomist*, I-II, p. 21; separate publication under the same title, Belgrade, 1912

Stanarević, N. (1924) *Razvitak kreditne organizacije u Srbiji* (Development of credit organization in Serbia), Zagreb

Stassinopoulos, E. (1966) *The History of the National Bank of Greece*, Athens (in Greek)

Štiblar, F. (1992) 'The rise and fall of Yugoslavia', paper for the *Annual Conference of British History Unit*, Leicester, April, pp. 1–26

Štiblar, F. (1994) 'Finance and trade in interwar Slovenia', paper at the *Conference on Interwar Banking in Central Europe*, Prague, May, pp. 1–25

Štiblar, F. (1994) 'The Former Yugoslavia: economic disintegration and outlook from Slovenia's point of view', paper prepared for Panel Discussion at Woodrow Wilson Center, Washington DC, May, pp. 1–13

Štiblar, F. (1995) 'Universal banking in Slovene region', in A. Teichova et al., *Universal Banking in the Twentieth Century*, Aldershot: Edward Elgar Publishing

Štiblar, F. (1994) 'Changes in the Yugoslav and Slovene financial system after 1919', paper presented at the Conference of European Banking History, Budapest, November, pp. 1–17, published in Štiblar F. (1995) *Slovenski finančni sektor med svetovnima vojnama*, a book from the conference *Veliki preobrati v slovenski zgodovini*, Celje, March

Štiblar, F. (1996) 'Restructuring of banking sector of Slovenia', OECD and WIIW Conference, Vienna, December

Stigler, G. (1971) 'The theory of economic regulation', *Bell Journal of Economics and Management Science*, 2(1), pp. 3–21

Stojadinović, M. (1929) 'Ratni dug prema Francuskoj' (Pre-war debt to France), *Politika*, 25 February

Stojadinović, M. (1929) 'Naši predratni i ratni dugovi Francuskoj' (Our pre-war and war debts to France), *Bankarstvo*, April, pp. 149–53

Stojković, J. (1994) 'Srpsko akcionarsko topioničarsko industrijsko društvo 1913–1945' (Serbian Smelting and Industrial Joint-Stock Company 1913–1945), master's thesis submitted to the Center for Interdisciplinary Studies, Belgrade University

Sturdja, M.D. (1983) 'Haute banque et Sublime porte. Préliminaires financiers de la guerre de Crimée', in Jean Louis Bacque-Grammond and Paul Dumont, *Contributions à l'histoire économique et sociale de l'Empire Ottoman*, Leuven pp. 451–80

Sundhausen, H. (1989) *Historische Statistik Serbiens 1834–1914*, Munich

Teichova, A. (1989) 'Industry', in M.C. Kaser and E.A. Radice (eds) *The Economic History of Eastern Europe, 1919–1975*, vol. I, Oxford: Clarendon Press, pp. 222–322

Thobie, J. (1977) *Intérêts et impérialisme français dans l'Empire Ottoman (1895–1914)*, Paris

Thobie, J. (1982) *La France impériale, 1880–1914*, Paris: Megrelis

Thobie, J. (1988) 'La France, la Grèce et les Balkans dans les années Trente', *Balkan Studies*, 29, pp. 3–28

Thobie, J. (1991) 'European banks in the Middle East', in R. Cameron and V.I. Bovykin (eds) *International Banking 1870–1914*, New York and Oxford

Todorova, M. (1997) *Imagining the Balkans*, New York and Oxford: Oxford University Press

Todorović, M. (1913) 'Plasman stranog kapitala u Srbiji' (Foreign capital investments in Serbia), *Ekonomist*, II, pp. 212–14

Toniolo, G. (1994) *One Hundred Years, 1894–1994. A Short History of the Banca Commerciale Italiana*, Fiesole

Tosti, A. (1989) 'Denarni zavodi v Sloveniji po prvi svetovni vojni, Bancni Vestnik', Ljubljana

Treptow, K. (ed.) (1996) *A History of Romania*, Iasi: The Center for Romanian Studies, The Romanian Cultural Foundation

Trgovinsko-zanatlijsko-industrijski šematizam Kraljevine Srbije za 1911. godinu (Professional directory of trade, crafts and industry in the Kingdom of Serbia for 1911)

Trgovinsko-zanatlijsko-industrijski šematizam Srbije za 1986–7 (Professional directory of trade, crafts and industry in Serbia for 1986–7)

Tsakalotos, E. (1991) *Alternative Economic Strategies: The Case of Greece*, Aldershot: Avebury

Tsoukalis, L. (1993) *The New European Economy*, Oxford: Oxford University Press

Usunov, N. (1927) *Die fremden Kapitalien in Bulgarien*, Berlin

Valaoritis, I. (1902/1988) *The History of the National Bank of Greece, 1842–1902*, Athens: National Bank Educational Foundation (in Greek)

Vickers, M. and Pettifer J. (1997) *Albania. From Anarchy to a Balkan Identity*, London: Hurst and Co.

von Hegedüs, R.E.G. (1917) *Geschichte der Entstehung und des Bestandes der Pester Ungarischen Commercial Bank. II. Band. 1892–1917*, Budapest

Williamson, S.R., Jr (1991) *Austria-Hungary and the Origins of the First World War*, Basingstoke: Macmillan

Wilson, J.S.G. (1986) *Banking Policy and Structure: A Comparative Analysis*, London: Croom Helm

Woodward, S.L. (1995) *Socialist Unemployment, The Political Economy of Yugoslavia, 1945–1990*. Princeton, NJ: Princeton University Press

Xanthakis, M. (1995) 'Investment banks: European and Greek experience', in T. Giannitsis (ed.) *Market Liberalisation and Transformations in the Greek Banking System*, Athens: ETBA-Papazissis (in Greek)

Yordanov, D. (1911) 'Pet godini na čuzdite banki v Bălgarija' (Five years of the foreign banks in Bulgaria), *Bankov pregled*, Sofia, pp. 13–14

Yordanov, D. (1914) *Kapitalite na bălgarskite akcionerni družestva v nadvečerieto na Balkanskata vojna* (The capital of the Bulgarian joint-stock companies on the eve of the Balkan War), Sofia

Yordanov, D. (1919) *Vojnata i novite akcionerni družestva* (The War and the new joint-stock companies), Sofia

Zgodovina denarstva in bančništva na Slovenskem, Zveza zgodovinskih društev Slovenije, Ljubljana, 1987

Zolotas, X. (1958) *Monetary Stability and Economic Development*, Athens: Bank of Greece (in Greek)

Zolotas, X. (1964) *Monetary Equilibrium and Economic Development*, Athens: Bank of Greece (in Greek)

Zolotas, X. (1962) *The Role of the Banks in a Developing Country*, Athens: Bank of Greece

Zuckerkandl, K. (1911) 'The Austro-Hungarian Bank', in National Monetary Commission (ed.) *Banking in Russia, Austro-Hungary, The Netherlands and Japan*, Washington DC, pp. 35–118

Zysman, J. (1983) *Governments, Markets and Growth*, New York: Cornell University Press

Index

For Product Safety Concerns and Information please contact our EU representative GPSR@taylorandfrancis.com Taylor & Francis Verlag GmbH, Kaufingerstraße 24, 80331 München, Germany

Batch number: 10725973

Printed by Printforce, the Netherlands

INSPIRING A MEDICO-LEGAL REVOLUTION